Dear Mr. Nelson

Dear Mr. Nelson

Kenneth E. Nelson

Library of Congress Control Number: 2010909102
ISBN: Hardcover   978-1-4535-2528-9
               Softcover   978-1-4535-2527-2
               Ebook   978-1-4535-2529-6

This book was printed in the United States of America.

To order additional copies of this book, contact:
Xlibris Corporation
1-888-795-4274
www.Xlibris.com
Orders@Xlibris.com
78939

CONTENTS

DEDICATION

This book is dedicated to the several thousand teenagers who wrote spontaneous letters to me while I was speaking to their classes.

Each had his/her reason for quietly pulling a sheet of paper from their binder and penning their own story. Some wadded up their letters, half-written, and I would never know what it was they felt compelled to share with me, and then lost the courage to continue.

I accepted each letter handed to me as these young people exited the classroom, always hopeful that my follow-up written response would contain suggestions which could be used to make their lives safer, or better in other ways. Some would receive only my assurance that they were on the right track and needed to pursue the new direction they wanted their lives to take.

My opportunity to briefly enter each young life will always be cherished.

ENDORSEMENTS

"*Dear Mr. Nelson* is a must read for all educators and those in the Juvenile Justice system."

Nanette Rigby
Member of the Madera County Juvenile Justice Commission

"This book is going to be a wonderful tool to help students know they are not alone in this struggle between life and alcohol. It will be used as a tool which students, teachers, counselors and parents can turn to find help and advice."

Amy E. Andrews
Health Teacher, E. Union High School Manteca, CA

"The letters to Ken reflect the wonderful effort he made on behalf of thousands of young people. Ken has proven that there is no generation gap! His words of wisdom have touched the hearts and minds of many young people over the years . . . and I'm sure he's saved some lives along the way."

Donna McBride
Retired, SADD National Director of Field Services

OVERVIEW

Probably the only one of its kind ever written, *Dear Mr. Nelson* is backgrounded by twenty eight years of volunteer speaking for the organizations MADD (Mothers Against Drunk Driving) and SADD (Students Against Destructive Decisions).

Almost by accident, a single letter handed to the author following his presentation to a high school class resulted in a flow of more than 3,500 spontaneous letters from teenagers. The author doesn't attempt to explain why so many troubled young people apparently found him to be believable, non-threatening and trustworthy, worthy of laying out their experiences, failings, worries and pleas for help in hastily written letters composed while he was speaking.

Here are some of those letters, laid out in chapters identified by who was involved: Boyfriends, parents, siblings, close friends, aunts and uncles, etc. This is not a novel to be read in one sitting. From the chapter titles, readers can select the part that they identify with as teachers, counselors, parents, friends, and teens themselves.

INTRODUCTION

It wasn't my intention to become a twenty-year volunteer speaker for MADD and SADD. It certainly wasn't in my thoughts to become a sort of Ann Landers for teenagers. I just fell into the whole situation. One step led to another, and before long, the personal rewards were so great I couldn't stop.

Soon after I retired from work in 1980, California and the entire nation was applauding the effort of Candy Lightner, as she fought to put together Mothers Against Drunk Drivers (soon changed to Mothers Against Drunk Driving).

I watched the almost daily newspaper articles and pictures as Ms. Lightner forced attention of lawmakers and then garnered their support in the drive to take the crime of drunk driving seriously.

After more than a year of retirement, I'd rebuilt fences, moved shrubs, repotted plants, and painted all of the outside woodwork around the house. I'd even been the bricklayer for my older neighbor who claimed he could no longer tolerate the encroachment of his neighbor's Bermuda grass into his little rose garden. Together, we constructed a twenty-foot-long, two and a half foot high divider, laying over 400 bricks. I wasn't ready to jump into golf as a steady diet, although I enjoyed playing golf and still do. I was looking for something interesting but different!

At about the same time, my young cousin, a middle school teacher in Tracy, California, was tragically destroyed by a multiple-offender drunk driver while on his regular after-school bicycle ride around the Tracy countryside. This triggered my decision to try and get involved.

I took a $1000 check out to MADD's office, introduced myself to Candy Lightner, and told her I'd like to do something for her organization. My offer to write their newsletter was turned down, as well as one to handle their financial records. Ms. Lightner said she had those bases covered but that requests for MADD speakers were overwhelming her, and she asked if I'd consider doing some speaking for them.

I tried to not show my disappointment because I'd been a writer and editor of a business newsletter for the company I had worked for for many years, and had equal experience in budgeting and small-company management. Public speaking was a different matter, and although I'd made many brief talks in required situations, speaking was never something I relished doing.

However, I didn't want to go home empty handed and told Ms. Lightner that I'd try it for two years and would commit myself to giving 100 talks to organizations requesting MADD speakers during that period. I was asked to prepare a sample speech and to return in a few days to deliver my planned talk for review by some 'committee.'

Two others, both young mothers who had recently lost children in drunk driving crashes were present at the MADD office when I arrived. They had agreed to help fill in some of the speaker requests, as I had, and preceded me in delivering their proposed talks. Both broke down and asked to be relieved of any public speaking until they could better handle their emotions. As the only remaining volunteer speaker, I struggled through my talk and was asked to give my first presentation to a Lioness Club in a nearby town two days later. One of MADD's volunteer staff would accompany me on the first outing.

One particular side of being a spokesperson for a charitable organization especially troubled me, that of fund raising. I absolutely couldn't bring myself to ask people for money!

I resolved that conflict by telling MADD's people that I wouldn't be asking my audiences for contributions but that I also wouldn't accept a dime from MADD. I'd cover all of my own expenses. The Lioness Club did insist on giving us $25. That was the first and the last.

This approach worked beautifully as I dove into the start of regular speech making. Over time, not asking for donations gave me an unexpected latitude, a freedom in how I approached the alcohol-driving issues.

Service clubs and occasionally business organizations desiring a speaker on the safety problems involved, dominated requests for several months. It wasn't unusual to have a breakfast, lunch, and dinner assignment on the same day. The first high school, Burbank High in Sacramento, California, called MADD for a speaker in December 1981.

A twenty-minute film that MADD provided, titled "Until I Get Caught," although unsuited for short service club talks, found an immediate fit in my school programs. In the film, several teenagers were featured, keying in on one seventeen year old boy who was the driver in a fatal crash. The emotional outbursts of parents, police activity, and responses of the boy's teenage friends assured students' riveted attention in the driver education classes. I knew I couldn't hold young audiences' attention for fifty minutes. By showing the film at mid-point, my voice was spared, and the students saved from the agony of listening to me for the full time. School assignments for me meant giving four, five, and sometimes six programs during a day.

After three hundred thirty-six showings of "Until I Get Caught," and several trips to a repair shop for emergency splicing, the film was no longer usable. The demise of the film became permanent when some undetected pranksters shoved the wheeled-table carrying the projector down the steep auditorium steps while the teacher and I were at lunch in the school's cafeteria. The film had been stripped off and ruined.

Fate was on my side. I had received in the mail, gratis, a fifteen minute film titled, "A Call To Action." Although, it didn't have the same emotional punch, it contained current information and could hold students' attention. I could answer affirmatively if a fifteen year old asked expectantly, *"Does it have any good wrecks in it?"* I found value in acknowledging to my student audiences that the video was designed mostly for adult viewing, but had found that teenagers today are mature enogh to get a lot from those fifteen minutes. A realistic high speed crash into a tree gets a flood of gasps, then total silence as a somber voice intones, "twenty-five thousand people a year die in drunk driving crashes." A dancing cartoon figure depicts the effect of rapid intake of alcohol; a liver explodes. Candy Lightener, MADD's founder, and several notables are pictured and quoted. It is surprising how profoundly correct they have proven to be, twenty years later. Few students take naps during this time.

A national insurance association that had sent the film replaced it once and then provided a video rendition which I had copied several times during the almost four thousand showings over a period of eighteen years.

Calls from high schools soon came in a flood! I'd always pictured myself as a potentially good teacher and had even contemplated going back and getting a credential after fifteen years of work in private industry. That never happened, but here was my chance to 'act like a teacher,' and yet not have to knuckle down to the time discipline required.

By late 1982, those of us speaking for MADD in my area seemed to have filled most of the requests that would be coming from service clubs. Most calls now were from high schools, wanting speakers for driver education classes, and for assemblies. MADD's chapter representatives soon handled all of the service club requests; high school calls were relayed to me.

SADD (Students Against Driving Drunk, and in 1998 changed to Students Against Destructive Decisions), had been founded in 1981 and was getting a lot of well-earned publicity. I began asking students to put their name of a piece of paper if they wanted some information about SADD, and I would send a little brochure to some of them and hope that they would contact SADD and maybe start a club on their campus.

Although I did several dozen assembly programs, I was never comfortable and left each time feeling my performance had been rather ragged. Kids at the assemblies came there expecting a rally atmosphere, where they could sit with their friends, talk, yell, and cheer. In individual classes, I could look directly at the young faces, ask questions about their feelings on issues, circulate appropriate printed articles and leave, assured that I'd made an impact on their lives. I always ended my early programs strongly urging my student audiences to consider starting a SADD club on their campus, although I had no forms or paperwork to give them.

A letter from a SADD attorney was hardly what I expected from my early efforts. In his letter, the man reminded me that I had no authority to speak for SADD and that I must immediately cease representing SADD. The attorney suggested that I could become qualified if I came to Marlboro, Massachusetts and took a training course. I was needlessly annoyed and angered.

My written response was prompt and brief. I reminded the attorney that I was a free person and that I wasn't representing SADD in any way, but was suggesting that students do start SADD clubs on their campuses. My clincher was to advise the man that I really didn't relish flying long distances and that I was beyond teaching. There was nothing further from him.

Almost immediately a helpful flow of information began coming from SADD. During the fifteen years following I gave over three thousand presentations to high school audiences, and enrolled fifty thousand students as SADD members.

Although I met only a few of SADD's main office personnel during that period, many of them were generous in their written compliments. Every several years an attractive plaque would arrive in my mail, commending my efforts to save young lives.

The highlight came in 1998 when I was invited, all expenses paid, to attend SADD's four day conference in Washington, D.C. To the cheers of three hundred student leaders from all over the country, and their advisors, I was presented their second only Lifetime Achievement Award.

I was fortunate to meet SADD's founder, Robert Anastas, in 1983 or 1984, when he came to Modesto, California, to speak to an assembled group of high school students and teacher leaders. Mr. Anastas was briefly standing alone, following his long presentation, so I went up and introduced myself. I told him that I'd been doing volunteer speaking to high school groups in Northern California and had been suggesting they form SADD chapters.

He asked what my purpose was in attending his meeting. I told him that I wanted to see how he approached his audiences and to get some ideas to help me.

After a short pause, his smiling comment was, *"If you've given three hundred speeches and they keep asking you back, you don't need any help from me!"*

I had watched carefully how effectively Anastas drew teenagers from his large audience. He challenged them to speak out on their love for each other and to take positive actions to prevent their friends from drinking and then driving.

During the next dozen or so visits with classes, I tried to more directly involve members of my small audiences, setting aside ten minutes at the end of each hour for the purpose of getting interchanges and answering questions.

Too often, though, there was little response, and we were left staring at each other. I concluded my class hour was better spent leaving time only to respond to hands raised during my program and to answer those questions as they arose. I found I was no Dr. Anastas!

It wasn't long before the first spontaneous letter was handed to me. That gave me a route to pursue, and an exciting opening for a more helpful involvement via the teenage letter writers:

✍

Mr. Nelson,

I know drinking and driving is very bad for you. I am 18 years old. I've been drinking and driving for a long time. I have no way, I think, that I will ever stop before I kill myself or someone else. If there were something I could do, I would, but I think I would not do something when it comes up again.

I don't like going out and drinking every weekend, but it is what everyone is doing, and I know that it's wrong, but there's no way I can stop it.

I'm known as the partier at school so everyone expects me to drink, so it is very hard. I hope you can understand what I am trying to. Plus, my mom doesn't know that I do this till last month. I've been coming home two weeks in a row now when she was up. I don't like having to go out and drink, but it is just something I think I cannot help or stop.

Please try to understand, I am not a loser or a drunk.

Mark

It came as a surprise to have an older boy hand me a neatly folded sheet of binder paper when the history class at a mountain area high school filed out of the room at the end of my presentation.

I quickly unfolded the paper and realized it was a full-page letter. My plea of *"Wait a minute, please!"* went unheeded. The writer was quickly disappearing in the stream of exiting students.

Mark's letter was a first. Although I'd been a regular MADD/ SADD volunteer speaker on the issues of drunk driving and alcohol abuse for almost three years and had addressed many dozens of high school audiences, no one before had written a letter to me while I was speaking with them.

The six minutes before the next class allowed me time to read the boy's letter. He didn't think very much of himself. What could I have said to an eighteen-year old senior even if he had responded to my call for him to wait?

By two-thirty, I'd completed the last of the five programs scheduled for that day. What to do about Mark's letter had popped into my mind numerous times while I was speaking. At one point, I completely lost my train of thought and stood staring blankly at the class for ten seconds while I recovered.

I discarded the idea of discussing his letter with the teacher or a school counselor. Mark had written his story in confidence, it seemed. Instead, I would write to him and send the letter c/o his school because he had included no home address.

What did I write to Mark? I have no recollection twenty-five years later. Although, I continue to make copies of most of the responses I write to teenagers, all of them are destroyed after a couple of years.

Very likely, I applauded his honesty about his situation. I might have acknowledged surprise over the fact that his mother had only recently discovered his drinking. I'm not surprised anymore. Among the thirty-five hundred spontaneous letters I've since received, most of those relating to teenagers' drinking contain the confession that their parents aren't aware of it, and the writers don't want them to know.

I doubt that a suggestion was made that he seek help from a school counselor. Mark had made his problem very clear. Now that his mother knew, hopefully she could influence him to make a change. At eighteen, he was legally an adult in many respects. As a strictly lay person, no solution was obvious to me.

Several years later, I did call the school and was able to reach the history class teacher during his prep period. He remembered me, but said he'd lost track of Mark. He recalled seeing an article about some run-in with the police and was pretty certain about a jail term. Mark's wasn't a success story, I'm afraid.

Additional letters were handed to me during the immediate weeks following. I was excited. The students were so candid and open about the problems they were facing. I wanted to make the best use of their letters.

Without giving it sufficient thought, I began circulating some letters exactly as they were handed to me, making certain only that I didn't pass them around in classes at the same school.

An almost immediate 'backfire' caused me to change that practice. From then on, I began typing the letters received and eliminated all the identification except the date, the nearest big town and the student's first name. I found the situation that prompted this change potentially serious but fortunately laughable.

A boy from a foothill school had handed me a letter telling me how he had recently taken charge of a drinking situation involving his older brother.

His story was that his older brother (smaller in stature that he) was drunk at a party and threatening to drive. The writer had manhandled his brother, stuffed him in the car trunk, and had driven the car home safely himself, even without a driving license.

The following week, I circulated this letter at a local school, along with a few other letters. I wanted to impress upon the class the need sometimes for friends to take strong measures to prevent driving after drinking.

It was only days later that I received a heated letter from the original writer: *"What right did you have to show anyone my letter? Who gave you permission? It was all a big lie anyway. Now, I'm in big trouble with my older brother!"*

Apparently, a good friend of this older brother attended the school. He recognized the names and had immediately told his friend about the content of his younger brother's letter.

I watched the mail with apprehension for several weeks, fearful of criticism from the boys' parents, or worse. None came. I learned a permanent lesson.

By 1984, I was averaging two hundred fifty lectures a year, given primarily to individual high school classes. While the demand for speakers at service clubs was decreasing, calls from high school teachers and principals were surging. Statistics had shown that drinking and driving was the single greatest cause of death for the 15-19-year-old age group.

I was slowly learning how to keep my young audience's attention. Teenagers go to sleep with too many statistics. Circulating typed, easily readable letters written spontaneously by others their age, proved to be a major help. This, of course, triggered many teenagers' need to tell their own story. If there was a 'five-speech day,' sometimes I was flooded with ten or a dozen letters. Occasionally, there were none.

In 1986 I selected another letter, this time from a high school girl, as one to give special attention. It had a common thread with so many that I was getting.

Dear Mr. Nelson,

My mother has been a heavy drinker ever since I can remember. I love her very much. I've tried so many ways to help her, but I can't. I don't mean I've given up; I'll never to do that. I mean, I can't help her. She has to help herself. But I'm so scared something's gonna happen to her. She's all I have. I don't want to lose her to something as unnecessary as drunk driving.

Also, when she gets drunk, she tends to fight with me a lot and sometimes hits me. Over the years I've learned to just leave the room and don't listen because all she'll do is make me mad. I've told her how I feel, but she only gets mad.

My mother is one of the greatest people, but when she's drunk, she's someone I don't want to know.

Thanks for caring!
Melanie

Mark's letter, and now Melanie's, became two that I read aloud during the early part of each presentation. I then circulated as many as ten pages of typed letters, always assuring my audiences, *"It doesn't bother me at all if you are reading while I'm talking to you."*

With experience, I'm now able to study my young audiences while speaking with them. It is almost predictable when a particular teenager is thinking about writing his/her letter. Their attention to what I'm saying becomes almost an unblinking stare. This is usually followed by them quietly opening their binder and extracting a single sheet of paper. Another letter is underway!

All of the teenager letters included in *Dear Mr. Nelson* were written ten to twenty-five years prior to this publication. The authors are now young adults. To eliminate any possible identification of the writers, names of all towns, schools, and dates have been removed. Only first names are used and all of these have been changed.

The value of these letters to new readers, parents, teachers, counselors, and today's teenagers has not been diminished by time, but the privacy of the letter writers has been permanently protected.

Kenneth E. Nelson pictured receiving the 1983 Volunteer of the Year Award from Mothers Against Drunk Driving (MADD) President, Ms. Candy Lightner.

The author had promised Ms. Lightner, MADD's founder, that he would try to help out by accepting at least a hundred requests for a speaker over a two year period. Suddenly, he found himself racing around northern California and western Nevada, answering calls from Rotary, Lions, Soroptomists, Optimists clubs and others, plus many high schools, until the two year tally reached three hundred and forty speeches, resulting in the award given by MADD. Nelson's wife, Betty, now deceased, strongly supported his volunteer work and several times accompanied him, but occasionally asked her husband, "Aren't you overdoing this just a little bit?"

CHAPTER ONE

"I'd like to tell you about my father.
He's a forty-two year old alcoholic."

Dear Mr. Nelson,

While listening to you talk about the accidents that happen because of people (too often teenagers) driving drunk got me to thinking. I myself don't drink. My dad was a heavy drinker until '78 when he went into a hospital for alcoholics, and stopped drinking. At that time it didn't faze me what he did, but now I'm very glad he stopped drinking. When I think that he stopped drinking because he knew he was an alcoholic, it makes me very proud of him, and makes me remember to say "No" to people offering me alcohol. It also makes me feel safer to be in a car with him, especially when he's teaching me to drive a car. I also know that if I ever get drunk and needed a ride home, my dad would understand my problem and be able to help and not scream at me. I also, at this moment, pledge myself to join SADD and try to get my parents and friends involved, too. It's a smart move to make.

Arthur

Dear Mr. Nelson,

Hello, I'd like to tell you about my father. He is a forty-two year old alcoholic. He comes home at least once a week drunk and at least once a month he falls down the concrete stairs. He was also shot in the right eye, by accident though. At that time, he was dealing cocaine and heroin. But back to the subject, he has damaged three of our cars. We don't live together anymore. He once almost killed my mom. My sister and I suffer through this, too. I am only thirteen years old and yell at my dad when he comes home drunk when I'm at his house.

> *Thanks a lot,*
> *Jackie*

Mr. Nelson,

My dad was in an accident with a drunk driver, and he lived but the drunk driver died. My dad knew it wasn't his fault, but he now has to live with looking into that truck and seeing that man take his last breath.

He doesn't have any physical scars because he had his seatbelt on, but now he has those emotional ones.

I thank God it wasn't my dad, but it was someone else's dad. He had a commitment with his family, and he blew it and almost killed mine! It's not fair. You can call a taxi for free. There is no reason for this.

The problem I have is driving with my boyfriend's father. He always has a few drinks before we go out, and I hate myself for going with him. I am just as guilty as he is. He isn't drunk, but his reactions are still slow. Please help us find a way around this situation. Thank you for your time.

> *Veronica*

Mr. Nelson,

My dad is a drunk (alcoholic). I tell him he should get help, but he doesn't think he's an alcoholic, but I know he is. It hurts me to have to see him hurting himself when he drinks because it's starting to hurt his body. My mom said he gets really sick. That scares me. I feel like crying a lot when he drinks because it's getting worse and worse. I wish he could go get help, but I know he would never admit it. Please help me in telling my dad to get help. I don't know what to do. Help, I'm soooo scared.

> *Louona*

Mr. Nelson,

I'm writing because I'm concerned. My dad is a steady drinker, and he tends to drive even after he has had one accident while he was drunk, and he was the one who got hurt. When he gets drunk, he also tends to get very upset over some of the littlest things and sometimes tries to hit us. I like to party, and I sometimes drank, but I quit because I know how it is and I know what could happen. I really want to find out about SADD. Thank you for coming.

> *Kevin*

Dear Mr. Nelson,

My name is Kim. I've grown up around people who are alcoholics. Do you know what it's like to know that all of your parents' friends are going to kill themselves one day and maybe someone else? It makes me so mad that I can't help them because they don't listen.

My dad is also an alcoholic, though he doesn't think he is. He drinks so much sometimes that when he comes home he just goes to bed. He sometimes aggravates me so much I can't stand it. He'll sleep for a couple of hours and wake up and doesn't even remember what he's done. I just thank God he has never killed anybody yet, and I also thank God I don't drink.

I think I don't drink because of what I've seen happen to my dad and all of his friends. I just hope one day he will quit drinking altogether. Maybe someday my dream will come true because I love him so much.

Kim

Dear Mr. Nelson,

I, myself, am not an alcoholic, but I have lived with one all my life. My father was an alcoholic. He never got in a wreck, but he used to come home super drunk and beat on my mother and me. My mom always called the cops when she could, but he always got out the next day and came back. You couldn't even reason with my father. He knew everything. We were always afraid. Finally, two years ago, my parents separated and then divorced. I never see my father now, and I feel it's better that way. I want to help any way I can with SADD because we teenagers are the future.

Leslie

Dear Mr. Nelson,

My father used to be an alcoholic, and he used to get in all kinds of accidents. He was in a band, and I guess that's where it started. My father has been put in jail. The longest time was for six months. He learned his lesson, and he doesn't drink anymore.

I thank God that he is heavily into religion now, because he used to hit us and do real bad things to my mom. I'm glad it's in the past.

Mr. Nelson, could you be so kind as to tell me something? People say that if one of your parents drinks, then the chances of you drinking are high! Could this really be true? Mr. Nelson, I'm scared. I don't want to drink.

Lourdes

Dear Mr. Nelson,

I know how it is to be around drunk people, and I hate it. I think that there are more things in life than drinking. My father was a heavy alcoholic, and it irritated me. My parents always fought because he'd come home drunk. My father couldn't take stress, so he went to the bottle. I didn't want to go home after school because I hated to see my parents fight.

One night my parents got into the biggest fight of the century. My dad went mad. We threatened to leave him, and he ran into the bedroom for his gun. He said, "If I can't have you, no one can." We ran. Later that week when our family got back together, he gave up the bottle. He had bought a fifth of whiskey and dumped it down the sink.

From that day, he hasn't touched another bottle. I wish other people had the power to stay away. We still don't know if he drinks while he's away, but it sure feels good to be a family again. Keep up the good work. Sooner or later, the world will understand how bad the problem is.

Trina

Of the family members mentioned most often in teenagers' letters, fathers have to be at the top of the list of those abusing alcohol. The father's drinking triggered a family breakup in most situations described. There is very little hatred indicated on the part of the young writers, just dismay and heartbreak, but seldom loss of hope.

A significant number of letters do indicate happy endings. Fathers have given up alcohol. The family does actually get back together and becomes functional again. Having a 'recovering alcoholic' in the household sometimes is only a temporary blessing, and the family endures several periods of the father 'falling off the wagon.'

You might think that after years of physical or emotional abuse, or both, by an alcoholic father, hate would become a dominant feeling. Although some letters express an almost hateful situation, the same writers seem to immediately revert to a plea for a chance to love that father.

Only recently has the degree and length of abuse suffered by many families come to light and been recognized for its seriousness. How many families bottled it up for years and years? I'm sure the teenagers feel some relief from being able to put their feelings on a sheet of paper for me to read.

How would you, my readers, respond to some of the letters you've just read? You'll find many more letters involving fathers in chapter FIFTEEN.

If the writers can't change a father's behavior, how can they best live with it? These teenage writers deserved an answer that gave some hope or understanding.

After approaching each of the early letters from various directions, I settled on a standard set of paragraphs to include in many responses:

"You can be sure that your father wakens each morning after being drunk and hates himself. He likely promises himself that he's going to quit drinking altogether or at least cut way back. But it doesn't happen with your father, at least not yet.

Please don't allow yourself to argue and fight with your father when he's drinking. You can't win! You only end up with more hurt feelings. Just stay out of his way!

There will be times when he's completely sober and wants to talk with you about himself. Do tell him then how much it hurts you to have him drinking the way he is. Don't press it, though. He'll hear you, but he may not want to show it. A father doesn't want to hurt his child, and this approach might push your father into taking a serious first step to get off alcohol."

Veronica's letter in this chapter hinted of the breadth of the list of victims from a single drunk driving crash. This child's perception may be right on target there.

CHAPTER TWO

"I'm going to be 15 tomorrow, and my friend and I both have alcoholic and drug problems."

Dear Mr. Nelson,

I'm writing to you because I'm a partial drinker. I'm enrolled in this class because my license was taken away after an accident. My uncle is an alcoholic. We have sent him to Starting Point twice.

After the loss of his two-month-old baby, he attempted to kill himself. I, myself, am trying to quit. I called AA twice but hung up. I'm afraid I might become an alcoholic. I am trying to quit. I appreciate you coming to our class. Thank you.

Kevin

Mr. Nelson,

I'm 15 and have been drinking since I was ten. My parents have sent me to Raleigh Hills twice for help, but I drive and drink. What can I do to stop myself? I am not concerned about my safety but the safety of others. When my brother was 19, he was with some friends and was in an accident. He was the only survivor. He blamed himself for this and committed suicide a month later. I wanted to be just like him until then. I am afraid I will be.

James

Dear Mr. Nelson,

I'm 15 and will be 16 in June. Both of my parents are heavy drinkers, and my older brother drinks but not as much as my parents. I can't do anything to stop them from drinking, but I always try.

My mother and I don't get along, and my father and I aren't on good terms, I've driven with them when they have been drunk, and it's scary. I can't handle my parents, and their actions are influencing me. I drink a little but I'm not an alcoholic. I have a little brother, and I don't want to see him start drinking. Can you give me some advice on what I should do?

Sincerely,
Jim

Ken Nelson,

Hi, I've been drinking since I was 14. I am 15 now. I started with friends just as kind of a game, but it has gotten worse. My cousin drinks. I go over to my cousins' and most of the time I look forward to drinking. Every time I start to drink, it gets easier and easier to pick it up. Every time I drink it seems to take longer for me to get drunk or buzzed. I can say "No," but when I say "No," it is harder for me to say it. I know that soon I'll be really addicted, and I won't be able to say "No."

I would like for you to send me some information on drinking and driving. I'm in a Health Safety class, and this class has started me to think about what I'm doing to myself. Soon, I will be driving, and I know that if I don't help myself, I will be drinking and driving. I have problems at home, and I use drinking to take me away from my problems at home, but I know it is a problem itself. Please don't tell my name.

Chris

Dear Mr. Nelson,

I'm a fifteen year-old boy. I started drinking just at parties. Then, that's all I wanted. When I got off school all I could think about was how to get drunk. Some people, like my friends, say I have a problem, but I always deny it. I just tell them I hardly drink at all.

I would like to tell whomever that you should never start drinking. It's just not worth it. I feel kind of guilty because I know I'm already headed downhill, but still, I never do anything to change that. I wish alcohol was never invented. I hope I can cut this off now, and I'm really going to have to try. No more parties! Parties started it all. Just be cool; then, you can't stop. It sucks. Why is it so hard to control?

Thank you for listening to me. You're doing a great job. I never would want to hurt anyone cause I have a problem.

Dylan

Mr. Nelson,

    I'm 16 years old as of last week and drank from fifth to ninth grade. It took four years and nine deaths for me to stop.

    I really enjoyed your presentation and found it very informative. There is one thing I would like to bring to your attention, probably not the first time you've heard it. It seems to me peer pressure is mentioned a lot these days. I know there is a peer pressure factor, but I think it is moving more towards not drinking.

    Whether the people drinking admit it or not, they, it seems to me, would rather be able to be non-drinkers. The most respected students in this school don't drink at all. I hope this movement continues, and I would like to be a part of the growth of non-drinkers. Thank you. Please respond.

Sincerely,
David

Mr. Nelson,

    I'd like to say thanks for you coming to talk to us today. I'm someone who drinks when I go out, but I wont drive with anyone who has been drinking. I have made a deal with my mother. It goes as follows: If I go to a party and have been drinking, and I can't find someone sober to drive me home, she'll come pick me up, and no questions asked, and she'll call me or a friend if she's been drinking. I've called her twice, and she's called me a few times.

    I would like to see more kids sign the life contract. I feel what you're doing is great, and you should continue it.

Edgar

Mr. Nelson,

    I do not drink a lot, but when I'm with my friends, I do drink. I'm in the 10th grade now. As a freshman, I was in a small car accident. We didn't hurt anybody, but my friend hit his head. He had a cut in his head. Since then, I try not to ride with my friends when they drink. I still drink and go to parties, but one of us stays sober. In the end, it works out okay. Thank you for your time.

Jay

Mr. Nelson,

    I'm 15 years old. I was formally introduced to alcohol last year. I really never thought much about it at first until I lost one of my best friends to it. Justin was drunk, but he wasn't driving. His older brother was driving, and he was also drunk. After Justin died, I began to look at my life. Alcohol had totally consumed my life. I couldn't, for the life of me, remember the last time I was sober.

My father is a sheriff's deputy, and my mother used to work at a state prison. My father's father died because alcohol ate his liver away. My mother's father is an alcoholic. But even because of that, they have never let alcohol take control of them.

I decided that I was not going to die that way, or kill an innocent person because of my negligence. I went through no rehabilitation program. I used good old-fashioned will power.

Now, I go to parties, only I don't drink. I drive drunk people home so they don't end up hurting themselves or someone else. Some people say I'm a little strange because I don't drink, but it doesn't matter to me anymore. I'm saving lives, and I'll keep it up, no matter what it takes! Thank you for caring enough to come to our school.

Tony

Dear Mr. Nelson,

I'm going to be 15 tomorrow, and my friend and I both have alcohol and drug problems. My friend is having problems at home with his parents' fighting. I drink because I get stressed at school and haven't had the parenting of a great father for ten years. I do believe that I'm getting addicted to alcohol.

I run cross country and play soccer on my school teams. I want to stop this problem, but I think I need someone to help me besides myself. I feel I hurt my mother and am going to be a bad influence on my little brother. Although my mother doesn't know, it's painful for me to do this.

Please write back, but if possible, through my teacher, so he can hand it to me.

Sincerely,
Steven

Dear Mr. Nelson,

I really appreciate you coming and talking to our Driver Education class. I would like to talk to you about my father. He was an alcoholic. I have helped my dad go to Alcoholics Anonymous four times. After the last time, he was put in the local correctional facility because he had four DUI's.

I've grown up with his alcohol problems. When he got out of the correctional facility, he went to AA for the last time. It has now been one and one-half years, and from what he was telling me, he has never touched a drop of alcohol since. I am very proud of him, and it is because I never gave up on him.

Just to let you know, I plan on signing up as a member of SADD at the end of today. I have not lived with my father for eight years and have not seen him for four years. I am very proud of him, and I'm glad that someone like you has devoted his time to help eliminate the use of alcohol by anyone and everyone.

Thank you,
Dan

Dear Mr. Nelson,

I don't think I have a drinking problem, but if it keeps going on then it could get bad. I don't want that to happen. I'm only 16 years of age. The problem isn't drinking; it's that I do a lot of drugs; not a lot, but almost every day.

When I do drugs, that is when I drink. There are a lot of people in my family who do have a problem with drinking. I don't want to turn out like them because I have seen what they have done, what they have, and what they do in life. They have done nothing, and they have nothing, only their drinks in their hands.

I don't want be like them. I know what's right, and I know what's wrong. I also know when to stop and when to go on doing what I'm doing. I smoke a lot of weed every day, but when I drink, it's mostly on weekends. When I drink, I drink hard stuff.

I'm not happy about any of that. I wish I would never drink at all. I don't know if I'm asking for help because I think I could stop on my own. I would love to keep writing to you, and I know that there are a lot of people like me, and I would like to try to help, so, if you can, write back to me. I would love to hear your feedback.

Thank you for coming,
Adam

The boys in classes I address, ages 14, 15, and 16, find it much more difficult to write about themselves than do the girls in the same age group. My experiences have been that I'll be handed eight to ten letters by girls for each one written by a boy. I do make it a point to include several representative letters from male students among those I circulate.

Keeping students' attention during a full class period is no small challenge. One device I found effective was to display a legal pad and announce:

"While the video is playing, I'll circulate this pad of paper for those of you who might want more information about SADD. We'll select two students from the list, and I'll send you letters with a lot of stuff about SADD that you can share with your friends, and I'll include a bumper sticker."

When I hold up the 'Friends Don't Let Friends Drive Drunk' sticker, expressions of approval usually are heard from several boys. Most, of course, like the prospect of getting a bumper sticker, whether they visualize pasting it on a friend's forehead or on a book cover.

My sticker probably won't end up on the family car bumper, as I might hope, or on the student's car bumper when their parents swallow the shock of insurance costs and the fear of their teenager being behind the wheel. The sign-up process does gain what I need, some boys to put their names and addresses on the pad that gets passed around the room. With girls, it's pretty automatic.

You'd never predict what single event brings absolute quiet and total attention in almost all classrooms. It's when I hold up that yellow legal pad and announce, *"While the video's playing . . ."*

Surprisingly, too, the absence of competing noises then carries through the entire class period, allowing me to reduce my voice a few decibels, most helpful on a day when I deliver five speeches.

As the students file out, I hand the teacher the completed pad and request that he or she select a boy and a girl to send the letters to. Initially, I asked teachers only to choose two students who are outgoing and influence others. Invariably, names of two girls were checked, by both men and women teachers. It was almost 100% that way and certainly wasn't what I wanted.

Now, it's always, *"Will you please check a boy and a girl for me to send the letters to?"* It works fine, and we don't neglect the boys. They're crucial, too, if the reversal in acceptance of driving drunk is to be achieved.

CHAPTER THREE

"I was really drunk, and one of the boys took advantage
of me being drunk, and to this day, I regret it."

Dear Mr. Nelson,

I go to parties every weekend, and my friends and I get drunk. I don't know why I do; maybe it's to be in the IN crowd. I don't like getting drunk, but I do. I don't like getting drunk because I do dumb things. I've never driven drunk but have ridden with people who have, and that's insane. What do I do? I don't want to be on the outside. I love my friends, but I don't like getting drunk.

My grandfather is an alcoholic, and everyone yells and tells him to quit, but he continues to drink. I yell, too, but why should I yell? I get drunk, too. I need help. Why do I do this? Why do I yell at someone for getting drunk when I do it? Please help!

Patty

Dear Mr. Nelson,

I'm 15 years old and a sophomore in high school. I usually drink on the weekends and get pretty drunk. Lately, I've been drinking more and more but no one really knows. People think I'm such a really good girl. They don't understand.

I drink a lot when I get angry, and I can't control myself when I'm drunk so I do terrible things! It gets pretty bad when I'm drunk and afterwards, I'm ashamed of myself and the mess I'm making of my life. I was so ashamed once, I tried to kill myself by swallowing a whole bunch of pills but, as you can see, I survived. I feel like a failure for what I do, but now I've realized I must help myself before anyone can help me. Thank you so very much for listening.

Cyndi

Dear Mr. Nelson,

I was recently in a situation where I was the only one who was not drunk, along with another guy who had a license. Our driver, by the end of the party, was not able to drive. I had to get the keys from him.

Mike and I had to drive everyone home, and I felt real glad because everyone could have been killed. I just turned sixteen today and will soon get my license. I'm afraid that one day someone drunk is going to drive me home. I usually drink because everyone else is. Please give me more information so I can learn to be a leader and not have to be in that situation. Thank you.

Jodi

Mr. Nelson,

I'm fifteen years old. I once was a heavy drinker and a heavy partier. I was like this for more than a year. I never got so drunk that I could not tell someone what had happened or where I was, but the point remains I drank too much.

One night, though, I did get drunk. Luckily for me, I had friends who cared enough to get me home. That was over four months ago, and I have not taken a drink since. I still go to parties, but instead of drinking, I find other things to do. In these past few months, I have met more people, made more friends, and had more fun than in that period of a year ago.

During that year, I gave up on a lot of things, such as sports, church, school, and most important, my family. I'm struggling to get back my interest in these things. I'm lucky I've got my mother's help and I've met a guy who's really willing to help me.

I'm lucky in another much more important way. I'm still alive and very thankful for that gift, so thankful that I now have the strength to say "No," so I'm sober and can help my friends like they have helped me. They don't understand why I stopped, but they seem deeply touched when I offer to help them.

I thank you for taking the time to visit our school, and sharing the facts. Thank you.

Julie

Mr. Nelson,

I drink to get drunk about once a week. It's fun. I know it's wrong, but life has been hard for me. My mom beats me up; my dad hates me, and I've been through a lot of things other teenagers never have happen to them. Up until last summer, I never drank. About three of my friends died last summer. How did

I escape? Drinking, and smoking green bud. My mom has requirements that I can't live up to. I know she doesn't like drinking, so that's what I do. I cause my own problems, but with the help of SADD, I am going to try and deal with my problems instead of fighting them. It's scary to know that someday, I could be a murderer.

Angi

Mr. Nelson,

I was put into a situation a few weeks ago where everyone at this party was drunk except me. I am 16 and only have a permit to drive. Well, anyway, I didn't drink because if someone needed to go home, I could manage.

One girl wanted to drive our family car home, and I said, "No." Well, she asked and asked and asked. I finally went out and reached in the engine and pulled on some wires until they came out. They were easy enough to fix, but I hope I saved at least one life that night.

I've given up drinking as of this year, and I have recently met a boy who also doesn't drink. We get along very well. I'm sorry I ever started drinking. I am definitely a living member of SADD. Sorry for being so dumb to drink.

Jill

Mr. Nelson,

Drunk driving is a hard topic for me to talk about. I'm 18 years old. I am known throughout some of the towns in my county as the biggest partier around. I have always been careful and cautious, and I try not to drive drunk. My parents are cool if I call them to come pick me up.

My brother is an alcoholic and has been one since he was a freshman in high school. He's 22 now. He has been in rehabilitation centers, but it doesn't do any good. He still drinks. I would very much like to join SADD, but I don't feel I could commit myself fully to it. I feel it is a good organization, and it may help a few people but I am beyond any help. The frustration I have gone through with my brother has taken away all my hope. Good luck with the rest of the students.

Carolyn

Dear Mr. Nelson,

My name is Ebony, and I have been drunk three times. My last incident was this last August. My friends and I had gotten drunk, and we were with a couple of boys. I was really drunk, and one of the boys took advantage of me being drunk and to this day I regret it. I promised myself that I would never drink again. I would like to tell you more, but the bell is about to ring. I would like to be a part of SADD.

Thank you for your time,
Ebony

Dear Mr. Nelson,

I have a friend named Arlene, and she is an alcoholic. She also smokes weed. Her mom knows what she does but just yells at her. The reason that I'm worried about her is because she doesn't see that she has a drinking problem. She believes that it's all in fun.

One time I had to try and carry her out of a public bathroom with her pants undone. Later on that night, I heard from this boy that he and three other boys had sex with her, and she didn't even know. Till this day, she still doesn't know what happened.

I tell her all the time that she has a problem, and she says that she can stop and that she will. But it's always a lie.

Thank you,
Amy

Dear Mr. Nelson,

I'm really glad teenagers are taking notice of what a danger drinking and driving is. I'm 16 years old and about a month ago, we had our junior prom. There were four of us. We went to dinner, to the prom, and back to a friend's house. We all sat around and got drunk.

At about 1:00 AM, it was time to go home, but my friend, Janet, the driver, was tipsy, and I was very drunk. I felt sure she could drive, but the real scary part was that I didn't even remember getting home. I woke up the next morning and didn't know how I got home. Since then, I've had one drink. I don't think I'll ever try that again.

Thanks for your time,
Jazette

Dear Mr. Nelson,

I used to go out every weekend and get drunk. One night, I was told to drive everyone home because they all were so drunk they couldn't walk. I only had two drinks, so I thought it wasn't affecting me at all.

As I started to drive home, I really had a hard time, but I told myself I was okay; I only had two drinks. To make a long story short, I hit another car when I was going 50 mph. I thank God no one was hurt. We could all have been killed. It shocked me out of drinking and my friends from drinking and driving.

Chantell

Mr. Nelson,

Some people say teenagers drink to be part of the "in" crowd. That may be true with some people, but I just do it because it's my own personal choice. I don't go around talking about how much or what I drank last weekend just to impress people. I drink mainly because it's just a way to relax and forget things one or two nights a week.

It's not very often I get drunk, just a bit buzzed. When everyone talks about not driving drunk, it's not good. I would think it's better not to drink at all and drive. Some people might think it's okay to drive just as long as you are not drunk. I can think of many times when I've been in a car with a driver who has been drinking. I look to see how well they are driving. If it's not steady or accurate, I might say something, but otherwise, I don't say anything.

Teenagers will always rebel; it's just the way it is. Thank you for coming and talking. You may not have totally changed everyone's view, but I think you had a big impact.

Thank you,
Maela

Dear Mr. Nelson,

I'm 15 years old, and I think I have a drinking problem. I get drunk often, but I really don't want to stop. My brother was killed by a drunk driver; he was only eleven. He would now have been twenty.

My real father was an alcoholic. Now he's dead. He died, but I don't care; I never knew him. It's just that they say these things are hereditary. My older brother is already an alcoholic. Maybe I am, too, I don't know. I am kind of worried. Well, what you said made me think. Maybe I'll get help.

Stephani

Dear Mr. Nelson,

I just finished reading the letter from Melanie. It reminded me so much of my past. When I was 7, my parents got a divorce. I ran away because my mother beat me. I left my three younger brothers.

I lived on the streets until I was 10 and then got involved in prostitution for 3 years. During those three years I had a number of abortions and became a heavy drinker and druggie/ smoker. When I was 14, we moved. I decided to go straight. It didn't work. I got back together with one of my ex-boyfriends. I got pregnant again and had the baby. I put it up for adoption.

I am now 16 and drink once in a while. I don't know if I'll ever be the same. Drinking did this to me. Please don't keep this confidential. I hope I can change lives.

Thanks for caring,
April

Dear Mr. Nelson,

I'm 15 years old and a sophomore. About four months ago, I experienced a car accident on the highway. I was very upset and had had about four beers. It was my second time drinking, so my buzz got to me fast.

I know I did wrong, but I'm a troubled girl who can't handle her problems. I'm the oldest in my home, and of course, I have more responsibilities.

About two weeks ago, I was with my friends at a park. I had too much to drink, and one of my friends took me home all drunk. She called my mom and asked her to come and get me out of the car because I didn't want to get out.

It was the first time my mom ever saw me drunk. My smallest sister and brother saw me like this. I was very embarrassed. Now my mother has lost her trust in me. I can't go out anymore. Please write back. I need help!

Sincerely,
Maria

Mr. Nelson,

Last summer, my friend and I went to McCloud. While we were there, my friend and I decided to get drunk. We didn't start out with the small stuff; we went straight for the hard stuff (Black Velvet).

While we were drunk, we lost our virginity. We weren't raped, but we really didn't want to have sex. That went on for the whole summer. Also, when we came down off the buzz, my friend got really violent. For me, I just got really silly. Everything to me was funny. This point is, I don't want to be an alcoholic. I just want to be normal.

Thanks for listening,
Sarah

Dear Mr. Nelson,

I am an alcoholic myself; well, I am recovering. My mother, step-mother, father, and step-father are all alcoholics. My father hasn't drank for five years. My step-mom is trying to quit, but it's not working.

I moved out of my mom's house because of the drinking, not because she was an alcoholic but because the alcohol was too tempting for me. My step-mom goes out and drinks and then drives home. I get real worried. I have been in a car accident involved with alcohol. I was lucky just to have a head injury, but another girl died.

She was my best friend. I'm only 15, and I'm an alcohol addict, and I'm not proud of it, but I am proud that I'm now clean and sober. Please send me more information on MADD and SADD.

Sincerely yours,
Heather

How many of you readers have seen your daughters or sisters in these situations? Did some of you even know that these events were happening until a much later date?

As the earlier letters flowed in, there seemed to be few common threads, with most writers, although their letter-writing was probably triggered by a letter they had read, apparently feeling their situation was an isolated event. But some, particularly as the number of letters I passed around increased, saw parallels, even mentioning other specific letter-writers.

Some were easy to respond to. I thought they would expect a letter from me, but maybe, that wasn't true. All of the girls who wrote again following receipt of my letter, expressed surprise and delight that I'd written back to them.

As a way of stimulating letter-writing, I would follow with a comment after reading aloud Mark's letter early in each talk. "*I wrote a long letter back to him, as I do to all students who write, . . . but I didn't get an answer.*"

It was easy to congratulate those who indicated they had recognized the damage done by their drinking and had made a positive statement about having changed. A two-page handwritten letter gave me room to develop one or two appropriate paragraphs that would fit many responses. For example:

"*Your life and your future are very precious, Julie. These are the years when you want to concentrate on your studies, make life-long friendships, and get involved in activities at your school. You can do these important things because of your personal commitment to not again allow alcohol or other mind-altering drugs to become a part of your young life.*"

I struggled for some time to write suitable letters to those whose continued drinking seemed to be a pattern they saw no reason to change.

I didn't want to try to scare or threaten them with dire consequences; teenagers don't scare easily! They will tune you out if you're not careful.

The candid revelations about hurtful sex experiences involving alcohol posed an even greater challenge. Were these girls exaggerating? Some seemed so casual in relating their experiences. Probably, I skirted around making specific comments or suggestions about future behavior. I felt that a mistake on my part was far too likely. I know now, having received more than a hundred letters from girls who outlined their experiences with 'sex' following drinking, how I handle each disclosure. Each is different to some degree and requires the most gentle approach. I can't tell them I understand their feelings, because how can I possibly do so?

The numbers of letters divulging regrettable sexual incidents involving alcohol have decreased steadily during recent years. My hope is that the problem itself has lessened. When one is handed to me I still avoid making direct recommendations, while doing my best to assure the writer that she can feel certain she is the same attractive and desirable young woman she was before the unfortunate event. I may even suggest that she might later look back and see it as just another learning experience, however hurtful it is right now. Then I keep my fingers crossed and hope I don't get another such letter.

Less frequent were letters from girls detailing experiences with over-dosing on alcohol. I could give them a more candid and direct response. An example of such a correspondence follows:

✍

Dear Mr. Nelson,

My name is Jennifer. About eight months ago I did something really stupid. I started drinking before school and during first period. I ended up passing out in class and my friends carried me to the office. I had alcohol poisoning. My blood alcohol level was .14%. I had to get my stomach pumped and I almost lost my life.

Since then I've been in several different rehabs. It changed my life. It made me think how bad it would be to lose your life at the age of 14.

Helping to stop underage drinking is the main thing, because if we stop that, it would help a lot more. None of my friends have drank since. My dad doesn't seem to trust me anymore.

Thank you!
Jennifer

☘

Dear Jennifer,

I wanted to send you this special note because you wrote such a thoughtful letter to me about your sad alcohol experience when I was at your school last Tuesday.

I like your honesty about what happened from your drinking. That had to be a real jolt for you and your parents. Fortunately, no permanent damage was done. You and your friends learned a valuable lesson about the poison effects of too much alcohol.

A girl wrote to me several years back from another school. She and a close friend attended a party. Her friend drank a lot and passed out. The boys decided to put the girl on a bed and allow her to "sleep it off." She was dead when the party ended and they checked on her.

Even I had to experience it once before I learned a lesson. I was 22 and a young naval officer, with very little experience with alcohol. I passed out and the other officers dumped me on a bed. I would surely have died except that I puked up everything. I'm sure the stench wasn't pleasant for my roommates when they finally escorted my date home and went to bed themselves.

Your life and your future and very precious, Jennifer. I hope you'll keep your determination to not again allow alcohol or other mind-altering drugs become a part of your young life.

It may take a while for your parents to regain confidence in your decision, but you can be sure that will happen.

I can tell from your letter that you're a good student. I know you will make a fine SADD member. You will be able to help many young friends in their decisions because of your own experience.

Will you write again and let me know how you're doing?

Your Friend,
Ken Nelson

And a week later in my mailbox, ...

☘

Dear Mr. Nelson,

Thank you so much for the wonderful letter. I'm halfway through your book. (Author's note: I had enclosed an extra copy of "Thoughts of a Boy Growing

Up"). Sometimes I wish I could write a book on my life and how hard it was to get through it.

Your letter meant a lot to me. It was hard seeing my parents cry and sit with me constantly in the Emergency Room. I'm so sorry for putting them through that.

It's sad how now-a-days kids and teens think that it is so cool to do drugs and drink alcohol. Thank you also for all the information you sent me. My mom was proud of me when she saw me reading all the papers.

Sometimes I wish that I could still drink. It seemed to take the pain away, but then I remember what happened and I also remember how much pain it brought into my life. I hope someday to talk to kids younger than me about the importance of life and that to ruin it with drugs and alcohol is stupid.

Write again when you have a chance. I love your letters.

Love, you friend,
Jennifer

Jennifer's next letter explained that her parents were getting a divorce and that she and her mother had moved to a different city. Her one comment about her father was that he had a serious medical problem and that "My father and I don't talk to each other anymore."

In my response I concentrated on complimenting Jennifer about the positive steps she had mentioned, but stayed away from what appeared to be a family conflict that was rubbing off on her. In two weeks another letter arrived.

✍

Dear Mr. Nelson,

About a week ago my best friend's sister died. She O.D. on Ecstasy. Her funeral was Monday. It was so sad. I'm now 15 and she was only 12. It's scary to know that kids keep getting younger and younger to try things.

I'm not sure what really happened. My best friend and I think that she (Mitzi) was trying to be cool. She was around us when we used to drink and do things. She saw what we went through, so I don't know why she would want to do something like that.

I got my first 4.0 GPA ever on my last report card! I was so proud of myself. Take care and write soon.

Much love,
Jennifer

Within a week I did write back to Jennifer, but there our correspondence ended. Was I right in reminding her that yes, her friend's younger sister should have seen what they went through and logically tried to avoid getting herself stuck in the same situation, but that maybe this 12 year old saw only the 'fun' part of getting drunk or drugged? Her fist 4.0 GPA allowed me to again express my growing confidence in Jennifer's future.

CHAPTER FOUR

"She won't change in order for her daughter
to come home. She chose alcohol over me."

Dear Mr. Nelson,

I really don't know what to say because I'm afraid for my mom. She's been drinking for about six years or more. When she first started she drank maybe two times a week but now she drinks every day, more than six beers a day. Maybe once in a while she doesn't drink, but most of the time, she does.

I love her very much, and I don't want to lose her. I tell her to stop, but then, she wants to drink more, and when she gets drunk, we always fight. I hate her when she's drunk. Sometimes I feel like it's my fault for her drinking. I don't know what to do.

I want to run away, but I can't because I know that my mom would probably kill herself because I am all she has. I love her, but I don't know what to do.

Thanks for caring,
Glorinda

Dear Mr. Nelson,

I know that drinking and driving is wrong. Driving is a privilege and a job.

I'm 16 years of age, and I've lived with my mother this last time for three years. Since I can remember, my mother has been drinking from the time she wakes up until she falls asleep. I love her with all my heart, but I can't help her anymore. I used to drink, and when I quit, I asked her to quit with me. But she said, "I'm not a drunk;" so I quit without her. I haven't had a drink in two years.

Thank you for caring about us,
Charity

Dear Mr. Nelson,

I'm 14 years old. My mom is 37 years old, and she is an alcoholic. She comes home after work and drinks. She is drunk at least three times a week. On weekends, she gets so drunk I have to drive her home from a bar. I don't know what to do. I wonder if it is me or not. What do you think I should do?

Doug

Dear Mr. Nelson,

I'm 16 years old, and I don't live with my mom or my father, mainly because alcohol has torn us apart. Since I was a little girl, both my mom and dad have been alcoholics, and my mom is the worst.

My dad has been dead for almost three years in October from alcohol. The doctors said he would have had a better chance of living, when he got in an accident, if he had a better liver.

To this day, I don't live with my mom. I've tried, but she would have mood swings, and at times I feel she hates me. I don't know the reasons she has to drink. She has had tragedies, but she's coped. I just think that alcohol is an excuse. I've talked to my mom about this situation, but every time she gets very angry.

She won't change in order for her daughter to come home. She chose alcohol over me. I'm very bitter, but I love her dearly, and without her I would be lost. Even though we live 100 miles apart, I get along better with her than when I lived with her.

When I think about what alcohol has done to my family, I wonder, and it makes me realize, what is the use of drinking? Do I want to be in the same position as my mother and father?

Thanks for caring,
Cassie

Dear Mr. Nelson,

You sometimes talk about MADD, but what if your mother is a drunk, and you try to control her and ask her to get help and she does, but she goes right back on the bottle? When she gets drunk, she gets crazy and doesn't know what she's doing. Sometimes I wish and pray to God that one day she will get help for her problem. I try to help her, but she never listens to me.

It makes me sad to see my mom's life go down the drain, and all I can do is just sit there and try to give her advice on getting help, but she doesn't listen. If she doesn't listen to her own son, then whom will she listen to? Death, maybe. I already know that it is killing her, but I don't want her to die this way.

I have a little brother (7 years), and he doesn't like it when she gets drunk. If I were old enough to live on my own, I would take my brother away from this madness my mom has brought on. She always embarrasses me in front of my friends. What should I do? Give me some advice, please.

Joe

Dear Ken,

I know how it feels to have someone in your family being an alcoholic. My mom was one of the biggest alcoholics. I used to hate my mom because she used to come in drunk, or wouldn't come home at all.

I wish I could have helped her, but there was just no way I could help her; she had to help herself. She doesn't drink now, but she used to, and it was very hard to live with someone who drank that badly, but as everyone knows, it runs in the family.

There are four girls in my family, and I think I'm headed towards being an alcoholic. Almost every weekend, I drink because it makes me feel good, and I can say anything and just let my feelings out. When I'm out, all I want is a drink or drugs. I don't take many drugs, but I do acid and weed. I seem to want them a lot, especially when I go to parties on weekends.

Well, anyway, I'm glad you came to the class and talked to us about alcoholism. I want to thank you, and I wish you would send me the information about alcoholism. Please write back.

Thank you,
Eva

Dear Mr. Nelson,

My mom drinks a lot. Every guy she's been with, especially the latest one, are all her drinking buddies. I have a drinking problem (just a little). I try to get a drink every time my mom has anything to drink. My older sister and younger brother both have drinking problems (worse than me).

I drink more now because I feel lonely and depressed. I know that's not the answer. People don't seem to like me for who I am, but for what I got (if you know what I mean).

My sister and brother have always come first. I've never really had the affection I need. The way I think I can get the affection I need, I can only get from a guy. What I mean is that he can give me affection and protection to make me feel safe.

My mother sometimes gives me a wine cooler, beer, or other things she drinks. I'm very confused about where my life is headed. My mom, brother, and I are all living with my grandma on my dad's side.

My mother never thinks or asks me what I want, or need, for that matter. She always comes first, then my sister, and my brother. My sister doesn't live with us, but she comes around a lot.

It's easier to tell you all this because you are not someone I know.

Please write me,
Kristi

Mr. Nelson,

I go to this high school, and I just moved here. I did because my dad died. My mom and dad were divorced, so I could have moved in with her. I have two brothers, too.

We decided to move out here because my aunt and uncle are more responsible than my mother. She does marijuana and cocaine. She used to drink a lot, and she got real sick, and her kidneys failed, so she went to a hospital and rehabilitation center. She doesn't drink anymore, but she does drugs.

She says she wants to see more of us since my dad died. He was an alcoholic when she was. But, I'm afraid to see her because I don't want her to get me into drugs, or even around them. I've already tried to talk to her about it, and she denied it! What should I do?

Thank you,
Elena

Dear Mr. Nelson,

My family has always had a problem with drinking. When I was ten years old, my mom married a man who was an alcoholic. He used to get drunk every day and night. He used to beat us, my mother, my brothers, and me. He was arrested many times, but my mom still took him back.

Now, we don't live with him, but it seems that every time my mom has a problem now, she drinks. I've tried to talk to her about it. All she said was that she wouldn't drink again, but you know how long that lasts.

I just need some advice to help me because I don't know what else to do. Please help me if you can. Thanks.

Jessica

Dear Mr. Nelson,

I wanted to thank you for coming and share, for a moment, something about myself. Last year, I was still living with my real mom and my stepfather. I had gone to a New Year's Eve party with my ex-boyfriend, and I was so blasted that I had passed out twice. Well, when I awoke the next morning, all of my clothes were off and so were my ex-boyfriend's.

Four months later, I found that I was pregnant, but I lost the baby. I still drink at times to the point where I get buzzed. I'm only 16 years old. I need someone who cares and has good advice.

Another problem I have is that there's not a day that goes by that I don't worry about my real mom, because her second husband, Brian, has an alcoholic and drug problem. She was so into this guy (and still is) that she let him beat up on both of us. She let him kick me out of the house two times.

On the second time he kicked me out, I went to live with my friend, and her parents asked for legal custody and got it. But, what hurts the most is that my mom allowed it!

Thanks for your time and an ear that would listen.

Sandie

Dear Ken Nelson,

My mom has been drinking as long as I can remember. I've talked to her, I've run away, and about three years later, she married a drug abuser. She still drinks a lot.

So now I don't live with her. I miss her. My sister is still with her. I'm so scared because my sister is in danger. I don't want my family hurt or dead. I want to see her and want to see my child born between now and then.

I live in a foster home. I've been in this foster home for ten months. Sometimes, I wonder if I will ever see my mom and step-dad stop drinking and using drugs. The reason why I had to leave my mom is because I didn't want to be like her when I get older. Thank you for listening.

Shelly

Mr. Nelson,

You just read us a letter from a girl who has an alcoholic mother. My mother is the same way. She is constantly drinking from the moment she gets out of bed in the morning.

I'm worried about her because she is not the same person I knew four or five years ago. I caught her hiding her beer and lying to my father and me about it. She won't admit that she has a drinking problem.

I wish I could help her, but whenever I say anything to her she wants to agree with me. For three years now, my life has been going downhill due to my mom's drinking. I love my mom, she means the world to me, but I'm beginning to get to where I can't stand her any longer.

I'm glad you came to class today because I needed someone to tell this to. I don't feel comfortable talking to people here at school because I have to see them every day. I'm really glad you came to talk to us, and I'm glad you're willing to listen to us teenagers who have problems talking to people.

I hope you can help me with my problem with my mom. I would really appreciate it. Please write back.

Sincerely,
Shelly

Dear Mr. Nelson,

I don't believe in drinking and driving because that's how my mother was killed. Alcohol and drugs were involved.

In March 1973, my mother (she was only 16) and father went to San Francisco with two friends. The guy driving was tripping out on drugs and started drinking. They crashed into an apartment building and killed the two girls on the passenger side. The report said the car was going 90 to 100 mph.

Sometimes, I wish it was my father because I never had a chance to know my mother. I was only two months old.

Ever since my mother died, I've been in foster homes. I've had two stepmothers and was an abused child all my life. My father is now a drug addict and so is my stepmother. My younger brother drinks and takes drugs.

That's why I'm for SADD.

Rhonda

Dear Mr. Nelson,

I've been thinking about what you said to me and my classmates. I really want to thank you.

I would like to tell you about a problem I have at home. It's really hard for me to say this, but I need to tell someone.

My mom has been drinking every day for the past few months. When she drinks she blames me for her problems, then we get into a big fight, and she takes off in the car. I have tried to help her. All she says is, "It's my life, not yours, so butt out."

I love her so much, and I don't want anything to happen to her. I do admit I drink, but only once in a great while. When my mom finds out, I get in trouble. I tell her she does it so it can't be that bad. Then I get grounded.

If you can, will you please help me?

Thank you,
Tina

Dear Mr. Nelson,

My mother is an alcoholic. I've been around alcohol all my life. When I was younger, I was proud to have this woman as my mother. I don't know how she got into drinking. I noticed as each year went by, she was becoming more of an alcoholic.

She left me, and sent me with relatives, and sometimes cruel, mean people. Through these years, I continuously tried to get her to stop. She started getting alcoholic boyfriends, of which a majority of them abused my brother and me both physically and mentally.

It's been over two years since I've lived with her. I couldn't take it anymore. The stress of everything that was caused by her alcoholism made me high-stressed and nerve-wracked. I live in a foster home now.

I felt that it would have to be her choice, and now she is trying to quit. I don't know how long she hasn't drank. I will never live with her again because of the bad feelings between us. I love her. Although I couldn't help my mom, I feel I can help someone else. I wish I could have helped her.

Thanks for caring,
Greta

Dear Mr. Nelson,

My mother is an alcoholic, but she won't admit it. She doesn't drink constantly, but even once every month is too much for her. When she starts, she'll never stop. She stays out all night, and I won't see her until the next day. Then when I see her, she always apologizes and says she realized she made a mistake.

If it were only me, I wouldn't care as much, but it isn't. I have four sisters but only live with one. She's only six. She deserves better than this life. But if it were only me and her, it could be handled.

I'm 15, almost 16, but I could take care of her while my mother is out. But now my stepfather comes in. when he comes home and finds my mother out drinking, he gets furious (not with me or my sister). He usually gives me some money and my boyfriend takes us to dinner, and my father leaves too, and goes out and drinks.

The next day, when I come home from school, my parents are either arguing or the cops have made it there. It's pretty embarrassing, but truthfully, I'm pretty used to it. The neighbors are even used to it.

My boyfriend and I are really serious and plan to live together in about two years. I want my sister to live with us. How do I tell my parents what's best for her? It really would be! My boyfriend thinks so, too.

Please write back and give me a little advice. It would be really appreciated. Sorry for taking up your time.

Thanks for everything,
Melissa

Dear Mr. Nelson,

I have a friend whose mother is a drunk. She used to want to commit suicide in order to get away from the hurt and pain her mother used to inflict on her. I talked her out of it after a while.

One night, I spent the night there after our homecoming game. She had been out all day with her husband. When she got home, she was really drunk and my friend was scared about what her mother would do to me. I was afraid. She was really loud. So, in order to be sure that we'd be safe, my friend and I slept outside.

I am still friends with this girl, but I haven't gone back to spend the night. Thanks for caring what happens to us.

Virginia

Dear Mr. Nelson,

I don't know you and you don't know me, but you seem like a very caring and special person. I noticed that some people shared a few problems with you. Now, I want to share something with you.

My mother and father got divorced when I was very little, and I lived with my grandmother. I lived with my grandmother for nine years, and off and on, I saw my mother and father. I was never really close to my mother.

Well, when I turned ten, I went and moved with my father and step-mom. My mom and I lost touch. She used to say she hated me. She used to tell me I wasn't good enough for her and that I wasn't her daughter. I used to think it was me, it was my grades, or I wasn't doing something right.

Just recently, I found out that my mother was on hard drugs and liquor. I had always thought that she didn't love me, but it was the drugs that were talking. I thought I wasn't good enough for her and that I wasn't her daughter.

About a week ago, I called her. We hadn't talked in over five years, and she told me she was off. I thought I believed her because it was my mother saying it and not the drugs. But then I realized she hadn't stopped at all. She shoots up every day and snorts. She got my older brother doing it, and now he's a nobody. How could she do this?

There is so much hatred that I have for her. I mean I guess I'm just extremely confused. I love her more than myself, but I just don't understand. Thanks, Mr. Nelson, for listening.

Cassandra

Dear Mr. Nelson,

My mom is an alcoholic. We always get into fights. She blames everything on me and always denies what she's doing. I want to help her, but I can't. It's almost as if she depends on me for everything.

I can't leave her, although, I sometimes want to get away and move to my grandma's, but she won't let me. You said we children are our parents' most precious thing. Well, I don't feel precious. I would like to know why my mom does what she does. I don't really understand it. Why can't she just quit?

I sometimes can't quit hating her for what she does. She parties all the time and always dumps me off at my grandma's. Sometimes, when she's drunk, she sleeps around with guys and never spends time with me.

I don't see my father, so she's all I have except for my grandma. I love her, yet hate her. Please send me more information so I can understand better. Thanks.

Carolyn

Dear Mr. Nelson,

This is really hard for me to accept, but my mom is an alcoholic. She was almost killed, when I was two, by a drunk driver, and now she uses alcohol to cope with her disability. She is paralyzed on the right side of her body. I don't know my father, so she's all I've got.

My mother had many boyfriends when I was younger, and she was severely abused. I was molested. My grandmother told me that the only reason my mom came out of her coma after the wreck was because of me. Now, I hardly want to be around her.

She stays out all night and comes home always with a new array of bruises and cuts and burns. About four months ago, she fell down an entire flight of concrete steps and split her head and got eight stitches. She scares me, and I'm going to try to be very careful. Thank you for making a difference, and keep talking to students. They'll never know unless they're told.

Angelique

Is there a more tender and more promising relationship than one between a mother and daughter? I'm sure that most young girls want to be just like their mom.

As I received and read each of the previous letters, it became clear that once the bond is established, daughters don't give up on their alcohol-abusing mothers. There seemed to be no length of time that wouldn't be bridged if only the mother would give up alcohol.

But until that happened, and those cases covered by the letters were too rare, the numbing feeling was consistent: *"She chose alcohol over me."*

Some girls, of course, did express anger and even hate, but all of this seemed ready to change if only their mother returned to being a 'mother.'

Some readers have expressed surprise that the letters I circulated indicate rather good spelling and grammar. How can that be when we read of such a need to improve those skills by the freshman-sophomore levels of high school?

I've opted to edit them for spelling myself, although some of my friends have suggested that I reproduce the letters exactly as they were written, to give them more authenticity.

When I hold up to each class the package of letters I'm about to distribute, I try to be honest with them.

"You'll note that the letters are all typed. I've done that so they'll be more readable. I've also corrected the spelling because some of the students just didn't spell well." I usually get some muted chuckles here. "I want you to concentrate on how you would handle each situation if it were yours, rather than puzzle over a word."

It is also my belief that if the students see words correctly spelled on the letters they are reading, it is quite possible they will be more accurate in their writing.

Immediately after placing two pages of letters on the front desk of each row, I continue the program with the assurance, . . . "It doesn't bother me a bit if close to a third of you are reading while I'm speaking."

A question most often asked by adult readers of the teenage letters is, "What on earth do you say to these kids? You're not a psychologist or a counselor. Do you think they do any differently after you write?"

Here is another sequence that will provide my readers with some encouragement. You might say that "Half a loaf is better than none."

✍

Dear Mr. Nelson,

Hi, my name is Mitzi. I'm 15 and in 10th grade. Alcoholics run in my family. My dad was a drunk but isn't anymore. My mom and younger sister (who's only 13) are major drinkers.

I started drinking about a year ago. I've also tried drugs, and I'm afraid that I'm not going to be able to stop. I've also started smoking.

All of my friends drink. I've only been really drunk a few times and only drink on weekends, but I see that my mom, my sister, and I need help. If you know any way to help us, please write to me. Thank you for your time.

Sincerely,
Mitzi

✍

Dear Mitzi,

I wanted to send you this special note because you wrote such a thoughtful letter to me about your family's alcohol abuse problems when I was at your school last Friday.

The brightest spot in your letter was that your father is no longer a drunk. I'm sure it wasn't easy for him to give up drinking, but he's proof it can be done. Hopefully, your mother is thinking of doing the same.

I'm especially worried about your and your younger sister's drinking. Thanks for being so honest about what is happening.

You may be beginning to realize that alcohol is a very treacherous drug, Mitzi. What almost always begins as so much 'fun' soon becomes a very bad habit. From there it's often only a short step to some tragedy involving a car, or to the start of a lifetime addiction to the alcohol.

You're right in saying that the three of you do need help. I hope you'll be as honest with a school counselor as you have been with me. They can give you some really helpful suggestions about how to start getting away from alcohol. Will you do that for me?

Your life and future are very precious. These are the years when you do want to concentrate on your studies, on making some really worthwhile friendships, and getting involved in some of the interesting activities at your school.

You can do these important things if you find a way to make sure that alcohol or other mind-altering drugs don't control your young life.

I know you'll make a wonderful SADD member. Once you get this drinking behind you, you'll be able to help many young friends in their decisions because of your experiences.

Will you write again, and tell me what you plan to do?

Your friend,
Ken Nelson

✍

Dear Mr. Nelson,

Thank you for sending me the information I wanted. It helped me a lot.

My mom and I are having our first counseling session together this Thursday so we can work on this problem together!

My sister, on the other hand, isn't doing so well. She just got out of juvenile hall a week before Christmas, and she's already messing up with drugs and alcohol. She still goes with her gang rules and friends. I don't know how I can help her. I've tried to talk with her, but she just acts like she doesn't need help.

Do you know any way I can help her? I'd appreciate any help or info you could provide. Well, thanks for caring.

Love always,
Mitzi

Mitzi didn't respond to the third letter that I penned to her. There was likely little for her to add about her younger sister's woes. My only new suggestion was that Mitzi stick by her sister, not to give up on her. On the other hand, I felt it prudent that she not make excuses for her sister, that her best route was to be loving but firm. She and her mom were showing the way. Her sister couldn't help but observe the positive changes, the decision to change must be hers.

I make it a point to always assure my writers who have expressed 'hate' for their alcohol-abusing mothers, that this is an understandable and acceptable feeling on their part. It is critical too, that I remind these very young daughters and sons that they can't possibly be the 'at fault' person in some of the awful situations they describe, as many feel they are.

These teenagers also need assurances that changes can take place in an alcoholic's or drug addict's life. Hope must never be totally lost!

Although I caution about the negative consequences of arguing with a drunk person, I do assure the writers that opportunities will surface where dialogue may be helpful: "There will be times when your mother is completely sober and seems to want to talk seriously with you about herself. That will be the perfect time to express your worries and your need to have her 'be a mother again.'"

CHAPTER FIVE

"My parents don't know I've started drinking again,
and I'm not sure how I should tell them,
or even if I want to tell them."

Mr. Nelson,

I'm 16 and a junior. I am an alcoholic. Like every other teenager, I thought I was just drinking to have a good time and to fit in. My friends and I used to drink every weekend and occasionally during the week at school. My entire sophomore year I dedicated to partying.

As the year progressed I got drunk more and more often. I even changed what I drank. I used to just drink beer, but I didn't like having to drink five beers before I felt something so I moved on to harder stuff. I started drinking rum, brandy, Schnapp's, but found my favorite, vodka.

At first, I had to chase it with coke, then moved to a beer chase and finally just drinking it straight. My friends and I kept it in the trunk of one's car. We'd buy a fifth a week (we always had buyers). As long as we had it, I'd drink it, in class, after class, in between, anytime, and gradually, all the time.

I became known for how much alcohol I could hold, and back then, I was quite proud of it. I could out drink a lot of guys. All my friends drank a lot, but I drank the most. When we were together and drunk, we'd all joke and kid about being alcoholics. That's when I thought it was a joke.

I consider myself very lucky. Less than a year later, I moved back with my family, away from my friends. I finally accepted my drinking as a serious problem.

That night, I was drunk off my ass, and I don't know why, but I thought about some of my relatives. My grandma—an alcoholic, my aunt—an alcoholic, and my uncle—an alcoholic who died, drunk and shot in the head by a friend who was also drunk. I was more scared than I had ever been in my life. I didn't want to face my family. I wanted to die.

Luckily, I was with a friend who truly cared and recognized I had a problem. She called my parents, and they came. As soon as I saw my mom, I cried in her arms and asked for help. It was her brother who died, and she told me she'd do anything to keep me from making a mistake like he did, not admitting to alcoholism.

Now, I'm happy and going through counseling. I haven't drank in 54 days. I feel strong, and I know I won't drink again. My family and friends have supported me the entire time. I've found a reason to live. I just hope other teenagers do, too, before it's too late.

Your time is appreciated,
Allexis

Mr. Nelson,

Your presentation was great. The way I feel about drinking is that everyone has to die some day and all of my friends drink. I care about all of them a lot, but once that beer can is open, or that bottle top is removed, it just doesn't matter anymore, because you are a totally different person starting then.

Drinking just means accepting the devil to come into you and make you do bad and weird things. Is that as fun as people make it out to be? I'm someone who's been there and knows.

Kayla

Dear Mr. Nelson,

I'm fifteen years of age and have illegally driven drunk three times in my freshman year. In elementary school, my friends and I always said that we'd never do anything of the sort, but when the times came, it was almost impossible to resist. Only once has someone tried to stop me, and I listened. It was funny because we weren't good friends at all.

People just don't know how hard it is to say "No" when you're at a party. A couple of friends who I go to parties with don't drink, and I'm envious towards them. Now I believe I've reached a plateau with it and just decided not to drink again. I've gone to many parties since and have not drank. Also, I've realized girls like it better when you're sober.

Sincerely,
Brian

Dear Mr. Nelson,

I'm a seventeen-year-old sophomore, and I have a problem. My parents say it isn't alcoholism, but after drinking for eight to ten months, I would say that it is. I go out with my friends to party and other things. On the way home, I keep thinking that my friend will crash or even one very scary word, DEATH. I have tried to stop, but I keep starting again. I want to live, but not in a hell hole.

Scotti

Mr. Nelson,

You're a great guy! I used to drink a lot! I used to drink so bad that I would black out. Anything would make me drink. I would get mad and upset, and I would get drunk.

Then, one Monday, I came to school and found out one of my good friends had died. Then, I realized, god, that could be me one of these days.

I can't say I don't drink anymore, but I don't drink that much anymore. My other problem is I don't know how to say "No" to my friends when they are going to drive me home drunk.

Could you write to me and help me out?

Thank you,
Seana

Mr. Nelson,

My name isn't important, but I'm writing this letter to let you know two things. I don't drink anymore. Once I did. I wasn't an alcoholic or anything.

I learned my lesson the hard way, though. One night, I got drunk with some guys. All I know is when I woke up I had a headache. Three months later, I found I was pregnant. I don't really believe in abortions, but that was my only choice. I wouldn't have known who the father was anyway.

My point here is that drinking is a big mistake. Take it from me as a teenager. Most teenagers are so hard-headed they don't want to listen. Teenagers usually end up learning the hard way. It's good you are making an effort.

Louneesha

Mr. Nelson,

I, myself, am an alcoholic! My family has a great history of being alcoholics. I've been suspended for three days because of my being drunk during school hours.

My parents know that I have drinking problems and because of it, we (my parents and I) don't have a relationship. That really bothers me. Plus, my best friend has the same problem with drinking. Thank you for coming to our school.

Laurie

Dear Mr. Nelson,

Hi, my name is Julie. I had a drinking problem until just recently when my mom and dad found out. They got really angry with me, and I got into a lot of trouble.

I haven't had a drink of anything for a month now. I'm really proud that I can finally say "No!" I think it's great that you go and talk to us young people. I'm moving to Nez Perce, Idaho in three weeks. Please, could we keep in touch? I'd love it if we could write back and forth to each other.

Julie

Dear Mr. Nelson,

The bell is going to ring in a few minutes so I have to hurry and get to the point. I think I'm an alcoholic and a druggie, and I like it. Sometimes, I want to stop, but I can't. I love it. I'm scared. I want a way out!

I've tried to commit suicide several times, and I'm afraid I'll try again. I'm trying to turn away from harming myself. I punch things for my frustrations.

I resort to drugs and alcohol almost every day. I'm falling down the tubes. Please help me!!

Thanks,
Autumn

Dear Mr. Nelson,

I'm writing to tell you what happened to me when I was drinking. I used to go out every weekend and get so drunk that I couldn't even walk. At first, it was no big deal, but then it started problems at home, and I got kicked out of my house because I started drinking more often than every weekend. It started being every other day.

I got to the point where I tried to kill myself. That didn't stop me. Just recently, I tried to kill myself again, and I had been drinking. This time, it took a big affect on me. I'm getting help so I am stronger. I haven't yet gone home but am living with my aunt. These are only half of the things that happened.

Thanks,
Mandee

Dear Mr. Nelson,

I'm not one of those people who believes that they should go to parties and get drunk for the hell of it. I've been seriously drinking since I was nine to get my problems of the past off my mind.

I tried to stop last year in March, but it only lasted until September of this year. When I'm sober, I have time to think about my problems at home, what I have to look forward to, and what my mind seems to make me remember.

Everyone today says "Just say no," but that's much easier said than done. Being a teenager is one of the most difficult things to deal with in life. All I can say is that I hope most people are strong enough to deal with it. So far, I'm not.

Thanks,
Kristi

Mr. Nelson,

I'm 16 and a sophomore. Two of my friends and I are drinking quite a bit. As of now, we're trying to quit, although it's very hard. Peer pressure plays a big part in our drinking. I really don't know why I drink, but I guess I do it to fit in. My parents don't know about this, and I'm afraid of what they would say if they found out. Since I've been drinking, I've been lying to my parents so I can go out and party.

Rhonda

Dear Mr. Nelson,

My boyfriend and my mother are both alcoholics. My boyfriend drinks every day. He's 23 years old, and he's ruining his life. He's admitted to me that he's an alcoholic, but to no one else. He's even promised me that he'd quit, but he never does. I want to help him, but he's so pig-headed he won't listen to a word I say.

Sometimes, I feel like if I left him he would quit if he really loved me, but it wouldn't help. I don't want to see him ruin his life. I want to help!

Now my mom is worse. She's been in the hospital for her alcohol problem. The doctors told her to stop drinking, but she can't. I've tried to help, but she won't listen. She won't listen to anyone, so I'm never home anymore to see her.

I drink with my boyfriend a lot, but I'm trying to quit, and I'm hoping he'll see that you can have fun without drinking. I don't want to become an alcoholic. Will you please write to me, and give me some hints on how to help my boyfriend?

Thank you,
Sidney

Dear Mr. Nelson,

I live with an alcoholic father and a recovered alcoholic mother. They don't have much to do with one another. My 29 year old brother moved out two and a half years ago. He drank constantly and was on hard drugs.

I drank occasionally in 8th grade, just enough to make me silly. By last year, I became a drinker. I only liked the hard stuff. I was drinking before school, sometimes during lunch, after school, and from Friday after school until Sunday nights. If I wasn't at a party, I was throwing one.

I wouldn't remember a thing. Guys knew I wanted sex when I was drunk. Along the way, I picked up the title "slut." It was funny to everyone. I began cheating on my boyfriends, but never got caught. I seemed to be drunk constantly.

One guy I was seeing was a druggie and drank. He said he wouldn't stay with me unless I quit drinking. I was surprised and hardly believed him.

When he and I got together, we both quit everything. I've given myself a new reputation. I have good grades, get along with my parents, and feel good. Ten months later, he and I are still together. We do drink occasionally but make sure we stay at one place for the night. We don't go to parties.

My friends hate him for the way I now am. They still drink and don't understand. I'm left with friends but not good friends.

My sister is only 12 and is worse than I was. I'm really scared for her.

Sonji

Ken Nelson,

I'm a 16 year old sophomore. I have been drinking since I was 11 years old. I've always hung around older people because my brother is now 20 and their main thing on weekends is "Let's go get drunk." I was young, so I said, "Sure, why not?" They would always tell me, "You can't hang around us unless you're going to be like us." That meant always getting drunk, and I think my brother is never going to stop 'cause my mom has a really bad problem with drinking. She is 37 and drinking her life away. I'm always trying to talk to them about drinking, but they always change the subject. What do I do?

I'm always having to drive people home 'cause I drink the least, but I don't want to drink at all. I hate it, but I want to hang around my friends. I really wish I could help them; I just don't know how.

Can you please write me and help me, and tell me how or what I can do before all of us die from trying to be cool like everyone else. I think you are a real understanding guy.

Jennifer

Mr. Nelson,

I guess the reason that I'm writing this letter is because I'm worried about myself. I seem to get a craving for alcohol all of the time.

My father is an alcoholic. He has been forever. His father is, too. I am really concerned. I try to ignore the craving when it comes, but the only way it goes away is by alcohol. I do believe that I'm going to become an alcoholic.

I don't want to end up getting drunk every day. Now, I drink casually every other day. A lot of my friends are older and are alcoholics already. I find myself with them when I drink, too. I feel I will never change for the better.

Thank you for being here and listening,
Kelly

Dear Mr. Nelson,

I'm 15 years old and come from a family with a history of alcoholism, and I'm really scared I might become a part of that history. I have been drunk many, many times, and everyone warns me about alcoholism, but I just don't seem to listen.

When I was about 10 years old, I got drunk for the first time with a bunch of people I didn't even know, and four strangers took advantage of me, or so I was told. I'm not actually sure what happened. All I know is I regret even getting a taste of alcohol.

I love the idea of MADD and SADD. I guess you wish you could find a way to get rid of alcohol, but I know that is impossible. Could you send me some information about SADD and a way I can prevent myself from becoming an alcoholic. Thank you.

Yours truly,
Aleesha

Dear Mr. Nelson,

I'm in the 10th grade at this school. My father is a very heavy drunk. Every weekend, he goes and spends all of his money on alcohol. When he is not drunk, he is a father, but when he is drunk, he is an abuser.

Luckily, he had to move out for committing a very stupid mistake with me. I just wish he'd stop drinking. I don't know what to do to help him, but I think I'm now going towards that direction.

Just a month ago I left school to be with some friends. When I saw they were drinking, I started to drink. I also wanted to drink because I was depressed. Now, every time I'm depressed, I want to drink.

I think I need help. If you can get me some help, please do.

Thank you,
Betty

Mr. Nelson,

I have a big problem. My dad is an alcoholic. I'm scared that I'm going to be the same way because I don't know how to say "No." My friends don't help.

I want to know what I can do to be more strong and learn to say "No," and how to tell my friends that they should learn to say "No," and how to also tell my friends that they should chill on the booze, because they all love it.

Should I look for new friends or just learn to say "No"? I don't want anybody else to know about this. I don't trust anybody else, not even my family.

Tanya

Mr. Nelson,

I'm glad you came and talked with us, but it was not you that made me think. It was one of the girl's letters. You see, I understand what she is going through.

All my life I have been raped by two family members. But, now we live here, away from them. My mother knows and I am getting help, but what I'm writing to say is that I thought I could do every thing on my own.

This letter got me crying and thinking a lot more. All of my friends drink and I do every once in a while, but I will make sure that someone I trust is around. I won't spend the night in a friend's house. I haven't spent the night at anyone's house for about two years, so I guess you could say I'm a messed up little girl.

People all of the time think there's something wrong with me. I mean, don't get me wrong, I have lots of friends like other people, and I hate that. But life goes on, so as you know I'm just writing to say thanks and you got to me.

Michelle

Dear Mr. Nelson,

My name is Fawn. I'm 15 years old and realizing my life is falling apart. My father was an alcoholic for most of his life and my brother (18) has been drinking heavily for a year or so now and it scares me. It has torn my family apart many times. While growing up with my brother we never got along, and now that he's moved out of the house and back to Colorado, I'm afraid I'm going to lose him for good.

I had drunk alcohol a couple of times. I never really liked the taste of it, but now it's like I'm realizing that my dad drank when he had problems he couldn't handle. That's basically when my brother and I started drinking. My brother started drinking little by little when he was fourteen. I didn't drink then. But when I was 14 years old I started drinking after I had to tell my mom I was raped by a friend of my brother who was drunk.

After my life had started falling apart, I'd listen to my dad saying, "Well, when I drink it doesn't hurt anymore," or my brother say, "When you feel good, nothing can bring you down," so I tried it.

I didn't want to care anymore, and I still don't. But I discovered that it hurt 100 times more when you wake up in the morning, not with the hangover, but with the hurt I started out with. Even though I know what it feels like, the first thing I say is, "I want to get wasted so bad," and nine out of ten times I do.

I'm afraid I'm going to do serious damage to myself and my family that I won't be able to fix, but what really scares me is that since I've lost so much and hurt so bad, I really don't care who I hurt, even if it is me.

What kind of person does that make me, uncaring, confused, selfish? I don't want to be like this, really I don't. I'm just tired of the pain and all.

Love,
Fawn

Dear Mr. Nelson,

I don't have a drinking problem and I hardly drink at all. I know "hardly at all" sounds like I'm lying, but I'm not. I am willing to quit but it's not the quitting that's hard, it's the friends you have who say it's cool.

The hardest thing to do at a party is to say "No" to alcohol. I've been trying to stop completely but it's just really hard to stop.

Sincerely yours,
Vince

Mr. Nelson,

I really enjoyed listening to you. My parents split up about a month ago after being married for nineteen years. Lately, since then, I have been drinking a lot more than I ever did before.

I'm afraid that I'm going to lose my girlfriend if I keep it up, but sometimes I think that she and alcohol are all that I have now. I love her a lot but I'm afraid I'm going to get drunk and do something with another girl.

I am going to have to quit drinking. Please write and help.

Sincerely,
Joel

Dear Mr. Nelson,

In one of the letters you passed around, a person asked why anyone would want to drink if they know it's bad for them. I want to answer that.

I've been drinking ever since I was a baby and could hold a bottle. My whole family drinks and some of them have been stopped for drunk driving. I myself have a hard time not drinking when I see alcohol. I know it's very bad for me but my body wants it. I don't drink regularly, but it's still a problem for me.

Maybe when you talk about teenagers drinking because of peer pressure, you might want to talk about drinking because their parents give them alcohol, like my mother and myself.

Sincerely,
Melissa

Dear Mr. Nelson,

That first letter you read really got to me. I know how this boy feels. Just this summer I started drinking and now I don't think I can stop. It happens so quickly

I first noticed that I had a serious problem last weekend when I woke up with a guy I didn't even know. I'm very scared and I don't know what to do. I'm a very shy person and don't make friends easily, but when I drink I'm a whole new person. I'm not Megan anymore.

It really frustrates me because I want to be outgoing all the time, not just when I'm drinking. After every party I tell myself, "No more drinking," but the next weekend I'm holding a beer.

It scares me most because my friends are really cool and they never offer anyone alcohol. I get it myself. More than once I've gotten in a car with a drunk driver to "make a beer run." I don't know what to do! If my mom ever found out, she would kill me.

Thank you,
Megan

Dear Mr. Nelson,

I've had plenty of problems with alcohol. I had my first drink when I was nine years old. I'm now fifteen. It was a very heavy screwdriver.

I often drink, not at parties, but with my family. My aunt takes me to bars and clubs. I don't want to say "No" because everyone will get on my case for being weak. The worst thing is my aunt pushes me the hardest.

I was at her house once and she made me keep drinking. She kept giving me more and more beers. I've never thrown up but I've done things I now regret.

I had sex for the first time with a boy who was drunk and kept pressuring me every time I saw him until one time when I was really wasted he got me into bed. I have no idea if I'm pregnant or not now, and I'm very scared. I'm just so scared and I really wish I had had the strength to say "No." Thanks so much for listening.

Lolli Rose

Dear Mr. Nelson,

Hi, my name is Desiree. I know that it's bad to drink and drive. I also know that drinking is bad altogether. Even though I know it's wrong, I drink fairly often, about two or three times a week. I do it because I think that people who care about me don't understand what I'm going through.

I do smoke pot and drink. I just broke up with my boyfriend. My parents are divorced, and I'm getting in more fights with my friends and siblings.

I've tried to get help but no one tries to help me except one or two of my best friends. They help, or try to help me stop.

I've been drinking for about two years. I have been smoking pot for about one year and five months. Doing both (drinking and driving and smoking) don't mix. It is hard to stop.

My parents don't know about any of the stuff I do. But, since I have nowhere else to turn to, I'm turning to you. Please help me!

Sincerely,
Desiree

Dear Mr. Nelson,

I'm 16 years old and have been drinking for three years. I'm embarrassed that I have to drink every weekend. I used to drink only a little. Now I can drink four Bacardi Breezers at a time. I spend almost all my paychecks on alcohol.

I find that when I'm drunk I have sex more freely. I've lost my boyfriend who I've been going out with for three years. He's a freshman in college now. It started with my only drinking one beer and he didn't mind. Now I drink Everclear, vodka and Schnapp's. He could not stand how violent I got when I drink.

My boyfriend and I are getting back together but I'm having problems because I'm known as a partier and everyone expects me to party. Help me so when I go out on weekends, I will be able to say, "Hey, I know where I live," instead of having to ask where I live.

I would join SADD, but this organization needs someone who can uphold what they represent.

Write me, please,
Lynn

Dear Mr. Nelson,

My mom is a really bad alcoholic. Ever since I was born she has been drinking. When I was younger she would always beat me. When my father left he used to send her money to buy my food and clothes. She didn't buy any of that, she bought liquor.

I hate her for everything she's done to me. I have run away because of my family alcohol problem. Now, when my mom and step-dad are away, I sneak liquor from them. I don't know what to do. I don't want to become an alcoholic. Can you help me?

Thank you,
Ann

Dear Mr. Nelson,

I have a problem that I can't get rid of. My step-dad is an alcoholic and is addicted to marijuana. He sells it, too. My dad is very verbally abusive with me. My little sister lives with us, too, and she's his real kid. He treats her like a queen and I get treated like a slave.

My mom doesn't get involved anymore because she knows nothing will change. I'm real nervous around my dad and am always in my room. That makes my parents more angry with me.

I was raped by two friends this summer and having to deal with all of the legal stuff and counseling has put stress on my family. I've run away before, and was forced back home. I've thought about suicide but I could never go through with it. I hope to get out soon. Please send a response.

A troubled sophomore,
Heather

Dear Mr. Nelson,

Right now you are talking to our class and the things you are saying are really touching me, mostly because I'm in a situation similar to the ones you're talking about. Right now I really don't know if I have a drinking problem or not. All I know is whenever I'm around drinking I end up drinking as well, even when I say I'm not going to drink.

I'm a sophomore here at this school and everyone thinks drinking and parties go together. Last year in junior high I was sure I had a drinking problem. I used to come to school drunk almost every other day. My parents found out and said that I shouldn't drink because my dad's side of the family all have drinking or drug problems.

My parents don't know I've started drinking again and I'm not sure how I should tell them, or even if I want to tell them. I'm scared and confused. I'm not able to drive yet since I'm only 15 years old but I'm scared that when I start driving I'm still going to be drinking, and maybe with a worse problem.

I can't really talk to my friends about it because admitting that you have a drinking problem is embarrassing. People would think that I can't "handle" my alcohol or something like that.

I'm not really sure why I decided to write to you. Maybe I got the feeling that you understand and really care. I trust my counselors but they would all be disappointed in me. My grades last year weren't real great, and this year they're bad again. I had A's and B's before I started drinking and all drinking has done for me has ruined my life, and it's getting worse. Although I realize it's messing my life up I keep drinking, so I guess that means I have a problem.

Please send me some information on drinking and alcoholism and drinking and driving.

Thanks for listening,
Jennifer

When are personal hand-written stories related to teenagers serious enough to warrant alerting school counselors?

That was a debate I soon had with myself. I showed several of the letters in question to some of my family and friends, and asked what they would do if they were in my shoes. Their reactions were positive enough to make my decisions easier. After studying a letter, their comments were consistent.

"Can't you see that this boy (or girl) is crying out for help? I'd surely let a counselor handle it."

School counselors everywhere seem to be busy people. Sometimes I waited almost half an hour for one to complete the interview he was conducting. At the start, most school counselors were reluctant to give me their time. I would watch the secretaries standing in the doorway of the counselor's office trying to explain who I was. Mr. Nelson certainly wasn't a parent. Why would a white-haired older man need to talk with a counselor? What could this information have to do with any of the students assigned to me? What was he selling?

After a few minutes in their offices, and a tedious explanation that I was merely a volunteer guest speaker in that particular class, and had been handed a letter that I thought needed a counselor's attention, the receptions became friendly, though still questioning.

"Why would one of our students write to you?"

Further explanation was needed to assure each counselor that my having letters written while I was speaking to a class had become rather normal. I acknowledged that I wasn't really sure why the teenagers opened up to me, but I was glad they had. I would explain that part of my program included the circulation of prior letters received from students at other high schools, and that this unquestionably had stimulated his student to want to tell her story.

Over a period of fifteen years I probably took no more than 150 letters to school counselors. I came to know and respect one or more counselors from each school that I regularly visited. Soon I was given an almost immediate audience. They were gracious, and openly welcomed the opportunity to address their student's expressed problems.

My only request of counselors was precise from the start. They must wait until I had responded to the student in writing, and had alerted the teenagers that I was asking his/her school counselor to get in touch with them. I normally would ask that the counselor wait a week from the time of my visit to allow their student time to receive my letter and read it thoroughly.

After a few trial wordings, I designed two paragraphs that became a standard part of my responses to these young writers, once I chose to involve counselors.

"I've read your letter through several times to make sure I understand what you are telling me. Thank you for your honesty. I do feel that you're trying to carry much too heavy a load on your shoulders.

I ask that you don't hate me for doing this, but I'm going to ask one of your school's counselors to talk with you and give you some suggestions that might help. You will find that they will be confidential. I can't stand by and call myself a friend, and not do something to try and help."

Only once did a teenager write back and complain about my alerting her counselor.

"I didn't give you permission to show my letter to anyone. I wrote it just for you to read. Besides, it was embarrassing to have my name called over

*the loudspeaker to come to the counselor's office immediately. My friends kept
asking, 'What kind of trouble are you in?'"*

I immediately wrote a second letter to the girl and smoothed over the
situation as best I could, again assuring her that I had only her best interests
at heart, and hoped that the problem she had described earlier had been
resolved. Nothing further came to me regarding that event. I did take a
few minutes the next time I was in the area to stop by the school and
asked the counselor if he, next time, would consider a note and lay off the
loudspeaker.

Only once, also, did a counselor refuse my request that she wait until
the freshmen girl, who had written to me during a class presentation that
morning, would have received my response by mail.

My day, at a California wine country school, had ended with the
completion of the fifth period class. Students had an additional fifty
minutes of work before dismissal.

The counselor had studied the letter, and I could see that she was
disturbed. However, I proceeded with the normal routine of requesting a
waiting period until the freshman girl would have received my letter.

"I'm sorry, Mr. Nelson, but now that you've shown me this letter,
my hands are tied. I must follow the law and notify the police and the
Children's Protective Service immediately."

My writer had told of a beating she had suffered at the hands of a
drunken step-father the night before. She wrote of being fearful of going
home because her mother was away and she was certain her father would
be drinking again when she got home.

In desperation I asked the counselor to at least wait until I could
compose a letter to the student, and promised to have it completed within
thirty minutes so it could be hand-delivered to her prior to the end of the
sixth period. The counselor tucked me away in a quiet office with several
sheets of typing paper and an envelope. Within the half-hour my penned
response to the scared girl was folded and in the envelope, and I on the
way home.

I thought of little else on the hour and half drive home. There was no
further word from the student or her counselor.

CHAPTER SIX

"Because of that drink I had, I lost a lot,
my virginity, my pride, and my self image.
I feel I don't have anything anymore."

Dear Mr. Nelson,

I have been listening to you very well and found it to be very interesting. I'm a peer counselor here at this high school and have gone through a lot of counseling for a lot of people with drinking problems. I was just wondering if you could give me some clues on what I should tell them.

And another thing, I used to drink a lot, and lately my boyfriend and really close friends have been drinking a lot. So I quit because there needs to be someone sober at a party who will be able to make sure someone will not drive drunk, and save a life.

Thanks a lot,
Rachel

Dear Mr. Nelson,

Within the last year, my mother was diagnosed with cancer and I became pregnant at 14. This caused my father to drink more than usual.

Because I was pregnant and putting my baby up for adoption, I was living at a maternity home. While I was there I got a letter from my mother saying that my father had admitted he was an alcoholic.

My father and I aren't very close but I love him a lot. Sometimes he's really hard to talk to. I've also been tempted to drink and do drugs to help take away the pain I feel for the loss from giving up my baby.

Would you please send me some information to help me along, and some advice for me to give to my father?

Thank you for being here.

Jessica

Mr. Nelson,

I have just heard the letter from 1984 and was shocked how much this man sounds like my friends and me. I'm in 10th grade and am 15 years old. I've been drinking for about three or four years. I am not afraid to die but don't want to die a drunk.

I came very close to dying a drunk when I was thrown from a truck after a weekend of drinking. Fortunately my mom doesn't know, and now that I'll be driving soon, I also know I'm going to get drunk at a party and will try to drive home.

I really want to stop, but I can't. I'M ADDICTED. This is the first time I've been able to admit it. I have always thought I could stop on my own, but now I see I need help to stop. Now, I've also started smoking.

Thanks,
Jason

Mr. Nelson,

I do drugs on weekends. Every once in a while I get buzzed. I have not asked myself or looked in the mirror, but sometimes I wish I could be good.

My mom left me three years ago and I live with my dad. I've tried to forget it and let my mom know I love her no matter what I do. I go to school to make a change in my life. I have given up friends because I don't want those kinds of friends anymore. I tried to tell my friends before, but they didn't want to hear me. They push me away and ask me, "What's wrong with you? You've changed!"

I don't go out anymore. I stay home and look at my TV or do homework that I have. I am 15 years old, and have been like this for two months. I started at 11 years old.

My big brother went to jail because of it. I wish he had stopped and talked to me. I would have listened to him. My mom and dad never knew. Thank you for listening to me and what I said.

Love and happiness,
Melissa

Dear Mr. Nelson,

I don't like to admit it, but I'm a drug addict who can't spell well as you can tell. I also drink a lot of alcohol. I'm not sure what to do. I really don't know. Sometimes I come to school high or drunk. I don't know why. My friends do it, so I guess that's why I do it, but now it's out of hand.

Even if my friends get high or drunk, I do it just for the heck of it. Sometimes I worry about it.

My mom's boyfriend is an alcoholic and he's gotten into many fights when he was drunk. My mom takes his side. He has stabbed me two times and he still lives with us. I have called the police and even though he stabbed me, he is now back.

I hate him. Don't let the teacher see this, please. I need help.

Got to go,
Mark,
A troubled pothead.

Mr. Nelson,

I really don't know where to start, but whenever I go to a party I drink a lot. I let people drive me home who have also drank too much. I never blank out and always remember the next day what happened while I was drinking, so I'm saying I'm willing to go home with someone who's been drinking.

My sister and I have had parties at my house while my parents are away. We had about 13 people once, and we had two gallons of vodka and punch, plus wine coolers and Jack Daniel's. We were all drunk, guys and girls. Everyone spent the night because no one could drive home. Plus it was 4:00 in the morning before we stopped drinking.

The thing about it is, I like drinking everything and I will drink whenever I can. My parents don't know I drink. I totally deceive them because I have a 3.7 grade average so they think I'm really good.

I'm just afraid one of these times I might get hurt. I've already almost got shot because some of my friends and I broke into an old lady's house to go swimming. A neighbor came over with a shotgun.

In June we're moving to Oregon and I'm going to be out of place and probably will be drinking more.

Thanks for coming and caring about us. There are so many adults who don't care.

Thank you,
Sharon

Mr. Nelson,

Hi. Thank you for coming to our class. I need to tell someone. Last year when I was a freshman, I wanted to go to a party in Tracy. I asked my parents, of course. They said "No." Well, then I asked to spend the night at my friend's house. They let me do that.

When I got to her house we decided to go to the party anyway because my parents wouldn't know and hers said "Yes," so we went. There were lots of people there and they were all drinking. I saw this fine guy who I wanted to meet, but I had a boyfriend and he was going to be there later.

This fine guy started talking to me and that was exciting, but then he gave me something to drink. It was alcoholic. Well, I got drunk and started acting differently. I didn't really know what I was doing. That fine guy walked me into the bedroom because I needed to lie down because I didn't feel good, so we went in there.

Well, he took advantage of me. He actually raped me. My friends all heard me yelling but didn't bother to check on me. Later on my boyfriend came. I haven't told him or anyone yet. I'm too scared because it was my fault.

I want all girls to read this so it doesn't happen to them.

Brandee

Dear Mr. Nelson,

I just read all the letters you passed around and one of them almost made me cry. It was about the girl and her friend's uncle raping her.

Something of that sort happened to me. It was New Year's Eve of 1991. I went to a party and started drinking. I kept drinking and soon became very drunk.

I had sex with two guys that night and one of them was my best friend's boyfriend. I have denied the whole thing to everyone for four months now. I don't remember any of it. One day my best friend's boyfriend and I started to talk about it. He said that he forced me. I couldn't believe that he would do that to me, but he did. I don't want anyone to know about it, especially my best friend. I regret the whole thing terribly.

I can't really look at my best friend or her boyfriend (ex-boyfriend now) in the eyes. I don't want that to happen again. I still drink, but not as much. I know I shouldn't, but I do like the taste of beer and most hard liquor.

I'm moving on Friday and I hope your response gets forwarded to my new address.

Your pen friend,
Tara

Dear Mr. Nelson,

I'm not sure if I have a problem or not. It also scares me to have to admit that I might have a drinking problem. I go to parties every weekend I can. If I don't get to go to a party I get really depressed and have a hard time finding other means of entertainment. I know that I can have fun without drinking but most of the time I don't want to. I have come home drunk five times. My mom got really upset and grounded me for weeks at a time, but I went out and drank again right after I got off restriction.

I don't feel that I can talk with my mom about this kind of thing because she gets too upset. My friends are worried about me because they sometimes think I have a drinking problem. Whenever I have a party and there is alcohol, I have to drink. I cannot leave it alone.

The problem is, I don't want to. Sometimes I can't remember what happened the night before, and that scares me. It takes me a lot more alcohol to feel anything than it did when I first started drinking. I don't want to stop drinking, but I'm thinking maybe I should lay off for a while. Please help me.

Thank you,
Kari

Dear Mr. Nelson,

I'm not a drunk, but sometimes I feel I want to drink because this real good looking girl drinks, and she likes it a lot. She needs help. She's not addicted, but she does drink when she gets a chance. I'm afraid I'm going to lose her. I feel she'll get in a drunk's car.

I don't know why I'm telling you this. I guess it's because I care for her so much but I don't know how to help her. She tries to quit, but at parties when she's offered, she can't refuse. Please help her out.

Thanks,
Mike

Dear. Mr. Nelson,

I'm not sure if I'm an alcoholic or not, but I drink most every weekend. I don't drink heavily, and I don't drink for the high. I think I drink to be "in." It's not that I don't like drinking, because it's kind of fun to party and play beer games.

I don't drive yet (legally), but I'm against drunk driving. I've only driven a couple of times, but I have walked a lot. I'm kind of lucky because my mom understands and will pick me up most of the time. She's nice but sometimes it's *hard to collect up enough courage to call her. I've never driven drunk and I've only stopped someone from driving drunk once.*

I'd really enjoy being a member of SADD and I hope you will contact me.
Thanks,
Tom

Mr. Nelson,

Ever since I moved back into my house, my mom has let me out every single weekend. Ever since New Year's I've gone to kickback parties or just out to drink. I don't think I have a problem with alcohol because I've never really needed it, but it scares me.

One time we'd been drinking for at least six or seven hours straight and we were out of town. On the way back the driver's boyfriend kept playing with the wheel and covering the driver's eyes. I was the only one who was still awake and was very scared.

Well, this all comes down to this weekend coming up. I am supposed to go out with at least three girl friends and five guy friends. Out of the three girls other than me, I know two of them drink. Out of the five guys, they all drink, and I'm only sure that three out of five smoke pot.

We are supposed to go to Sacramento, about one hour from here. We're then supposed to go to some cruise, then to a party and then back home. I'm not sure if I'm scared, but I think I am.

Well, thanks for listening. If you were me and you hadn't been drinking, but you don't have a license, would you still insist on driving the car home?
Lidia

Mr. Nelson,

I know I'm not perfect but when I'm with my friends or cousins, they want to drink, so one time I tried a wine cooler. I thought it was good. It made me feel good, also. I knew it was wrong, but I really didn't know what to say.

Well, the same thing happened a few months later, but this time it was hard liquor. I didn't like the taste, but I drank it anyway. Just a couple of days ago I was at my cousin's house again. We went to her friend's house. There was Budweiser there. They were all drinking and they said, "Come on, have some, it's okay." I ended up drinking four cans.

I was drunk off my butt. We were walking home and I couldn't even walk straight. If I don't want to drink anymore, I think I could stop, just like I did with cigarettes, but when you're with friends, you feel left out. Now, I know that it's true if your friends don't like you for yourself, then they're not your friends.

My mom doesn't even know I did these things, but I have this conscience that bugs me all the time about it. I think it is okay if you drink once in a few months.

Well, I hope to hear from you soon, and hope you have some information and suggestions for me.

A person who's worried about her reputation,
Dana

Ken,

I hope you don't mind me calling you Ken. Well, I lost my uncle to a drunk driving accident. He was an alcoholic like most of my family.

I know it's dangerous to drink and drive, but often I would drink and party with my mom. We used the excuse, "I'm with my mom. It can't hurt anything," but it did.

Now I can't see my mom without supervision. Still I get drunk and still I get in cars with drunk drivers, because I do not know how to say, "No, don't drink and drive."

I'm sorry,
Katrina

Dear Mr. Nelson,

My whole family background is filled with alcoholics, all the way to my mom. I have even had alcohol on several occasions. I strongly believe against drunk driving.

Last weekend I found out how easy it is. Some friends and I had about three or four beers, and I didn't think. I just got in the car. It was so easy, and I am so mad at myself.

My dad found out about me drinking and took no action. This made me even more angry, so I made a Contract for Life with my mom.

Jerry

Mr. Nelson,

I'm 15 years old. I've been drinking for a while, six years or so, but not heavily since the start of this year. I've been trying to quit. I haven't drank for two weeks or so. I know this isn't much, but I feel like it's a start. I've been in cars where the driver was drunk.

I've done marijuana, cocaine, crank, and speed, but only once or twice each. I know it's bad, but I'm not addicted or was ever totally screwed up, either. I've decided lately I haven't wanted to do any of them.

My grades got very low and I felt stressed. I guess that's why I turned to this stuff. I need to change, I know that. My name is Sarah and I am an alcoholic/ drug user.

Sincerely,
Sarah

Dear Mr. Nelson,

Thank you for coming. You seem like a very caring person. I have been really confused lately. My mother and father broke up about two years ago. She was feeling very bad so she turned to the bottle. My mother has a new boyfriend now who is an alcoholic. They've been going out almost every night now. I'm scared. I really love her, but I don't know how to help her.

I had a very scary incident happen to me. It was only about a week ago. My friend came over last Sunday night with a bottle of brandy. He kept on saying that it was "cool to drink." I did. I had my first blackout. When I came to, he was on top of me. Then I blacked out again.

I wish that I'd have said "No" to him when he offered me a drink, but I didn't. I give a lot of speeches about abortions and capital punishment around schools. Maybe, instead, I should give them on alcohol. It affects everyone.

I love my mom even though she drinks. She thinks that it only affects her. This is not true, it really affects me, too. I was curious last week as to why my mother drank. I found out! Yea, getting raped and having a blackout is really fun! I hope that teenagers will listen when people talk about the effects of alcohol, but they, like me, are curious. A lot of them, like me, will find out the hard way.

Please write back and also, send me some stuff about SADD.

Amber

Mr. Nelson,

I'm 15 and I feel like I'm going on thirty. I'm not sure if I'm an alcoholic, but it would be safe to assume. My life has been the pits. The last three years have been the worst. I've wanted to commit suicide many times, but I won't let it get to me.

When I moved in with my dad he beat me, so I started drinking. Well, that wasn't enough so I started drugs. I was in the 7th grade then.

I came back to my mom in the 8th grade. I quit drugs when I came back up here. I can't talk to my mom because everything was so perfect for her. She was gorgeous and popular in high school. How can I tell her I'm treated like crap?

Things started to pick up at the beginning of this year, but now they're worse than ever. So I wont commit suicide, I drink. People can be so cold and heartless. I've waited for things to look up, but they won't, so I drink because I'll never commit suicide.

Love doesn't make the world go around if no one's giving it. Don't let anyone see this letter until my complete name is taken off of it. Thank you for coming. Please write back.

Laura

Dear Mr. Nelson,

When I was 12, I started drinking with some of my friends. At first it was just a game, but then it became an everyday thing. In junior high I would take it to school with me. Mostly I drank it during lunch time. The rest of the day just drifted by.

Then one weekend I got really drunk with my friends. We started drinking about five p.m. and didn't stop until two in the morning. After all the beer was gone, almost everyone went home and to bed. But there was this guy I know whose name I won't say, but I was really drunk, and he raped me.

The next morning when I woke up my best friend told me what happened the night before. Ever since that night I haven't taken another drink. When this happened to me I was almost 15 years old. I haven't drank now for two years.

Heather

Mr. Nelson,

I'm 15 years old and very confused. I feel like I'm in a situation as the kid in the first letter. I drink, but not just on weekends. During the week, before school, lunch time, and after school, I drink.

On weekends I usually have a car, but of course, no license. I do drink and drive. To be honest, I'm scared. My dad is an alcoholic and my mother is a full-on drug addict. I don't know where my life is. At this rate I'll end up just like my father. I hope I don't. I would really appreciate it if you would send me some information.

Justin

Dear Mr. Nelson,

I'm 15 years old and I, myself, feel as though I drink too much. I have a 19 year old friend who is a drunk. I love him and fear for his safety and other peoples' safety. My father is a drunk and so is my grandfather.

I know that drinking is bad, and I should not do it, but if I don't drink, all of my other friends call me "stupid," etc. I want to help my friend out but I'm not sure how.

I just finished reading some letters. I, too, was a victim of rape after drinking too much. Please send me some information about SADD.

Thanks for caring,
Sara

Dear Mr. Nelson,

I've just read some of the letters you passed around and they brought back a lot of bad memories. I am 16 years of age, and I've only been drinking about one or two years continually, just socially before that.

From September to December of 1991 I had a bad drinking problem. I would leave school before I even went to the first class and would go to a friend's house and get wasted. One day it got a little out of hand. Some people who I really thought were my friends raped me. There were four guys and the girls who were there just left me. It wasn't only alcohol, though, it was also crank. I hardly remembered a thing, but I woke up with my clothes ripped off me. I was also beaten up that day.

I'm really glad you came in today. I hope you keep teaching students about alcohol. You're doing a good job.

Thank you,
Carrie

Mr. Nelson,

My name is Michael. I'm 15 years old, and I'm in 10th grade. Every weekend I go out and drink. I seem to still be so drunk the next morning when I wake up, I can't remember anything.

The odd thing about it is, I like it. I just can't stop drinking. It's a very fun experience towards me.

I know not to drink and drive. I was just 15 when I first experienced drinking and driving. I was in my mother's brand new minivan taking my cousin home. We ran off the road and flipped over. Thank God nobody was

*hurt. That's also my last time drinking and driving at the same time, but I'm
still going to drink.*

Your friend,
Mike

Dear Mr. Nelson,

*I would like to thank you for coming to our school today and talking to
us. I've read most of the letters you passed out. I'm 16 years old and in the 10th
grade. I would like to share something with you and, hopefully to a lot of people,
so they won't drink too much.*

*The first thing I'd like to say is that I've made up my mind about drinking,
because, in my freshman year I got majorly drunk with my step-dad. I drank
way too much. That night I kept passing out and coming to. I remember that
every time I came to, my step-dad was trying to take off my clothes.*

*I remember telling him to stop but he wouldn't. Then he hit me and must
have knocked me out. One of the times I came to he was raping me. I tried to
push him off but he wouldn't stop. He just hit me again and said, "Shut up, you
bitch! Can't you just let me have my fun?"*

*I turned him in to C.P.S. and I got pulled out of my home. I've been in a
foster home for nine and a half months now.*

*My mom wouldn't believe me, and she said that she didn't ever want me
back. She is now in Sacramento living with my little sister and my step-dad.*

*Also, three days after my sixteenth birthday, a guy I've liked for three years
got me plastered. He mixed some drinks together and told me it was a shake,
and it didn't taste like it had any alcohol in it. I believed him and kept drinking
and drinking until I couldn't walk.*

*Then we had sex, and I didn't want it to happen this way. Now he doesn't
talk to me. He's 17 and going out with someone four years younger than he is.*

*I feel like I'm a target for guys who just want to have a good time in the
bedroom.*

That's NOT the kind of a person I am. Please write me back.

Thank you for caring,
Melissa

Mr. Nelson,

*Hi, I have a problem with drinking. I am very ashamed of it. It started
when I was nine years old. I wasn't doing it that much, but gradually I got to*

doing it every weekend. I've been in a car accident, but it wasn't that serious. The person driving was drunk. I'm scared that my drinking will end up taking my life. I'm trying to quit but it's hard when there's peer pressure. Also, whenever you go to a party, it's available.

In three days it's my birthday, and I will only be 15 years old. My cousin is throwing a party. I will do my best not to drink but I need support. I'm very interested in the SADD club. I'm also very thankful you came to our school and talked. I've known many people who have lost their lives from drinking and driving.

Oh, my mother doesn't know, and I'm scared she'll find out before I quit. Well, that's about all I have to say.

Love always,
Debbie

Dear Mr. Nelson,

Hi, my name is Shawnda. I have a drinking and smoking problem. I get drunk sometimes, but mostly I just drink one or two beers a day. Mostly on weekends, I get drunk. I can't stop, I love the taste.

As for smoking, I usually go through one pack in three days. I take my mom's cigarettes when she stocks up. My mom always tells me she hopes I never start smoking. How do I tell her I already did? Or do I tell her? Will you please help me make this decision?

I have faith. I think I can quit both if I want to, and I want to.

Thank you,
Shawnda

Dear Mr. Nelson,

I always said to myself that I was never going to drink, and yet, I was wrong! Just in February I had a lot to drink, as a matter of fact, too much.

I found myself having sex with a guy who I cared for very much, my boyfriend. But I never intended to have sex with him! Now, because of that drink I had, I lost a lot, my virginity, my pride, and my self-image.

I wish it would never have happened. My whole life has changed, and I feel very sorry for myself. Sometimes I feel as if I want to drink again, but only because of depression. I feel like I don't have anything, anymore!

Sincerely,
Shiloh

Once I circulated the first letter from a girl student who had experienced an unfortunate and unexpected event with sex and alcohol, the floodgates seemed to open. It was apparent to me, watching as the pages of letters moved from desk to desk, that "the sex letter" was commanding more than normal attention. Often, one girl would hand the pages to one seated across from her, and point to the particular revelation, at the same time shaking her head. The impact on the girls of seeing others' bad experience in print was evident.

My intent was not to overwhelm my classroom audiences with revelations of these especially hurtful experiences. If I were circulating ten typed pages containing a total of twenty-five letters, I made it a point of not including more than two of these letters of sexual abuse.

The boys' reaction was muted. With little change in their expression except for an occasional rolling of eyes, the letters would be passed along. I'm sure that most of these young boys had listened to some of their older friends brag about their escapades with girls. There was no hint as to whether the male students were envious or if they considered those friends as being jerks. Occasional questions asked to me in classes never addressed the matter of sex and alcohol. I'm satisfied that the health teachers did cover that area well, and that perhaps the circulated letters stimulated thought and helpful dialogue.

Looking back on the value of regularly including copies of these letters involving sex, rape, and alcohol, I would predict one certain gain. It reinforced the conviction of the boys in my audiences who didn't feel a need to pressure their girlfriends for sex, and hopefully assured them that they would be looked up to by these girls. I don't recall any letter where the female writers told of having a further relationship with the boy who took advantage of them.

Pregnancy and abortions were noted as the consequences of several rapes and otherwise unwanted sex advances. My readers might ask how many or what percentage of the girls chose to give birth and keep their babies. There had to be some. On a single occasion I reluctantly agreed to talk with a special class of pregnant girls. My worst fears were realized when I stood in front of 12-15 visibly pregnant fourteen, fifteen and sixteen year olds. I had figured out nothing pertinent to say; I couldn't be critical; I couldn't be helpful.

I did ask how many became pregnant in an alcohol-related event. Most raised their hands. Also, I felt okay in asking how many planned to continue school after giving birth to their child. Again, most hands went up. I didn't ask if they knew who the father was, or who was going to have the burden of child-care while the girls continued their classwork.

I considered taking the letters about forced sex to counselors, but that step was taken only once. My readers will note that some girls, though few, said they had exposed their troubles, with names, to their parents or authorities. That was their option. Responding to these dozens of letters from teenage girls who had opened up to me about these regrettable actions never became easy. Probably the best approach was to recognize in my letters the pain each of the writers was feeling. Beyond that it seemed imperative that each girl be assured they were every bit as worthwhile as before they were taken advantage of. Also, I generally would add:

"You will later look back on this very hurtful event and realize you've learned a lot and can avoid suffering through this pain again. You need to be as honest with your younger friends as you have been with me because you can help them steer clear of these awful experiences."

CHAPTER SEVEN

"I have a boyfriend who drinks and always gets loaded.
He always takes his problems out on me."

Dear Mr. Nelson,

I have a very special person in my life; he is my boyfriend. He started going out and drinking with his cousin and brother last school year. He's eighteen years old. I have told him not to drink and drive, but he doesn't seem to listen to me. He is a very sweet guy and I love him more than life itself. I never want to see him hurt.

He is young, and he has a lot to live for. We have been together for three years and this is the most difficult problem we have ever had. I would appreciate your suggestions.

Thank you for your support and caring for us! We need more people like you to help us out.

Tina

Mr. Nelson,

I'm writing to you because I have a problem that nobody else seems to care enough about to try to help. I'm not an alcoholic. I don't drink but my boyfriend does. He hasn't admitted to me that he has a drinking problem other than his old line, "I have a drinking problem . . . two hands and one mouth."

I believe he is an alcoholic. He's been out drinking thirteen nights in a row and plans to go out again tonight. He doesn't believe he can change, but he says he'll try anything for me.

This is a massive problem for me. My boyfriend is going to be 16 years old in November and will be driving so I need to start action right away. I cannot find help for my boyfriend in my family because they simply tell me to get away from him.

My boyfriend wants help and if it comes from me I believe he will take it. He doesn't know his father, but is often accused of being "a drunk like your father," which doesn't help.

Please send me some information about SADD, and some hints as to how to deal with my alcoholic boyfriend. Thanks for your concern. Please help!

Ina

Dear Mr. Nelson,

I enjoyed your comments today, and I can really relate to the letters. I'm 15 years old, and I've gotten drunk at a couple of parties and everyone seemed like it was not a problem. We were all bombed and singing and, ya know, just partying.

I felt really bad the next morning about what I'd done. My ex-boyfriend went and got drunk, I mean drunk, every weekend, and I didn't like it at all. I told him I didn't like it, and he said, "Okay, I'll quit," and everything was fine for a while. When he started getting back into his drinking habit, I again talked to him about it and he admitted, "I'm an alcoholic," like it was no big deal.

But it was. I had a lot of relatives who were drunks, 'had' being a main word because three died in car accidents and two of liver disease.

These letters have really made me think and put some problems in perspective. Thanks.

A friend,
Christine

Dear Mr. Nelson,

What you are doing is a great idea. I wish my brother would have stayed in school and maybe he would have heard someone like you speak.

Two years ago when my brother had just turned 18 he was killed, and his friend of 21 was paralyzed from the waist down. All were drinking, but my brother was the one driving so the other guy didn't get into any trouble.

Now, I'm going out with a guy who is legally of the age to drink, so it's around, but I make the decision every day to turn it down so I can keep straight, avoid arguments, and be able to talk him out of dumb things.

He does listen because I've seen a lot of alcohol abuse. My real father was an alcoholic for 32 years of his life. He's been sober for nine years now.

Both of my parents (mother and step-father) now drink a lot and it really affects them. I never know what to expect, sometimes nice and sometimes off the wall. They don't hit me 'cause I'm too aggressive and I'll fight back. Well, I'm writing a book here.

Thanks a lot,
Dawna

Mr. Nelson,

My ex-boyfriend drinks on the weekends, just enough to get a good buzz, he says. He tells me he won't drive if he's drunk. It really scares me because it's not good for him. His mom has decided not to let him go out this weekend. She is scared for him, too, but no one can force him and no one can change his mind.

I think he doesn't want to drink, but he won't listen, and he won't let me help him try to get over it. That is why I broke up with him. I felt helpless. I wanted to help him, but he just won't listen.

How could I help him? I couldn't just stand there and watch him throwing his life away like that. I love him too much to simply do nothing. Maybe I can help him better as a friend, but how?

Kimberly

Mr. Nelson,

I'm really glad you came to our school. My ex-boyfriend drinks a lot. When he starts he doesn't know when to stop. I broke up with him 'cause I did not want to compete with the alcohol. I told him he had to quit or at least cut down, but I don't know if he listens to me. I care about him very much.

How can I help more?

Thanks,
Aubrey

Dear Mr. Nelson,

I know someone who has a drinking problem, and I tried to help him quit his drinking, but he will not stop his drinking. What should I do about it? Sometimes I stayed at his house at night. Now, I do not stay there at all. He will not stop drinking at all. He drinks at least six beers a day. I don't want him to die.

He drinks wine at night. I've been trying to help him stop drinking wine. He's been drinking for as long as I've known him. He will not stop drinking because he is addicted to it.

Because I know what could happen to people who drink, I would like to be a member of SADD.

Your friend,
Jason

Dear Mr. Nelson,

I think that you are doing a fine job. I never noticed that so many teenagers have a problem with drinking, but when I think about it, a lot of my friends have problems with drinking and drugs. I, myself, used to be that way, but later I realized it wasn't worth it.

Although I don't have a problem now, I have a friend who does. He's my ex-boyfriend. We broke up because every time we went out he would drink or smoke some weed. He treated me differently when he was intoxicated.

I've tried so many times to talk to him. He repeatedly says that it's not a problem and that he can quit whenever he wants to, but I really think he's addicted. He even does rock now. Even though he's not a boyfriend anymore I still care a great deal about him. He tells me he drinks or does rocks to calm himself and to get rid of any stress from his family and friends. He's been doing this for almost five months now, and it worries me. He doesn't realize where he's headed and I'm afraid it's too far.

Since he's the youngest of four children, he tends to be spoiled. When he doesn't get his way he turns to alcohol or weed or drugs.

I'd really like to help him and prove that he has a life to live instead of throwing it all away, but I don't know how I can help. Since I'm his ex-girlfriend, he tends to neglect me and misunderstands me when I try to talk to him. I always hope that he changes, but he doesn't. Things just get worse. Sometimes I think I am the reason he does these things.

I'd like to help him before he goes "overboard!" What should I do? Talking just doesn't cut it. Help me, please.

Sincerely,
Michelle

Mr. Nelson,

I'm a 16-year-old girl, and I want to commend you in what you are doing, but I have a question.

I go to parties all the time with my friends. My boyfriend (the guy I'm seeing) always drinks like a six-pack of Mickey's and other stuff, but you can never tell when he's drunk. He is the one who drives everyone home.

I never drink at all. All I drink is Pepsi, only because my dad is an alcoholic, and I don't want to turn out like him.

I love my boyfriend so much; I would give him the world if I could. It scares me, though, wondering if I'll ever make it home. My question is, how do I try to get him not to drive when he drinks? He would get really mad at me if I word it wrong, and I don't want to lose him.

It may be a common question but actually it is a very hard one if you really think about it. I love my boyfriend a lot, and I want him here with me, but the way he is it's easier said than done!

Jessica

Mr. Nelson,

My boyfriend drinks, and he says it's not that bad. I, of course, think it's a bigger problem than he thinks. I've never seen him drink because he knows I don't like drinking. I wish I could get him to realize how much harm he is really doing. He's an athlete, and I know he would be better if he didn't drink.

Have you ever dealt with this kind of a situation? Do you have any advice for me? I care about my boyfriend very much, and I hope to help him in some way. Please help me to help him. Thank you for your time in class. I appreciate it very much.

I think the banner should read, "Friends Don't Let Friends Drink."

Thank you again,
Christine

Dear Mr. Nelson,

Thank you for sharing your knowledge with our class today. I am 17 years old; my boyfriend is 23 years old. He's been drinking for quite a while, and of course, he drives while intoxicated. I love him very much and don't want anything to ever happen to him. He has the attitude that he is immortal and that he'll never die.

Four of us were in an accident in February that was due to drunk driving. The driver, my friend's boyfriend, was going too fast to make a corner. We rolled the truck, and I was ejected through the window! As of today I'm still hurting from this. My boyfriend continues to drink!

Thank you for your time,
Misty

Dear Mr. Nelson,

It was really nice of you to come and talk to my driver's ed. class. I'm not a person who would go out and get drunk.

I have a problem with my boyfriend. He's 22 and I am 15. I know there are lots of "possibilities" in our age difference, but he is a person who I know *really cares about me and his family. I hate to say it, but he seems like a normal person who gets drunk every once in a while.*

I'm scared. I really care for him and don't want him to drink at all. I have tried telling him to stop, but a week later he would get drunk again. Last Friday he promised me he wouldn't get drunk that night. Well, he broke his promise.

How can I talk to him? I want to tell him I'm writing to you. Then if you would write back I will tell him your advice that I should give him. I'm really scared for him, and if anything happened to him, I don't know what I would do.

I know he cares, and he doesn't do this constantly, but to me it's still a problem. He can drive and does have a car. He doesn't usually drive when he's drunk, but it's still a point that I don't want him to get drunk every week or two. Please give me some advice before it's too late.

Thanks for caring,
Jill

Dear Mr. Nelson,

I have personal reasons for having joined SADD. My boyfriend is a drug addict and alcoholic. He doesn't do drugs anymore, or alcohol, but he's still an alcoholic.

My family is a family whose social life is drinking alcohol. I never plan on drinking but my grandparents expect me to. I think I can stand up to them, though. I love my boyfriend and my family but it's hard to play both mother and friend to a bunch of people. Sometimes I feel I have to grow up too fast.

I don't mean to be a crybaby, but please give a little support to the people who practice a safe lifestyle. I know that you care, and that's great. I say a prayer for the SADD club each night. I hope that we can make a difference. Please write back with information.

Thank you so much,
Marjorie

Dear Mr. Nelson,

My boyfriend and I have been dating for six months. He drinks and smokes pot sometimes. It really scares me because he just got his license. He lives in Sacramento so I see him maybe twice a month. We talk about drugs, and he knows how I feel. He says he won't force me to do anything. I'm not scared of that.

It's just that now he has his license, and he has driven drunk once. I am just scared that if I'm not there, he won't listen to his friends, and that something might happen.

I do go to parties and I do drink, but I don't drink too much. I'm really scared that I might lose him. I already lost my uncle because of his drinking problem.

Please let me know what you think I should do.

Sincerely,
Jennifer

Mr. Nelson,

I'm 17 and I don't have a license. My boyfriend and I drink every time we go out. I've taken his keys away but he's much stronger than I am, and he always ends up getting his keys back. The last time we went out we hit a tree. Luckily, neither of us was hurt and no one else was either.

He doesn't understand that when I take away his keys or try to talk him into letting someone, who wasn't drinking, drive, it's for his own good as well as the good of other motorists. He says the next time I try something like that, he'll leave me there. I'm really concerned about him. I'd like to know if there's anything I can do to make him realize exactly what he's doing. He's 20 and thinks I'm just trying to run his life. Thank you.

Terri

Mr. Nelson,

I have a boyfriend who used to drink every day of the week, but I got him down to drinking only on weekends. He still drinks too much. He drank before he went to work this morning.

It makes me really upset to see him drink his life away. He was going to meetings to help him stop drinking, but the meeting didn't help. He said sometimes when he got home he would drink because the meetings made him mad. He drinks and drives all the time. I try to make him stop, but he only listens to me sometimes.

I'm not going to give up on him now. I'm still going to try to help him with his drinking problem.

Eileen

Mr. Nelson,

Hi. Sitting here listening to you talk, I find it very interesting and would like more info on SADD. I have a boyfriend who drinks. I mean, he drinks a lot! He also does drugs. Ever since I've been going out with him, I've started to drink more and do more drugs.

I don't know if I want to stop. My mom is an alcoholic. It kills me to see her do it, too, but she doesn't care.

My boyfriend wants to stop everything. He is 15 years old. I'm 16. We both admit that we have a problem.

I lost my best friend when I was a freshman. I'm a junior now. It still hurts. I want to help and be helped, but I'm just too scared to ask.

I think I really needed to get this out. Thank you for listening, Mr. Nelson. I have talked to my teacher before. He helped, too, but I just can't seem to get off the stuff.

Sincerely,
Shauna

Mr. Nelson,

My boyfriend and I broke up last year. After we broke up he began to drink. I sort of felt responsible, but I know now I wasn't. I used to write him letters about quitting even though we weren't boyfriend/girlfriend. After a while he began to stop drinking, and then he started to drink again. One night he got in an accident and I called his mother and father, who I was real close to.

After I told them what was going on, we never talked again. I really miss Mark (boyfriend), but he's not the same anymore.

I got drunk once but found I was highly allergic to it, and haven't drank since. In some ways I wish everyone was allergic to alcohol.

Last year was a hard year for me. I wish we had more programs like MADD and SADD. Thanks a lot.

Kelli

Mr. Nelson,

Hi, my name is Michelle. I have a boyfriend who drinks and always gets loaded. He always takes his problems out on me. He goes to parties, and he can never stop drinking! I can't leave him, he means everything to me. What should I do? I don't drink or do any kind of drugs.

Love,
Michelle

Dear Mr. Nelson,

I'm 16 and have a very large problem. I met a boyfriend named Chuck when I was 13 years old. We started dating and fell in love. I've been with him for three years. We've recently stopped dating.

He has been stopped three times in the last four months for driving drunk. This hurts me and upsets me. I care for him very much and have often tried to help him stop drinking, but he just goes right back to the booze! I don't feel like I have to live my life with someone who is killing himself, but doesn't want to admit it. Please help me with some advice. It would be very much appreciated.

Concerned,
Rhonda

Dear Mr. Nelson,

I'm 15 years old. I don't drink that often, but my boyfriend (recently my ex-boyfriend) does. He either drives drunk or is high on pot. It really scares me. We are still really good friends even though we're no longer boyfriend and girlfriend.

I try to tell him that what he's doing is wrong, but he doesn't seem to care about himself. He never drove drunk with me in the car. His name is Tim, and he's a 17 year old senior. I'm afraid I'm going to lose him forever.

He feels he has nothing to live for because he isn't going to graduate. He doesn't seem to understand that the reason why he isn't going to graduate is because of his getting stoned and drinking. I really care for him. He's not a bad person, just confused. Thanks for coming. You may share this with other students so they can make the right choice, not the one Tim did.

Gratefully yours,
Terri

Dear Mr. Nelson,

I'm a member of SADD here at our school. I firmly believe that people shouldn't drive drunk or ride with a drunk driver.

Yet, last Saturday I got in a car with someone who was driving drunk. This was a guy whom I like a lot. I wanted to tell him that he shouldn't drive drunk, but he's the type who thinks SADD is stupid. He parties a lot and then drives home.

I am really worried about him, but I know if I tell him, he'll laugh right in my face. He (probably) even thinks caring about someone is stupid.

I don't want him to get in an accident, but I also don't want him to think I'm "un-cool."

I'm very glad you came to our class, and I hope everyone joins SADD. Please write back if you want to.

Thank you,
Heather

Mr. Nelson,

My name is Mona, and I'm 16. I don't have a drinking problem, but my boyfriend does.

He's always getting drunk on alcohol and marijuana. I love him a lot, but I'm afraid that if I say something, he'll compare me to all the other people who do tell him, plus I'm afraid he'll break up with me.

He's always urging me to drink and smoke with him, but I'm scared that my mom will find out. I drank a beer with him once, just to be a sport, but I didn't like it at all. If I keep turning him down he'll get mad, and I'm running out of excuses. I'm glad you came. Please help me!

Mona

Dear Mr. Nelson,

My boyfriend is an alcoholic. He's been drinking since he was 12 years old. I am now very worried. Whenever we have an argument he runs and drinks. He can't face any problem without being drunk. I am scared I'm going to lose him. I love him so much and could never bear losing him.

My parents know he used to drink a lot, but they don't know he still does. His parents don't know, and they will never know as far as he's concerned. His father's an alcoholic, too, and he gets very violent when he drinks.

Why does my boyfriend do this? Is it his whole life? Without it, I don't know if he could handle the stress of our problems. Please help me understand why!

I tell him it's bad, but he doesn't see it as a problem. But it is! It hurts me so bad when he gets drunk, and I can't handle it anymore.

I always tell him I'll leave, but I can't. He needs my help, and I can't run away. I need to help him.

Please send me info on SADD! Thanks a bunch.

Thanks for coming,
Tivvany

Mr. Nelson,

I have a friend, and his name is Greg. He has a very bad drinking problem. His problem is so bad he beats me, and I hurt so bad. He tells me he won't hit me anymore, and I stay with him 'cause I love him. I'm concerned that one day he'll hurt me so bad he'll put me in the hospital. I'm afraid.

Please help me help him control his abuse of alcohol, and help me to help myself.

Thanks,
Zerlina

Dear Mr. Nelson,

I lived with my step-father and mom when I was younger, and my step-father was an alcoholic. I remember times we were both afraid he wouldn't come home and/or he would come home after a few too many. A few years later I moved in with my real dad, and, just recently, he began to drink. Now, he's a member of A.A.!

I hate to say this, but I believe my boyfriend is also an alcoholic. He wants to marry, but I find it personally impossible because of my fear of alcohol. I don't only fear that he may become violent or that he won't come home one night because of an accident, but that my future children will have to grow up in the same atmosphere that I did. I don't want them to be afraid to get in the car with their own father!

Thanks for your involvement to help drunk driving stop.

Thank you,
Lana

Dear Mr. Nelson,

I'm a freshman here at this school. My whole family drinks. My mom drinks more than three times a week. She never looks drunk, but she gets real mean. My whole life I've gone to parties, some my friends' have, some my family, and I drink.

Sometimes I drink alone. Sometimes it helps. I've drank so much, and I hate the smell of it so much. One time I went to a small party and drank. The next think I knew, I was being raped. It was the most scary thing I've ever gone through.

Whenever I drink alone, I can't feel pain. I'm very suicidal, so when I cut myself, I don't feel pain. I have a very bad life and drinking helps me escape. However, when I cut myself, being that I can't feel it, I get tempted to cut deeper and deeper.

My boyfriend has convinced me to stop drinking. He knows I've been raped. Maybe I needed that to wake me up.

Written with love,
Jennifer

Dear Mr. Nelson,

Three years ago my boyfriend got into a car accident due to driving drunk. He drinks heavy. I've tried to get him to stop, but he doesn't seem to listen to me or anyone else, including his family. He's told me he would stop after this one beer, but I cannot remember how many times I've heard that before.

I feel that ever since he's been in his car accident, he thinks life isn't worth living, when in reality it's just beginning. How can I make him see this?

Sincerely,
Danielle

Several things jump out at me as I try to absorb the expressions of concern written by these teenage girls.

Worry about the boys doesn't end with the termination of the relationship. The ex-boyfriends appear to be the target of the girls' need to remain in the picture as friends, determined to help change the boy's behavior and save him from himself. It doesn't appear that most of the girls are trying to ingratiate themselves, hopeful of again becoming the boy's girlfriend. Feelings of the need to help are genuine.

Why are the boys not writing about the undesirable actions of their girlfriends where alcohol is concerned? It is not happening or is there a great reluctance to relate the situation on a piece of paper?

Some girls' hesitancy to approach their boyfriends directly and confront them about the need to change their behavior is disturbing, because any delay could so easily be followed by a tragic event involving alcohol. The girl's feeling of 'love' is so intense, as indicated by the frequency of the words: *"I don't know how I possibly could live without him."*

Once, a 17-year-old senior stopped me in the student parking lot at a California foothill high school following my presentation.

"My boyfriend is 21," she began, "and has a really bad alcohol problem. He drives us home after parties and I'm always afraid. I don't drink, but he does all of the time. We've been going together for over two years, and we really love each other. He told me that if I'll marry him he'll promise to quit drinking."

Perhaps I was more blunt than was appropriate. I told her that she would have to search a long time to find a man who lived up to such a promise, and that she could be almost sure her boyfriend wouldn't. I suggested, "Why don't you tell him that he has to prove himself first by staying completely off alcohol for maybe two years, and that then you'll seriously consider marriage?"

Her response to this suggestion was a frown, followed by an expression of fear: "But if I do that, he might break up with me."

I acknowledged that this might happen, but asked that she consider the other side. "You'll be eighteen soon and legally making all of your own decisions. Imagine the awful situation for you if you have children and your husband continued his heavy drinking. It would be a nightmare for you."

The student was on the verge of tears. I hastily pulled a small note pad from my shirt pocket and printed my name and address. I asked that she let me know of her decision. She nodded and thanked me for talking with her. I hopefully checked my mailbox for several weeks, but no word came from her.

The parents of these female writers of thirteen to seventeen must surely be aware that their daughters are involved with young men over twenty-one. If parents had voiced objections, none of the girls mentioned them in letters to me.

The legal access to alcohol by the older boyfriends is obvious and was casually noted by some of the girls. Nowhere though, was there an indication that any parent raised the question of the legality of a man of legal drinking age providing alcohol for an underage girl. The girls involved don't see it as a problem; they're in love!

'Being in love' as a fourteen to sixteen year old girl appears to lay the responsibility on the girl's shoulders alone of helping her much older boyfriend control or kick his alcohol problem. It's difficult to justify or even imagine such a completely unfair situation, but it's presented clearly.

I seldom raised the age difference question in my responses to letters where it existed because I felt it unfair to add this aspect on to the writers' already overloaded shoulders. Inwardly, and regrettably, I saw little hope of a successful ending to their stories.

CHAPTER EIGHT

"My grandfather is an alcoholic . . . He has to start a fight
or else he's not happy. He often hits my grandmother."

Mr. Nelson,

My grandmother died about three years ago. Since then my grandfather has been drinking. He's not a huge drunk, he just drinks till he passes out. My grandfather has really been trying not to drink, but he has failed.

Your presentation and thoughts helped me know how to get through to him to help him.

Concerned teenager,
Lisa

Dear Mr. Nelson,

I live with my grandma. Four years ago my grandpa died but not because of drunk driving. It was just natural causes. About a year before he died, he was an alcoholic. He used to get mad at my grandma and try to hit her. My grandma used to run outside and hide from him.

My grandma had to go to work one night and she wouldn't take me. I was so scared of him that I told her that I was going to walk to town. She picked me up and took me back. My grandpa beat me because of that.

I hated him for that. About a month after that, he stopped drinking. I was about nine years old. Now I'm 15, almost 16. I miss him so bad. I want him back.

My three uncles are alcoholics. My uncle Randall used to beat my aunt and my cousins. Now his two boys are alcoholics and beat each other. One of his two boys is a diabetic, and if my uncle keeps it up, he will die. The doctor said so.

Why in the hell do they do this? Now I find myself doing what they are doing, but my last time was New Year's Eve.

I want to help them, but they won't listen so why should I care? If they want to die, let them! But I love each of them so much. Help!

Sincerely,
Tommy

Mr. Nelson,

My grandfather is an alcoholic. I have to admit I've been drunk before, but I've never been to the point where every minute of the day I'm mean. My grandfather is at this point. I've always known he drinks, but lately it's like if I go to see him, nothing can be pleasant. He has to start a fight or else he's not happy. He often hits my grandmother.

This really hurts me due to the fact we're close. I want to help him and tried talking to my parents about it, but my dad (its his father) refuses to admit to it.

Please help me find a way to help him. Thank you for being someone I can talk to.

Thank you very much,
Kristine

Mr. Nelson,

My grandfather is a heavy drinker. It drives me crazy! Once, he was majorly wasted and he punched my lip when we got in a fight. After that, I decided I hated him, and was never going to talk to him again.

Then, we were fighting again, and he slammed the door into my arm, almost breaking it. I haven't talked to him since. It happened about five months ago. It's strange living with somebody you can't talk to!

Alcohol has ruined my family, and I don't think I'll ever start. Please send me some info on SADD.

Sincerely,
Amber

Mr. Nelson,

My grandpa was a very heavy drinker. I used to live with him and my grandma. I remember when my grandpa would come home, and he would get in fights with my grandma. My dad would always send me to my room, but I will always hear my grandpa's voice. He died one year ago from liver cancer because he used to smoke, too.

Sometimes I wish I could have stopped him from drinking and smoking, but I know I couldn't have done anything. I might, but I don't know. It makes me cry just to think about him. I know he wasn't a bad man, he just had a problem.

I hope you can understand what I'm writing about. I would really enjoy joining SADD. I think it is really good that some people care. Please, if you can, write back.

Love,
Heather

Mr. Nelson,

I grew up with an alcoholic grandfather. I didn't quite realize that alcoholism was a disease until people like you began to enlighten me. He lives in Wisconsin and every time he calls, he is crying. He says he misses us. You can tell that he's drunk. He slurs his words and acts very sad. My mom always ends up in tears because he only calls when he's drunk.

My dad's mom is an alcoholic. I just found out two months ago. She polished off two bottles of vodka in six days. She and my grandpa were visiting and I finally realized this one day.

My boyfriend has an alcoholic grandfather, also. My boyfriend has never touched any drug or alcohol is his life. Recently, I began drinking at parties. He found out and reminded me where alcohol can put you. I came to my senses and stopped drinking.

The scary thing is, I crave alcohol. It's hard to be strong, but it's been two weeks, and I haven't touched any alcohol. I was afraid I was going to be like my grandpa or grandma. Thanks to people who care, I'm clean and feel very good about myself.

As for my grandparents, it's too late. Now I want to inform people how alcohol hurts people who don't even drink.

Thank you,
Amy Sue

Dear Mr. Nelson,

I've been hearing a great deal about drinking. It applies very personally because my grandfather is an alcoholic. At this time in my life I have a hard time dealing with it. My grandmother, who is a drug and alcohol counselor for the hospital here, does nothing when he gets drunk. She just leaves. It's not a healthy situation. He's only what one calls a "situation alcoholic." . . . . he drinks when pain and stress get too much.

But every time he does, he hurts all of us. Even though I understand that, I don't know how to deal with it. Do you have any suggestion for me? I don't think I can help my grandpa, but I think I can help myself, and that's what I want to do.

Thank you,
Sarah

Mr. Nelson,

My grandfather has been a drunk all his life. Sometimes he will get so drunk he can't walk, yet he still drives his work truck to work.

He's been a drinker ever since my dad can remember. Luckily he has never been in an accident while drunk. He has several kids who are not from my grandma because he got drunk and, well, the rest I think you know.

Ever since I was ten I have tried to get him to stop, but he's so stubborn he won't listen I would like to know if you have any solutions for me to use. If so, please write back.

Sincerely,
Jeff

Dear Mr. Nelson,

Neither of my parents are alcoholics. They just drink socially, but alcoholism exists on both sides of my family. My grandmother, (Dad's mom) was an alcoholic. She was 'clean' for over 25 years. She recently heard that a glass of red wine will help her heart, so she decided to have a glass. Her heart was really bad so she kept drinking more. Now she is an alcoholic again. It's really sad. She thinks it's helping her, but it's not . . . . it's killing her. Sad to say, but she probably doesn't have more than a year to live.

My grandfather on my mom's side was also an alcoholic. He beat my grandmother, and sometimes my mom and her brothers and sisters. He never even attempted to get help. He was also a professional boxer, not a good combination. He had cancer and one day he overdosed on pills and was drunk at the same time. He crashed his car and died instantly. My mom said she wasn't even sad. In a way she was glad he wouldn't beat her or her family anymore.

I have friends who drink, but I don't because there's no reason to, and I have been affected by alcoholism too deeply. My point in writing this letter? Well, I'm not really sure, but thank you for speaking during your spare time and helping to decrease this huge problem.

Thank you,
Melissa

Dear Mr. Nelson,

I'm 15 years old and have grown up with an alcoholic in my family, my grandfather. Grandpa doesn't drink as much as he used to, but he always does. When my father and aunt were growing up, Grandpa would beat them, my dad mostly. I know of a few things he did, such as throwing him down the cellar stairs and strapping him to a chair and beating him with a flashlight.

My mother's ex-husband, Jim, was also an alcoholic. He used to beat her and my brothers. He never did anything to me because I didn't live with them, and my dad would have hurt him if he did. Because of Jim I really don't have a relationship with my mom. My parents got divorced when I was two or three, and Jim moved my mother and brothers all around.

It has affected my younger brother, Timmy, very badly. He has A.D.D. and is hyperactive. Jim is the only father he knew, and he doesn't realize that violence is wrong.

Thanks for listening and caring,
Jaymee

Mr. Nelson,

I never really knew my grandfather, but I've heard many stories about him. He was a decorated soldier in World War 2. After the war he became a successful photographer.

My mom loved my grandpa, but he had a serious alcohol problem. He was very abusive and an angry person. He even spent numerous times in prison for those problems. He wasn't always cruel and mean. I don't mean to bring out only the bad things in him, but these are the things that stand out in the stories that I hear.

The reason I really never knew my grandpa was because he was killed by a drunk driver when he was crossing the street to an Alcoholics Anonymous meeting. I'm really upset that I never knew him, but I am happy he was trying to get help. The fact that he did so many things to my mom's family, his alcohol abuse will always blacken the memory of my grandpa.

Kristian

Mr. Nelson,

After reading the letters you brought to our class, I thought I would write. My grandfather is an alcoholic but he doesn't look like some of the ones on a video we have seen. He comes home from work and drinks two beers, then he has a whole lot of brandy and water.

After that he will get in the car and he and my grandma will go to my aunt's house and play cards. I fear for his and my grandma's safety.

After your presentation, I now have the courage to go and talk to my grandma and grandpa about this problem. I would like them to be alive when I graduate.

Thank you a whole lot,
Joni

Dear Mr. Nelson,

Thanks for coming to our class. Well, I have a problem with my grandma's alcohol problem. I live with her now because my parents are gone. Ever since my grandpa died from drinking and smoking, my grandma has started to drink more and then she starts to accuse me of things.

Could you give me some advice? I would also like to learn more about SADD. Please write back.

Thank you for your time and caring,
Shelly

Mr. Nelson,

I know you have heard a lot of sad, heartbreaking stories. I would like to tell you a success story.

My grandparents had been alcoholics for years. When my dad was a child, most of his life was spent outside of or in the lobby of a bar. It wasn't unusual for him, that was all he knew.

After my grandma died, my grandpa became a really bad alcoholic. He came to our house drunk all the time, or he called. That's why we got an answering machine. I remember the fights. There was a lot more but memories are too painful.

I'd like for you to know my grandfather has remarried and doesn't drink alcohol anymore. He jokes about how his non-alcoholic beer tastes horrible, but I believe it's saved his life. I wish his new wife could do the same. She's really bad. She takes days off work to go to a bar.

Thank you
Andie

Mr. Nelson,

My grandmother and great-grandmother both died of liver poisoning when I was young. I didn't understand why, but now I know why. They both drank all their lives. Now that I think about it, I don't think that I wanted to know at a young age.

I've also seen what it can do to my mom. A few years ago my mom went on a drinking binge. It was at the same time my grandma and great-grandma died. I didn't understand. My parents were splitting up, my grandma and great-grandma died, and I thought my life was going to end as I knew it.

But now, as my mom isn't drinking anymore and my parents are still together, I learned from their mistakes not to drink. I am sad that I had to learn from my grandparents' mistakes. They had to die for me to learn. A lot of people sometimes have to learn that way.

Thanks,
Tammi

Dear Mr. Nelson,

I want to thank you for spending your time here at my high school, and I appreciate it very much.

I have many people in my family who like to drink, but only do it on certain occasions. My biggest worry is my grandfather. He's almost 60 years old and is still working. Every day when he comes home he has a cup of Jack Daniels or scotch, and my grandmother is tired of it.

Whenever I get a chance to visit, they're usually arguing because he drinks more than necessary and doesn't even realize it. I love him with all my heart and he is my last grandpa left, and I don't want to lose him, especially from drinking.

Once again, I would like to thank you for your time.

Robyn

Most of us are firm in our love and support of grandparents everywhere. They're a source of comfort, stories about old times and prime examples of honestly and good citizenship.

There are occasionally darker sides, seemingly related to alcohol or other drug abuses, as are related in many of my teenage writers' letters.

Most unexpectedly, one of only two phone calls I've ever had from a parent came from a highly-agitated San Francisco mother. She burned my ears almost nonstop for ten minutes about the content of a hand-written response I'd made to a freshman student who had written to me, in class, about her grandfather's situation.

This mother was absolutely incensed because she claimed I'd referred to her daughter's grandfather as a drunk.

"He isn't a drunk," she shouted over the phone. "When you don't have any facts, you don't have the right to say he's a drunk. You had my daughter in tears. How could you do such a thing? I'm going to call the school!," and then, she added unexpectedly, "She hasn't seen her grandfather in six years!"

I gleaned that her daughter was living away from home with an aunt. This girl had shown her aunt my letter, and the woman had called the girl's mother to read my letter to her.

The conversation ended with my giving the caller the teacher's name and the school phone number, and asked that she contact him. This mother needed to be reassured that I wasn't a monster who made little girls cry.

Afterwards, I dug out my copy of my response: *"I can understand your worry about your grandfather's drinking habits. It must be pretty awful for your grandmother to have to watch him each day turn from a nice guy to an obnoxious person once he's had too much to drink.*

I'm sure your grandmother realizes that it's futile to argue with a drunk person, but they say such awful things and repeat themselves constantly, that it becomes difficult not to argue back.

. . . I hope your grandfather decides to make some changes before his health is impaired too badly. Some time, when he's completely sober and seems to want to talk seriously with you about himself, do tell him honestly about your concerns. He will be listening to you!"

It became quite apparent that I didn't get the full picture of the girl/grandfather situation from her letter. If the granddaughter's only contact in six years had been via occasional phone conversations, as her mother indicated, her imagination may have played a part.

How did this mother get my phone number? She must have gone through the operator and tried each of the several similar listings until she got a "Yes" to her question, "Are you the man who goes to schools and talks about alcohol and drunk driving?"

It came as a surprise to receive so many letters with stories of grandparents' troubled alcoholic lives, and the distress felt by the young writers. My readers will have shared with me the expressions ranging from annoyance, to grave concerns, to fear.

The experiences were sobering to these teenagers, and perhaps even helpful in affecting their own decisions. So many had to literally watch their grandparents die from the alcohol abuse they couldn't or chose not to escape.

As a grandfather myself of seven loving, talented and savvy grandchildren, I can picture their dismay if our visits ever resulted in unwelcome or scary behavior.

CHAPTER NINE

"When you were talking to our class, I felt like you were talking just to me. I just wish you could have talked to my brother and maybe he would be alive today."

Mr. Nelson,

My sister is hooked on cocaine and her boyfriend is a cocaine addict and an alcoholic, and plus they have a 13 month old kid. I don't drink anymore, or do drugs, but I used to and I know all about it. I don't know what to do with my sister, her boyfriend and my nephew. Please send me some information on how to deal with my problem.

Bob

Dear Mr. Nelson,

How can you tell someone not to drink and drive? My brother used to drink and drive, and last Saturday he hit a side-bank on the road when he was drunk. He's not an alcoholic, but he just doesn't listen. He is 20 right now.

My sister used to be addicted to drugs but not to alcohol. I'll tell you it's not the way to go. She went to juvenile hall, got in fist fights with my mom, and ran away from home. It took her a few months to get over drugs. She could tell you it's not the way to go.

I'm not addicted to drugs, but I do smoke cigarettes and pot, but I shouldn't. It's not the way to go, if you think it's cool. I'm going to quit.

Sincerely,
Jason

Dear Mr. Nelson,

This summer I lost a very dear friend in a drunk driving accident. To be truthful, it was my brother and his best friend. All this time I thought to myself that it could never happen to me.

I somewhat blame myself because I was drinking with them that night, and I didn't take their keys. I've never really talked to anyone about this. My family still pretty much doesn't talk about it. If someone brings up the subject then my parents will change the subject.

When you were talking to our class, I felt like you were talking just to me. I just wish that you could have talked to my brother and maybe he would be alive today.

Thanks for caring,
Andrea

Dear Mr. Nelson,

My dad and older brother have always drank together, and now they're trying to pressure me. I tell then "NO." All my friends drink. My brother is on drugs, too. My dad and brother like to hit me sometimes, but I want to help them. I just don't know how to help them.

They call me names sometimes, and I'm starting to believe them. I wish they would just go away, or I can just disappear. I almost got away with suicide. Thanks for listening.

Sincerely,
Arianna

Dear Mr. Nelson,

I have a little problem with my brother. Over the last three years he has started smoking and drinking again. Five years ago he started smoking, drinking, and doing drugs. I thought he would never start again, but he has.

My dad told him if he ever started again he would have to find someplace else to live. I'm scared he will get kicked out of our house, or he will drive drunk and get hurt or killed. My grandma just died, and I wouldn't be able to live if my brother died. I love my brother, and he means a lot to me. Please write me back.

Love,
Melissa

Mr. Nelson,

Hi, this is Linda, and I'm afraid for my sister and I don't know what to do about it. Every night she'll drink more and more and sometimes she'll say, "I don't want my kids," or "I want to kill myself."

I don't know how to handle this. Please help me out. Just don't tell my mom this because she doesn't like to talk about it.

I would love to join SADD because I don't want to die young. I don't like to drink because it's not good for our health.

Linda

Mr. Nelson,

My brother is an alcoholic. He has gotten into trouble with the law over drinking. I was scared he was going to kill someone drinking because he has such an attitude problem. He ended up in Juvy. Now, he's in rehab for a year. He's already served five months. I talked to him the other day and he says he'll still drink when he gets out, as well as the other drugs he does.

I was an alcoholic for two years then got help, so now I no longer drink. I just left home to go live with my best friend whose four friends just died of drunk driving. Also, three were my friends. It hurts, but anyway I left, but my mother found alcohol in my room so she threw everything of mine in her house away, clothes, pictures, letters, etc. It hurts.

Over 90% of my family (on my mom's side) are all alcoholics, so we've experienced it all. That hurts as well. I will never drink except maybe once a year. When I get my license I'll be the sober driver for others. When I get older I wish to help others with drug related problems, be a juvenile probation officer or a police officer.

I think having a speaker coming to this school was a wonderful idea. It helps people relate to their problems. I think you're really a great person helping others the way you do. I bet a lot are thankful for having you care so much.

Please write if there is time for you. Also, please send more information on SADD or on helping others. Thanks a lot for helping.

Penny

Dear Mr. Nelson,

I am a 15 year old sophomore, and I have a younger sister, by one year, who's a freshman. We have heavy drinking problems on both sides of my family, but my parents were the ones who decided to go against it, and didn't drink. My dad was a social drinker, though.

My sister and I have both drank. As a matter of fact, we had our first drink at my 12th birthday party. I don't like to drink, though, because I'm afraid of becoming an alcoholic like some of my relatives.

I then find out my sister was hanging around people who smoke pot. I also found empty vodka bottles in her backpack. She started to ask me to search my house (I don't live with her) for vodka to give her. I told her we didn't have any.

I love her so much. She's the only real thing I have, and I don't know what to do. My mom said my dad drank too much, but I never saw it. Now that I live with him, I see it. He spends his days with my alcoholic cousin and comes home late at night drunk. He does this a lot, but claims he's only a social drinker. Please advise me on what I should do.

Don't write your return address on the envelope. Put it inside the letter. I don't want my parents to know I wrote this.

Thank you,
Malena

Dear Mr. Nelson,

My sister just turned 18 on November 29th. She goes out every weekend and sometimes during the week and gets drunk and stoned. I'm really scared. She's my only sister.

In the past year we really started getting along, and now I'm afraid I'm going to lose her. I would have had another older sister, but she died at three, so I'm trying my best to keep the only one I have.

I think she's getting it from my father. He is an alcoholic. He left my mom when I was two, but my sister is picking up his bad habits.

Please help me. What should I do? Also, can you please send me some info on SADD.

Thank you,
Laura

Dear Mr. Nelson,

My step-father drinks a lot sometimes, I get really scared, not for myself, because I can sort of handle myself, but I'm scared for my little brother and two sisters.

When my dad gets drunk he yells a lot and gets real mad and sometimes starts to swing and hit us. It got to the point to where one time I had to take the kids to a neighbor's house for the night.

Thanks for listening. So far you are the only one who really listened to me. Sometimes I think most people just don't give a damn.

Sincerely,
Brad

Dear Mr. Nelson,

I left my house because my sister was drinking, and she told me to my face that she was going to kill me. I didn't know what to do, so I left my house.

My mom didn't care where I was, so I stayed away for two days. Then one of my teachers thought I was kind of down, so she reported it to one of the counselors here at school. The counselor reported it to the nurse, and the nurse called me down and started asking questions. I didn't want to say anything. She gave me some numbers to call if I decided to leave again, so now I have places to go.

Thanks for caring,
Jean

Dear Mr. Nelson,

My brother is an alcoholic and a drug addict. I really love my brother, and I want to talk to him, but that's hard to do because he was drunk and doing drugs one night, and he murdered his girlfriend. I don't know what to do. I love him, but what do I talk to him about?

If you have any advice for me, please tell me. I need to know.

Thanks for listening,
Traci

Dear Mr. Nelson,

Along with so many other teenagers, I know someone who drinks a little too often, actually whenever he can get his hands on it, which is just about every weekend.

This particular person gets so drunk, he often passes out before even attempting to go home. There have been times when he and all his friends were drunk, yet they gave him the keys and gambled with their lives.

This person has greatly affected me and my family, for he is my brother. Many nights I've had to sneak him into the house, telling my parents he fell asleep and was too tired to walk on his own.

Now, I know that I shouldn't lie because it just lets him get away with it, and allows him more chances to play with his life, his friends' lives, and everyone's emotions. Also I find myself praying for his safety when he goes out and staying awake until he comes home. "He needs to be safe," I used to say. I used to feel that if I stayed awake, he'd always come home safe. I don't know anymore.

My parents have recently found out and have really come down hard. Their son, #1 he used to be, the best son anyone could have. Such a star that once in a while, their daughter, me, wasn't there.

He isn't allowed to do much anymore, but now, when he does go out, not only does he drink, he gets wasted on drugs, too.

I don't know what to do! My parents tell me if I find out he's doing this, which I already have, to tell them! I can't because he threatens to hurt me, but I feel he's already hurt me enough, and no more pain can actually be inflicted upon me . . . could it? Please help! Thank you.

Lyndra

Dear Mr. Nelson,

I have a father and brother who are alcoholics. My father has been an alcoholic since I was born. When he gets drunk, I do not like it because he hits my mother. He has changed somewhat since I talked to him. I feel that he really doesn't care for me.

My brother just became an alcoholic also, about two years ago. I'm really worried about him. He has a driver's license, and he drinks and drives. I think that one day he will hurt himself and other people.

Sometimes I just wish that a policeman will arrest him for drinking and driving, and take away his license. I'm really worried. Please write to me and give me advice to help my brother. If you can't, thank you for caring.

Sidney

Dear Mr. Nelson,

I'm really worried about my brother. He's 17 years old and a senior here at school. My brother is always getting drunk and smoking weed. I don't understand why he's doing this.

My dad had a really bad alcohol problem. My parents almost got a divorce over this. My dad drank so much that his doctor told him he would die if he didn't quit. I'm happy to say that my dad has quit for over four years after being an alcoholic since he was sixteen.

I'm really scared about my brother. I always talk to him about it, but it doesn't help, or stop him. My brother's already got a DUI and lost his license for a year. All he did was laugh about it. He thinks it made him look macho or something.

He always steals money from my parents. I don't think they're aware of it though. They do know he drinks. I don't think they realize how serious it is, though. I don't know what to do. I'm scared something's going to happen to him. He's getting worse and worse.

Thanks for your time,
Kristie

Dear Mr. Nelson,

My sister, who just turned 14 over the summer, has a bad drinking problem. See, when my mom says "No" to her about going to parties, she runs away from home and goes out and gets drunk. I'm really worried about her. Do you know how I can talk to her about it? Thanks for coming to our school.

Lena

Dear Mr. Nelson,

I have a 19-year-old brother, and I think he's on the verge of heading in the direction of the guy whose letter you read. I've warned him twice. About a year ago, my brother was a gangbanger. He had a really close friend who was hit by a police car . . . cut him in half. The driver was drunk (just buzzed). My brother still hasn't stopped. Let me see, he's had his driver's license taken away, and he was put on probation.

I go cruising with him, and when he drives drunk, I go with him sometimes. He goes to a lot of parties where there is alcohol. That doesn't help any. Myself, I hate alcohol. I don't like the taste.

I would appreciate it if you would give me some tips on how to stop him, or at least cut him down slowly. Thank you for talking about alcohol with us. It makes me dislike it even more.

Your Friend,
Jason

Dear Mr. Nelson,

Hi, I may not be listening well, but I know what you're talking about. My brother gets drunk a lot. I think I'm his little sister. I hate seeing him drunk. I know he's had sex with people he didn't know because he was drunk. He's only 18 and I'm 15. I really don't want to follow his footsteps, and I don't think I will.

I want my brother to stop and for my cousin, Josh, too. He's all messed up; he can't stop what he's doing. I think he's going to die by being in an accident on his motorcycle.

My brother does other stuff I won't name, but I will say it's bad. I try to tell him not to do it, but he does it anyway. I had to drive for him about a month ago because he was drunk or buzzed. Well, what could I do?

Angel is just a nickname. I don't want you to tell my parents.

Angel

Dear Mr. Nelson,

Hi. The only reason I'm writing to you is because my brother says I have a problem. But before I tell you about my so-called problem, I should tell you I don't believe I have one. So what if I drink every once-in-a-while? So what if I need a drink in the morning? It is just to get me going. It's not like I do it all day. I don't even get drunk. It just makes me feel better.

You see, my grandmother just passed away, and it seems as though a drink is the only way to get through the day. But don't get worried that I'm going to hurt someone by driving because I don't have a license to drive.

When I was 15, I was arrested for being drunk in a public place, and they suspended my right to receive a license until I turn 18. I turn 18 in seven months. I am kind of worried that I'll hurt someone, but I don't think I will.

Like I said, I don't have a problem.

Thanks anyway,
Kourtney

Dear Mr. Nelson,

I need some advice. My brother's fiancée is a drunk. She's also addicted to prescriptions. She's drunk most every day of her life, and she takes almost 20 pills a day.

My brother is in prison, so he's not there to help her. She won't let any of us help her. She says she's just fine, that there's nothing wrong. Every other week when we go to see my brother, I see the pain and worry in his eyes. I want to help her and take away my brother's pain, but how? What can I do? She's slowly killing herself, and she doesn't even realize it.

Is there anything I can do to make her see and understand? Please help.

Sincerely,
Katrina

Dear Mr. Nelson,

I'm going to be 16 in December, and my sister's a drunk. She married a guy who's a drunk. Every time he got drunk or did drugs, he would beat my sister, and sometimes he would try to kill her.

My sister divorced this guy, and he got put in prison. She said she was going to her "meeting," but every time I would baby-sit, I would find alcohol in the fridge.

Last Thursday my sister's ex-husband got out of prison, and my sister took him back. She wants the rest of the family to accept him if he can prove he's not a drunk or a druggie. Sometimes I don't think I can ever accept him back because he not only hurt my sister, he threatened my mom and my other sister too.

My sister used to talk about my dad. She used to say he was a drunk because he would have a few beers in his own home, but my dad never drove anywhere after he drank. I finally realized that the reason she said that was because she didn't want to face her own reality.

I used to drink when I went to parties until I realized what was happening to my sister. I never got into a car with anyone who was drinking. I don't go to parties anymore because I'm scared that if I go, I'll get drunk. I don't want to drink because I would end up drinking a lot because for some reason I love the taste of alcohol. I've never been able to figure it out, but that's why I don't go to any parties.

Mecina

Dear Mr. Nelson,

I'm a 15-year-old freshman girl who has an older sister who drinks. It hurts me to see her like this. Although she has attended AA, I feel it hasn't helped her any. Sometimes, after a meeting, she'll go out and drink. My mother knows about it, but that doesn't stop her. On weekends she won't come home until the next morning, and she's usually drunk. It scares me because I know someday she'll have too much to drink and never come home.

I also have a dad who also is a drunk and a druggie. My parents are divorced, so I don't have to see him come home drunk, but it hurts me inside. When I see them drunk, it helps me to say, "No" because I don't want to be like them.

Thank you,
Elizabeth

Dear Mr. Nelson,

Hi, I'm 15 years old. My "sweet 16" is coming up in a few days. I'm an alcoholic. I've been drinking since I was 12. For about three months, I've been trying to stop.

I never worried too much about it until my oldest brother, who has been drinking for three years, tried other drugs. My brother is now a major druggie, and I think it was because he first tried drugs when he was drunk.

I care so much for my brother, but when he's on drugs, he doesn't care about me. In fact, he treats me like crap. I can't even tell when he's drunk, high, or what anymore. I want to stop. I want my brother to be okay. I don't want to turn out like him.

I can't tell my parents, so I can't get help. I have to do it by myself, and I will. I just want my brother to be okay. Several weeks ago, he went to jail for embezzlement, and only a few days ago my brother O.D.'d on ecstacy. I don't want my brother to hurt himself anymore, and I will stop to show him he can. I feel like it's my fault that he is the way he is, and that's why I feel it's my duty to help him stop.

Thanks for just being there.
Allison

Dear Mr. Nelson,

Hi, my name is Teresa. I have a sister who likes to go out and drink a lot. She goes out all night and comes home drunk about three times a week. She doesn't drive drunk, though. My mother or other sister usually picks her up, but I'm still scared for her.

She's mentioned taking drugs. I didn't know what being drunk was like at that time because I wasn't around it, but one night my friends and I were introduced to it. We all drank because we wanted to by like the other guys. Since I had never drunk before, I was so badly messed up that I passed out on the couch.

When my sister came to get me, I didn't even know her. The next day my mother told me we were going to take a drive. We ended up at the hospital. I had an appointment to see a doctor. The doctor explained that as much alcohol as I had drunk could have killed me. He said I would have died if no one had caught me in time.

Since then my sister and I never thought about drinking again. I plan to join SADD. I also hope a lot of other teens learn just to say, "No."

Thanks,
Teresa

Dear Mr. Nelson,

This letter is about my 19-year-old brother. I'm really scared for him because he just turned 19 three days ago and he's a big alcoholic. I know how it is for him because my whole family used to do it. For my brother's life, I pray every night that the coming weekend he won't go and get a hotel to party in. By the way, for the last three weekends he rented a hotel. It's very sad because one time I walked into the hotel to ask him if I could get my jacket out of his truck. I walked in and not only was he drinking, but he was getting stoned with my best friend.

I've talked to my mom about this situation, and she told me that she's always tried her hardest to stop him, but there's not much she can do because he's over 18. I wish there's something I can do because I want my brother and I to do more stuff together before he kills himself either by alcohol or pot.

By the way, my brother dropped out of school when he was in the 10th grade. My brother was the best brother anyone could have before he started to drink. I know for a fact that if he stops before it's too late, he'll be the same brother. I love him a lot!! If you don't mind, I'd love to join SADD.

Thanks for listening,
Kym

Dear Mr. Nelson,

My brother is an alcoholic, but he won't admit it. I know there's nothing I can do. He doesn't live with my family. He lives with his friends.

I love my brother. I hate to see him like this. I've had to sober him up. He's real blunt about drinking. Although the drinking is generic, it doesn't excuse him.

I, myself, do not drink. The only thing I've done remotely close to drinking was a half-glass of a screwdriver (orange juice and vodka). I don't know what to do about my brother. He is only 17 years old, and already he has to go to AA. He won't admit his problems. I miss having him around.

Cassandra

Dear Mr. Nelson,

I hope you understand what I'm trying to say. It's my dad; he has been drinking since I was really little. My older brother has followed him with his drinking. I'm so scared of my dad driving with me in the car after he has been drinking. I am proud of my brother. He does not drive after he has been drinking.

I'm also scared of following in both of their footsteps. I am surprised that I have not followed them yet. I am about to cry, this is so hard to talk about, but I can manage. I'm only 16 years old, and my brother's 21, and he has been drinking since he was 17 years old.

I love both of them, my dad and my brother. They both don't want to admit that they have a problem. I know they both do. I don't want this to happen to me, so I'm doing the best I can to stop it from going on to one more generation. I thank you a lot for talking to our class.

Thank you,
Angela

Dear Mr. Nelson,

About a year and a half ago, my brother went to a party at his friend's house, and everybody got drunk and then went four-wheeling. My brother was driving his jeep with two people with him. None were wearing seatbelts. They ended up crashing by taking too sharp of a turn and went into a roll.

All three were thrown from the jeep. Jason, my brother, got banged up really bad, and one of his friends did, too. The third person got caught under the jeep and was dying. My brother tried doing CPR, but his friend was coughing up blood because his lung had collapsed. Now my brother has just gotten off parole for involuntary manslaughter and is going to get his license back in a few weeks.

Jay

Dear Mr. Nelson,

Thank you so much for coming here to talk with us. My sister drinks a lot, and she always drives. I tell her not to, but she doesn't take me seriously. My mom knows she drinks, but she won't talk to her because when she does, my sister gets really mad and says that my mom doesn't trust her.

My sister is over the legal drinking age; she's 22. She still lives at home and doesn't have a job. All she does is drink. I never want to be an alcoholic because I think it's a waste.

I've been drunk one time, and two of my friends ended up getting arrested, but I got away. I don't ever want to drink again, and I haven't, but before I drank a lot. That was close, and I never want to take a chance like that again.

Thank you so much. It's good to know that people care.

Melissa

Dear Mr. Nelson,

I would like to tell you that I'm having problems with my brother; he drinks alcohol. I hoped he wouldn't because it's bad for his health and body, but he doesn't listen to me or my mom. I'm afraid that he's going to do something to my mom, or kill her.

One example is that he beats me up, and then he acts like he didn't do anything wrong, so he wouldn't get in trouble with my dad and mom. My mom

*and dad are divorced. I don't know what to do. Can you give me something to
do? Please write back.*

Sincerely,
Monica

Dear Mr. Nelson,

*It is hard for me to write someone who has never met me or known my
family. Well, it must have started two years ago when my brother and sister got
into a car accident. My brother had been drinking with my sister at a party.
He decided it was time to go. My sister and her boyfriend got into the car with
him.*

*I guess it was going okay until he went too fast around a turn and hit a
bulldozer head on. My brother and sister were in the front. My brother hit his
head on the steering wheel, but my sister hit her head on the dash, and then the
seat hit the back of her head and crushed her head like a sandwich. She is still
in a coma. Bruises are all that her boyfriend got.*

*My brother is out and right back to where he was, drinking and doing
drugs. The reason I've written you this is because I've always said that I would
not be like them, but I have become like them. In fact, I'm supposed to go to a
party this weekend. I don't want to be the outcast. I want to be with my friends,
but I don't know if I want to do the things we do anymore.*

*Can you please write to me and tell me how to say "No" without losing my
friends? Can you send me more on SADD? I really need help.*

Thank you,
Amorita

Dear Mr. Nelson,

*I'm writing to you because I have a lot of family who drink, like my uncle.
Once he got so drunk that he wanted to leave, but my mom told him "No." then
he tried to fight my mom.*

*I've gotten drunk before, and I was riding my bike and almost got hit a
few times by a car. One day my sister got drunk, and she was taking a shower.
She was shaving her legs, and all of a sudden I heard my sister crying. When I
walked in, she was bleeding from her wrists. It looked like she shot herself; there
was blood all over the place. Because she was drunk, she might have died.*

*My best friend's mom died from drunk driving, and he still cries. Thank
you for helping us. Please write back and give it to my teacher.*

Your friend,
Jerry

Dear Mr. Nelson,

I was wondering if maybe you could help me out. My sister has a problem with drinking. It's getting so bad that the other day I saw three empty 40's in her room and a six-pack in the closet. My sister is almost 20 years old, and she has a baby girl. I'm worried because she goes out and parties with her friends, and then she thinks she's sober enough to drive home. I'm worried that something's going to happen to her, and that her baby's going to grow up not knowing what to think of her mother. Her father is the same way.

I've tried talking to her about it, but she is so stubborn she won't listen to a word I say. My mother and father don't know that her boyfriend sneaks into the house late at night and brings her beer. What should I do? I don't want to tell on her because then she'll never forgive me and never trust me again.

Thanks for taking time to listen to my problems. I want your advice.

Thank you,
Hannah

Dear Mr. Nelson,

Hi. My brother has a problem with alcohol. He has gotten his license revoked. He no longer can drive, at least for two years. He's still driving his truck. My brother has had several jobs, and has lost them because he would come to work very drunk.

I love my brother very much, but he lies to my parents, and asks for money for buying beer. I hope he gets caught driving drunk, so maybe they can stop him, but maybe it wouldn't help.

I'm glad you came to talk to us today. I appreciated the letters you passed around. They helped me know that I'm not the only one. Thank you.

Sincerely,
Nicole

One thing can be said for brothers and sisters looking at their sibling's alcohol or other drug problems, they may not have solutions, but their eyes are open. It's evident that most feel they see the situation more clearly than their parents.

Should a brother or sister tell on each other? Would it help address the alcohol abuse problem and open the way for a solution? For the most part, siblings aren't squealing on each other. They suffer a lot, but try to handle the usually increasing problem with words and hope. They don't want to lose trust or closeness.

You don't get the parents' viewpoints from these letters. If they were to speak out, we might find that they have become numbed to their son's or daughter's plight. In their minds they could feel they've pleaded, argued, and threatened for years and now see little hope for change. Have they lost the will to fight?

Most brothers and sisters are still looking for answers to regain the formerly loving and secure relationship with their sibling. What sort of an answer could I give that would be helpful? These teenagers desperately want to be encouraged, so I do that. How can you ask them to just walk away?

If there's an indication that there's an Alateen group functioning in their town or in one nearby, I almost always suggest that they ask around and attend one or two meetings.

My standard form of encouragement includes: *"I had a letter last year from another student at your school, and they told me that they finally went to several Alateen meetings and found that they can now handle their problem with an alcoholic family member much better. Would you consider trying that?"*

Once I had received a couple of positive responses, I felt comfortable and hopeful doing this. There are no great answers.

A letter arrived yesterday, with the envelope addressed to me in my own handwriting. A glimpse told me that it was from a teenage girl who had written to me several weeks ago while I was speaking with her freshman class. In my response letter to her, I had asked for more information and had enclosed a self-addressed, stamped envelope. Here is the sequence of letters:

November 13th

Dear Mr. Nelson,

Well, thanks for coming to our class and talking with us. I need to find a way to get my sister to stop drinking. I can't take her to some specialist because she won't go. What I can do is try to stop her from partying.

I have to blame this on my dad, because he is such a jerk that he would have her drink hard liquor and other stuff when my sister was little. Now, she's messed up. She can't help it. Just this morning she showed me her Mr. Pibb mixed with liquor.

I remember when I was little I almost got in a car crash because my dad was driving drunk. Now I don't see my dad, but he screwed up my sister. I will never forgive him because he screwed up my sister. Thank you so much.

Love always,
Victoria

✉

November 14th

Dear Victoria,

I wanted to send you this special note because you wrote such a thoughtful letter to me about your sister when I was at your school on Tuesday.

You can't be blamed for being angry with your dad for his part in your sister's awful situation. Am I right in guessing that this is an older sister? Is she still in high school or has she completed it?

It isn't often that I get letters from young family members telling of their father or mother pushing alcohol on their kids. Most times it does lead to the children's dependency on alcohol later on. It's so very harmful!

Your sister has a serious problem to face if she's at a point of "needing" alcohol to get her day started. If she was drinking just for the fun and good feeling, talking with her might prove to be just the way to go.

Do you think you sister realizes that alcohol is such a treacherous drug? Does she believe she can stop drinking anytime she wants to?

My basic feeling from what you wrote, Victoria, is that your sister has reached a point where quitting on her own may be most difficult. She has to want to awfully badly, and has to feel a great need to quit drinking.

Your own life and your future are very precious. These are the years when you want to concentrate on your studies, on making life-long friendships, and getting involved in activities at your school.

You can do these important things if you keep your own determination to not allow alcohol or other mind-altering drugs to become a part of your young life.

I know you will make a wonderful SADD member!

Would you write again, soon, and tell me more about what you're planning and answer some of my questions? I've enclosed an envelope, so you won't have to hunt for one.

Your friend,
Ken Nelson

November 26th

Dear Mr. Nelson,

Sorry it took me so long to write back. I've been busy. Things are starting to get better. It is Nov. 26th, and tonight my sister was in the hospital for drinking. She drank a half-bottle of brandy and took some drug that started with an "s." she threw up six times. She's better now.

She's sitting with me right now. She read your letter. She was touched. My sister almost died tonight. I don't know what I'd do if I lost her. Thank you so much for everything, Mr. Nelson, you have helped me in such a great way. Even though I only met you once, you will forever be in my memories.

My sister finally realizes I wrote a letter to you. She's probably thinking, "Oh, my God, not another counselor," but I don't care. Besides, my sister could have died two days before my birthday. I hope we really got to her about how bad this is.

She is my older sister and is a beautiful redhead with beautiful green eyes. She still goes to high school and also goes to a special school (a school for bad kids). My sister and I have a two-year age difference. We are so close. We really love each other, and I really care for her and want the best for her.

Well, I'm glad it's all over now. I think she's probably going to go back to it, but I hope she starts to do something for herself. Write back, please. Thanks.

Love always,
Victoria

I did respond to Victoria's second letter. She didn't write a third, however, so we lost touch.

Her observation that her sister was probably thinking, "Oh my God, not another counselor," prompted me to encourage exactly that route. I reminded her that I've received many letters indicating that continued counseling has helped others with deeply-embedded alcohol problems.

Victoria seemed to fully understand that her older sister's life was really at stake. I'm hopeful that maybe she did convince her that more counseling was a courageous, even though an understandably embarrassing route to take.

CHAPTER TEN

"My uncle and I used to be very close. He was the
only family member who truly understood me,
but recently my uncle started drinking heavily."

Dear Mr. Nelson,

My whole family is really good about not driving drunk. But my uncle, he drinks every day. It makes my family really worry. My grandmother worries the most. She can't sleep at night when she knows he's drinking. The way it affects me is that I live with my grandmother. I'm the one who takes care of her when she worries. It hurts me to watch her cry all night.

We've tried to make him stop before he dies or gets really hurt, but he won't listen to us. I hope you understand my problem. My uncle was in an accident a few weeks ago, but he wasn't badly injured.

Thank you,
Pricilla

Dear Mr. Nelson,

I have two alcoholics in my family. The one I'm worried about is my uncle. He lives with my grandmother who I love dearly. My uncle is unemployed and isn't really looking for a job. Whenever I go over to her house (which I'll do tomorrow), I'm afraid of him. He constantly yells at my grandmother. He makes her cry every time he yells at her. I've never seen him hit her, but I'm sure it's happened.

For a long time, I didn't know about his problem. A few months ago, I was in the family room watching TV and found a bottle of alcohol a quarter full. When I asked him about it, my uncle just said, "I don't have a problem."

I hadn't said anything about a problem. I know for a fact that is the reason his wife divorced him.

He occasionally hits my baby cousins. One's ten and the other's seven. The ten-year-old told me a while ago. They don't live with him now, though. I'm still scared when I go over there. I really want him to stop hurting my grandmother.

The other alcoholic is my grandfather. I'm sure he'll be dead within a year. If there is anything I can do, please tell me. Thank you.

Yours truly,
Marriah

Mr. Nelson,

My family and I are scared. My uncle is 29 and gets blitzed almost every day. He has to, to be able to go to sleep. My dad used to, but because of my mother, he stopped.

I want students to know that drinking stinks. My grandfather ruined his marriage because of booze. Also, his children would not associate with him. I detest this drug, and wish it would be banished off this earth.

Thank you for letting me ramble on. Please send me more information on SADD.

Jennifer

Mr. Nelson,

I'm 15 years old. I don't have a drinking problem, but I have an uncle who drinks a lot and now he is in the hospital. I told him, and kept on telling him, to stop drinking because one day he will die. Even my aunt is trying to stop him. It seems that no matter what we try, he still drinks. Now he's lost his license and his car. Can you give me some information on what to say to him and how?

Thank you for coming to our school. I also have lots of friends who drink a lot and are into drugs. Life is very difficult and lots of decisions to make.

Claudie

Mr. Nelson,

I don't know what to do about my uncle. He is always drinking. He went to the doctor's, for he started having seizures from it and he almost killed himself twice. He will be awake in one minute, then asleep the next.

I remember when I went to go visit with him and, in the middle of our conversation, he fell asleep. All of my family members are trying to help him stop drinking, but we don't know where to start. He already has cancer and could die. I can't go through another death without going crazy.

I had to go to six funerals this year, and I can't stand the thought of my favorite uncle dying.

Well, thanks for your time and for caring.

Sincerely,
Lisa

Dear Mr. Nelson,

I know very well that alcohol is dangerous. My uncle who lives in Nevada is having a big problem with it. I have not seen him in about a year, but I do care for him and wish I could help in some way. About two weeks ago, he had to go to the hospital because he almost died from drinking.

Although he came so near to death, he still drinks. He lost his job and verbally abuses his mother and physically abuses his wife. His mother has spent over three thousand dollars to send him to get help. He stays for about a week and then leaves.

I know he's under a lot of stress since his father passed away two years ago, and the responsibilities of supporting his family have fallen to him, but he shouldn't have to kill himself to try. I just wish he would get some help.

Please write before it's too late. Please send information about the programs that could help.

Worried,
Michelle

Mr. Nelson,

I'm just writing to tell you that my uncle is a very heavy drinker. Every day after work, he is in the garage, drinking. He has said he's tried to quit numerous times but can't. I just think he doesn't want to.

I'm the kind of person who thinks you can do anything you want to. My uncle had some problems when he was younger that I don't know much about. Those problems led him to drinking. He has already been caught twice driving drunk, and got his license suspended. That didn't help too much because he drives for a living, so he got a "worker's license."

I fear for my uncle and the lives around him. I really hope he doesn't turn out a statistic of drunk driving.

Thanks for your time.

Nicole

Mr. Nelson,

I am a 10th grader at this school, and I think that you are a great person for caring about other peoples' problems.

My family has a problem with alcohol. My grandma has six children and five of them are alcoholics. My aunt is the worst. She has been drinking for 13 years. I feel so sorry for her. She gets so sick, she sometimes coughs up blood. My cousins, one 15 and one 13 go through beatings every day. One time my cousin was beat so bad she had blisters on her back from the belt.

The reason I'm writing is that I care a lot about my aunt and I want her to get help. She's been in and out of rehab centers, but none seem to help. I know she can only change if she wants to, but I love her, and I don't want her to die. I would appreciate it if you would write me back and give me some advice.

Thank you,
Natalie

Mr. Nelson,

I just wanted to tell you that my uncle died because of alcohol. He was an easy man to love but was very depressed, and alcohol didn't help him any. He came over only once in a while to eat because he didn't eat a lot.

One day he was drinking a lot at his home by himself. He was sitting in his room with all the doors open and the music was on very low, practically a whisper. He was sitting there for a long time, drinking. He took one of his guns, put it in his mouth, and pulled the trigger.

They say he died because of a gunshot wound. I say he died because of alcohol. I miss him coming over, and I miss his smell. Thank you for listening to my story.

Tonya

Mr. Nelson,

My uncle who I live with drinks a lot, and he's really mean when he drinks. He doesn't drink beer, but vodka and other related beverages. To tell the truth, I hate that, and have asked him to stop or cut down. He does for a while, but then he has it back to the original level it was within a couple of days.

When he gets mad, he's scary, but he's even worse when he's been drinking. My uncle tries to pick fights with us, and I can ignore it most of the time. For my brother, it's harder to ignore the temptation to fight, so eventually it comes to blows, and I have had to pull them apart.

Once my uncle turned and yelled at me to get off, and when I continued to pull him off, he hit me in the jaw, and it hurt real bad, but I had to get him off my brother!

Thanks for caring,
Annie

Dear Mr. Nelson,

My uncle and I used to be very close. He was the only family member who truly understood me. But just recently my uncle started drinking heavily. He goes to numerous bars at night and gets extremely drunk. When he gets drunk, he likes to pick fights. He's a big guy, but one of these days he's going to go out and get drunk and pick a fight with the wrong person!

When he gets drunk, he comes to my house around 3:00 a.m. and crashes on my bedroom floor. I usually try and take this time to tell him how I feel about his drinking, but he just says, "I'll be fine." I even think he might be using drugs. Help! How can I talk to him? Please send some information.

Love,
Amy

Dear Mr. Nelson,

I'm an exchange student from Denmark. My family in Denmark often drinks a lot. My uncle is an alcoholic. He stayed at my grandma's house. He didn't pay anything so now she had to sell her house, and still has no money. Now he moved to my grandpa's house; he has no money, either. It really hurts to see his kids when they have to throw him out.

I don't like it when adults drink. When teenagers drink, they just get funny. When adults drink, they get wired. Over here, I live with a Mormon family, so I have experienced parties without alcohol. They are fun, too. But parties with alcohol are so much easier because everyone becomes your friend. In Denmark there is no drinking age for beer and wine. The drinking age for hard alcohol is 18. There is almost no drinking and driving among teenagers because the driving age is 18. Also, because there are of a lot of trains and busses.

Love,
Kristine

Dear Mr. Nelson,

I'm a sophomore, 15 years old. I thoroughly enjoyed your speech. My mother and father are both sober alcoholics, but the big problem is my uncle; he's a big alcoholic. He used to stay with my parents and me for a while, and he always drank Jack Daniels. I got mad because my parents had a rule that alcohol was not to be brought into our house, but they let my uncle bring it in. They said he could have it if he would hide it, but he wouldn't hide it. He would drink in front of me.

Now, whenever I see him I can't even tell if he's been drinking or not because he's so good at keeping a straight face when he's drunk. All he is doing is wasting his life away. Everyone in my family tries to help him but he won't listen. I would appreciate any help and advice you can offer.

Sincerely,
Joseph

Dear Mr. Nelson,

It's hard to be around someone who drinks. My aunt is like that. She drinks a lot! When she drinks, I hate her. I don't drink now and I never will. I've seen what it does to people.

She has been arrested many times, and if you ask me, she shouldn't be allowed to drive, let alone have a child. I fear that one day, either she or someone else will get killed for her stupidity.

She has a two-year-old little girl. I'm not so worried about my aunt as I am about my cousin. When my aunt drinks, she leaves the "baby" in her room, or has someone else watch her, usually someone she doesn't know.

Recently, my aunt started dating a man who drinks like she does. When he's drunk, he hurts my aunt. He's tried to kill her twice, but she doesn't think about it because she says she loves him! It makes me wonder what he'd do to that baby if he was drunk around her.

I love my aunt and my cousin, and I was wondering if you could help me to help them. My aunt doesn't drink as much anymore, but when she does, she gets drunk bad! I'm scared for their lives along with anyone who might be on the road with her when she's drunk.

Alcoholism is something that runs in my family. I know that I will never drink because I don't like the smell of alcohol. So, if I don't like the smell, I won't try it.

A lot of my friends drink and do drugs. If feel like such a pup around them. I feel like such a good little girl. I'm not saying my life is perfect. I have a lot of problems. As a matter of fact, I have clinical depression right now, at least that what friends and teachers have told me!

Even though my life is not going well, I will never turn to drugs or alcohol to solve my problems because I know it will only make things worse! Please help me.

Thank you for coming today.

A friend always,
Candice

Dear Mr. Nelson,

I've never drunk, but my uncle has. My uncle drank every day. There wasn't a moment when I saw him without a can of beer in his hand. My uncle is dead now. He didn't die from suicide or in a car accident. He died from cancer. He drank beer like water. He drank two 12-packs a day and they were non-stop.

I miss my uncle very much. He died from three cancer tumors, one in his liver and one in his lungs. The one that got him was the one in his brain.

The last words he said to me were, "I'm living proof of a man obsessed with alcohol. This is what it got me. Don't let it get you."

Sincerely,
Robert

Mr. Nelson,

I don't drink. I've never touched the stuff, but a long time ago, my grandfather did, and I watched him come and go, drunk. My mom threw him out several times, yet that still didn't stop him. He drove drunk, and it worried me a lot. He was the only grandfather I had, and I wanted him around when I grew up.

He doesn't drink anymore. He's been recovered now since 1988, my 6th grade year. He now has a liver problem, and they don't know if he'll live.

I had an aunt who was a drug addict and also drank. She abused me, and I hate her so much. I got help. She still does the stuff, so I heard, but that's her life.

I was raised that drugs, drinking, and smoking were wrong. My parents taught that. They are special, and I just thought I would tell you. Thanks for coming. If you want, write back.

Sincerely,
Shauna

Mr. Nelson,

I enjoyed your presentation, although I would never drink and drive because of the way I was brought up. I was brought up in the religion of a Mormon, and I strongly believe in it.

About four years ago, my aunt first married. She was in love, and I guess love blinded her from what was really going on in her marriage. Each night, on her husband's way home, he would stop off at a bar with his friends and have a few beers, then drive home.

When he got home, he would mentally harm my aunt. He would say things that he would never think of saying if he was sober. One night he stopped by the bar as usual, but he stayed a little longer and had a little more to drink. Then he drove home and on the way home, he misjudged a curve and drove off the ledge and died. I was glad for my aunt because she was finally out of a relationship that never would have gotten anywhere.

If I ever find myself in a predicament where one of my friends is drinking, then attempting drive home, I promise you I'll take their keys away from them, then drive home.

Write me back if you would like.

Thank you,
Shelly

Dear Mr. Nelson,

Two out of three of my uncles are alcoholics. One of my uncles has ruined his whole life due to alcohol. He has deserted his wife and only son. Before he started drinking, his life was wonderful. Now it seems like it's all over.

I've always wanted to talk to him, but I never knew the right things to say. His ex-wife now lives down the street from us, and she always tells me you can't talk to a drunk.

My other uncle is the same way, but now he's all screwed up with alcohol and drugs. I wish there was something I could do to help them, but I feel there's no hope. Even though I never see them, I always worry about them drinking and driving.

My uncle who is divorced is now with a woman who encourages him to drink. She always has a 12-pack waiting for him when he gets home. My uncles are both great people when they're not drinking, and I will never stop loving them. I just wish there was something I could do.

I worry about myself ending up the way they are, and I do pray it won't happen. I do admit, though, that I do drink at times but never do it when I'm too far to walk home.

My boyfriend is 16 and he drinks every weekend. I always tell him not to get into a car with someone who's been drinking, and he just tells me to quit being stupid.

I care about these people very, very much, and I don't want to lose any of them to drunk driving. Maybe some day there will be a way. Please, if you can, write back.

Your friend,
Jessica

Ken,

Hi. My name is Kimi, and I'm 15 years old. I have many friends who use alcohol and some family members, too. My uncle used to, after work, go to the bar next door to his work. He'd get drunk and go home. Then he'd take it out on my aunt. He'd beat her all the time and then she'd come to my house to get away from her husband.

She told him that if he ever came home drunk again, she'd leave him. He stopped, but recently he got drunk, and this time my little cousin saw his father beat his mother. He got so scared that he ran out of the house to a friend's house.

My uncle ran my aunt's head into a wall and kept hitting her. She and my cousin moved out, but they kept good contact with my uncle.

I also have a friend who was adopted and had an alcoholic mother. Now, she's becoming an alcoholic. She dropped out of school, has used lots of drugs, and has had a lot of experience with sex. She used to be a straight A student in junior high school, but not anymore. She's my best friend, but I know it's not right, so I don't do drugs or alcohol.

I don't want her to get hurt. What can I do?

Thank you,
Kimi

Dear Mr. Nelson,

I would like to say, Thank You for coming to talk to us today. I learned more about how alcohol affects peoples' lives. While you were talking, it made me think of my two uncles.

My oldest uncle is a recovering alcoholic. He has been clean and sober for two and a half years now. My youngest uncle drinks heavily. I just get so scared whenever I'm around him because I am afraid that one day he's going to be drinking too much, and he just might lose control and get into an accident.

I don't know what to do. I love my uncle very much and try to tell him all the time how bad alcohol is and that it's not good to drink and drive. He just ignores me, and sometimes I feel like giving up on him, but I don't because I don't want to see anything happen to him.

Well, thank you for your time and for reading my letter. Before I end this letter, I was wondering if it's possible to send me more information on SADD. I would really appreciate it.

Sincerely,
Anetra

Dear Mr. Nelson,

My name is Lorie. I have had many alcohol and drug users in my family. My uncle Dave was a really bad alcoholic, and when he drank, he got mean. He used to beat up my aunt and things, but then he died of cirrhosis. I loved my uncle very much, but sometimes I think it's better that he's gone. I don't know if that is wrong, but it's the way I feel.

My dad used to drink and drive a lot, too, but after his mom died, he got really heavily into drugs, so my two sisters, my mom, and I spent about five years running and hiding from him. He died last summer from cancer.

I love my dad. I always did, but he hurt so many people. I was wondering if I could get some information on SADD, and if you know something about drug abuse.

Thank you,
Lorie

Dear Mr. Nelson,

I have an uncle who drinks a lot. He gets mean and angry all the time he gets drunk. He drinks from morning to night on his days off, and he drinks all the time after work. I don't know what to do because he keeps denying it. Also, my Aunt Jeannie divorced him because of it.

I'm confused because of my friends. A lot of them drink and they say it's cool and everything. I don't know what to do because a lot of them say that I should because that is what almost all of them are doing. I have tried alcohol, but I didn't get drunk.

Thank you,
Charity

Dear Mr. Nelson,

My dad, uncle, and a whole lot of other people in my family have drinking problems. Recently I have moved out of my home where I lived with my mother and step-dad. When I left I moved in with my aunt and uncle.

My uncle is a heavy drinker. We always talk about me not drinking and driving, and anytime I get in a car with someone who drinks, I get grounded.

My other uncle got grounded from driving when he got caught by my aunt. The uncle I live with now drinks all the time. When he drives when he is drunk, he always preaches to me about "not drinkin' and driving."

The question I have for you is how in the world do I get him to stop? I would greatly appreciate it if you would write back and give me some ideas about how I can help him not drink and drive. Thanks for caring.

Misty

Dear Ken,

Last year you came to our class. I'm sorry to say that I'm here again! Last year I wrote you a letter about my cousin and my uncle, and the pain that he has caused. You wrote to me and helped me to face my fears.

Well, it has been a long year and not much has changed. My uncle is now very heavily into drugs and alcohol. On New Year's Eve, he went out drinking. He came home and dragged me out with him. I hated it. He brought me back home and left again.

About 7 a.m. the next day, he came home after taking my car out to pick up more alcohol and drugs. I was so scared when I found my car gone. I didn't want him to get in an accident and die. I'd already lost one boyfriend and almost a cousin to drunk driving. I wish he'd stop, but I don't think he will.

I know that I won't drink. I can't because I used to have a problem with it. But I realized that it was harming me and helping me do things that I wouldn't normally do. I think what you're doing is great. People need to know about the dangers of drinking and driving. Thanks for caring.

Love,
Dana

Aunts and uncles are wonderful people to have around! They're often close to the age of our mothers and fathers, but don't have the urge to be disciplinarians. Aunts and uncles can compliment us on our strengths and successes and somehow completely overlook weaknesses.

They're usually more numerous than parents, so their value is multiplied. They provide a variety of talents and often they can be a confidant when we find ourselves in a little trouble.

Too often though, it seems that an aunt or uncle has become the 'black sheep' of a family. As we read the letters, we have to feel the hurt and disappointment expressed by the teenagers. They understandably want their aunts and uncles to again be their heroes, not an abusive drunk that makes their family's lives miserable, and them an unwelcome guest.

As I sorted through the stacks of letters, it surprised me how few students wrote of their once favorite uncle or aunt ever getting off the alcohol or other drugs. It provided an opportunity to remind these young writers that there is a relationship between early drinking and subsequent inability to get off alcohol in later years. I sometimes suggest they ask their aunt or uncle to map the route to becoming dependent upon alcohol. When did they begin having 'fun' with alcohol or other drugs? I ask letter-writers not to raise this question as a criticism of their relative's early behavior, but to better educate themselves to understand reality.

The sequence of letters that follow suggests that the minds of our young people are alert and working.

✍

Mr. Nelson,

Hi, my name is Morgan, and I'm a 10th grader at this school. I would like to thank you for taking your time to come and teach us about SADD. I would very much like to get information about it.

I know about alcohol very well because in the eighth grade I would drink like every other day. I stopped my ninth grade year, but I'm drinking again this year. I am scared because I like it so much, and my uncle is 62 and is dying of liver and kidney failure. The doctors say he has three weeks tops.

I'm in the ROK (Reaching Out and Caring) program, and it is very helpful. I also go to other schools and talk about my experience with alcohol.

Thank you very much for taking the time to read my letter.

Love always,
Morgan

✍

Dear Morgan,

I wanted to send you this special note because you wrote such a thoughtful letter to me about your uncle and yourself when I was at your school on Tuesday. I'm sorry to hear about your uncle's situation. Unfortunately, when there is the level of damage you describe from his drinking so much for so long a time, his liver and kidneys are beyond repair. If the doctors give him three weeks to live, his condition is awfully serious.

You seem to be thinking seriously about your own use of alcohol, and that's a good start. I like the program you're in. You will be able to help many other young people, and hopefully yourself.

Your life and your future are very precious, Morgan. These are the years when you want to concentrate on your studies, on making lifelong friendships, and getting involved in activities at your school.

You can do these important things if you again build and keep your determination to not let alcohol or other mind-altering drugs become a regular part of your young life.

If you would have asked your uncle about it, he probably would have told you he began drinking as a teenager. Your bodies are developing rapidly at your age, and alcohol problems can set in very quickly. I read that most adult alcoholics today began drinking regularly as teenagers.

I know you will make a fine SADD member. Will you share the information I've enclosed with your friends?

Your friend,
Ken Nelson

✍

Dear Mr. Nelson,

Thank you for your support. My uncle who was dying from liver and kidney failure did die. He passed away on Christmas Day around noon. He is in a better place now!

When I went to see him a week before he died, his feet were very swollen. Each foot was as big as my head. It was very scary.

Since then I have made a promise to myself not to drink or do pot! I know that is not the right path, so I'm trying to turn around, but it's hard, and I need all the support I can get. Thank you for your support; it's a big help!

Well, I hope you continue helping young teens like myself. Thanks again.

Morgan

Although Morgan was another writer who I encouraged to continue to keep me abreast of her progress, this didn't happen. My feeling, and hope, was that the death of her uncle and the direct involvement with the ROK program would be a sufficient push to carry Morgan safely through the next several years.

When SADD adjusted their thrust from using the Contract For Life, involving parents or other responsible adults as a live-saving tool for getting children home safely from parties if the son or daughter had been drinking, to one of a firm 'no use' policy, it was appropriate for me to change part of my presentation. I settled on an approach that I hoped wouldn't cause my audience to 'tune out' and the letters to stop.

My new speech included something like the following exchange:

"If any of you here today believe that you hear me say it's okay for teenagers to drink, it isn't what I intend to say. Because no thinking adult, in our society at least, is going to come out and say it's alright for our young people to use alcohol. Why not? Well, you might find two reasons acceptable. First, it's against our nation's laws to drink before we're twenty-one. Now, I realize that isn't true everywhere. I've talked with a number of exchange students from European countries, as I'm sure some of you have. They tell me that in many of those countries the legal drinking age for beer and wine is sixteen, and for hard liquor it's eighteen, and those age laws aren't rigidly enforced. Here in our country, though, congress set a minimum drinking age of twenty-one some time back.

We all like to think of ourselves as being good citizens. That's very important to us, as it should be. Good citizenship calls for us to obey our nation's laws. If we don't agree with them, we change them by voting, not by ignoring them.

Second, it's a health issue. The more I read and study the situation, the more I'm convinced that most of our adult alcoholics today began drinking regularly as teenagers. It seems that very few people who wait until they're twenty-one to begin regular drinking, ever become alcoholics. There's something about your systems at your age that makes you awfully sensitive to alcohol. Your bodies are developing, they're changing almost daily, and addiction seems to set in quickly from too much drinking. You don't even realize that it's happening. I ask only that you do consider these two reasons for not drinking when you're at a party and the discussion comes up."

Immediately following this changed part of my program has proven to be timely for introduction of the letters, and I do so as follows:

"I've brought along some things that you might like to read. They are letters from teenagers like yourselves."

Throughout the twenty-five years of appearing before high school audiences, I must have asked for a show of hands five hundred times on two very direct questions. The first, "How many of you feel that the minimum legal drinking age in this country should be kept at twenty-one," and the second, "How many of your feel that it should be lower, like in many European countries, for example at eighteen?"

I don't recall a single time when the vote wasn't strongly in favor of keeping the age at twenty-one. Our young people aren't dumb. They're the victims of being teenagers, very emotional, very much wanting to be a part of things, and sometimes too easily influenced.

Occasionally, a hand shoots up to ask me if I drank as a teenager. My answer is, "No, but I do drink some now." Then half-jokingly I tell my listeners that, as a teenager, I didn't have to face the alcohol use decisions that they do now, and that it was different for me.

"My family had a small dairy that required us four boys to milk, clean the barns, and feed the cows each morning and night. There wasn't time to think about parties. My father made it even easier. He got the four of us together one time and said, 'If I ever catch any of you drinking or smoking before you're twenty-one, I'll beat the hell out of you.' We believed him."

The surprised looks, and outright laughter from many, eased any tensions that might be building. Subsequent letters from students indicated no strong support nor disagreement with the legal drinking age question.

CHAPTER ELEVEN

"I hate to think I lost my best friend to alcohol. She has a lot
of problems in her life, and I was always there to help her,
but I guess she just doesn't need my help anymore."

Dear Mr. Nelson,

*I really enjoyed your discussion in my driver's education class. It made me
stop and think how serious alcohol is. I myself am not a drinker. I learned three
years ago a very serious effect of liquor.*

*I was twelve years old at the time and was always very trusting. You could
tell me anything and I would believe it. It was New Year's Eve and lots of
parties were going on. My mother wouldn't let me go to any of them. My friend
asked if I wanted to go to the bowling alley with her and her uncle. She was 14
and her uncle was 27.*

*I asked my mother, and she said it was okay as long as I was careful. When
I got to my friend's house, I was faced with a subject I had really never thought
about, alcohol. My friend was drinking a little, so I got curious and opened a
wine cooler.*

*Her uncle had bought about five four-packs of wine coolers plus a few
six-packs of beer. It seemed that every time I finished a wine cooler, I wanted
another. I lost count after the seventh.*

*We did go to the bowling alley. I remember I kept falling. My friend and
I were both bombed. One the way back to my friend's house, I fell asleep while
my friend proceeded to vomit all over the truck door.*

*I decided to spend the night at my friend's house, so we stopped to ask my
mom if it was okay. My mother looked at my friend and me and said, "I hope
to God you learn your lesson." I guess it was pretty obvious we were drunk. I did
get permission to sleep over at my friend's house.*

Her uncle drove us home, and he was pretty buzzed, too. We decided to sleep on the living room floor. I walked into the house and passed out. When I came to, my friend's uncle was on top of me. Since I was so drunk, I was weak and couldn't get him off me. I kept blanking out, so he succeeded in raping me.

I never had the guts to turn him in or tell my mother. My mother got her wish. I learned my lesson. I hope other females read this before it's too late.

Please write back to me. Even though it has been three years, I still want to find a way to tell my mother.

Thanx,
Jenni

Mr. Nelson,

Hi. I know this may not seem too bad of a problem, but it kind of seems like it to me. I'm 15 years old, and last May I met this guy (he's now my boyfriend). He's the greatest guy I ever met. He never pushes me into anything I don't want to do. I never really knew he drank until one night I went over to his house and he started drinking.

Then he goes and offers me some. I didn't want him to think like, "oh, my God, she's like a total straight girl never does anything wrong," so I went ahead and drank with him. Then, after a while, it was like we both changed, and we were all over each other.

I know it will probably happen again! He still drinks and his parents don't even care. It really bothered me a lot when he told me that because I know they'll never help him. They let him worship Satan when he was younger!

What I really want to ask is how I can approach him now, a year before he joins the Marines, and tell him I don't want him to drink? I know he'll do that when he joins the service.

If you can write back, please don't send it to my house. Please send it to my school, and have them give it to me.

Thanks,
Beci

Dear Mr. Nelson,

I have a really good friend who drinks almost every weekend. I really want to help him, but I don't know how. He doesn't care about anything. My friends aren't with him when he drives drunk, so I wish I could help.

He personally doesn't care about life or anything. He barely has anything going for him. He gets F's, and his parents don't care, so now, he doesn't care.

I've talked to him a lot but he says, "What in life do I have to live for?" I'm really confused. Please help me!

Love,
Michie

Dear Mr. Nelson,

Thank you for coming today and discussing the dangers of drunk driving. My friend and I have always had to make the decision to get in the car of a person who is drunk.

We do not want to, but our parents would not come home to get us in the middle of the night. In the first place, they don't know that we drink, and the second place, we really sneaked to those parties.

We like to drink, but we feel guilty doing it.

Sincerely,
Jean & Becky

Mr. Nelson,

I had a good friend who was driving home from a party one night and was drunk, not really drunk, but drunk enough. He continued on driving and later went off the bridge. He was a good friend, and I miss him very much. He's been gone a couple of months.

He had a girlfriend, and she was pregnant. She since had a little boy. I wonder what she's going to tell him about his daddy, my friend.

Thanks for listening,
Joe

Mr. Nelson,

About two years ago, I went to a party with my best friend. It was supposed to be a "safe party," but it wasn't. There were alcohol and drugs. My best friend and I drank and did some, well, a lot, of drugs. About two o'clock in the morning, the guys who threw the party took me over to her house. I guess I threw up the stuff or something, otherwise I probably would have died.

My best friend did die. The guys didn't tell me, either. They just threw her body in a ditch 20 miles away. They didn't tell me! The next morning her parents asked me where she was, and I couldn't remember what happened. I told them we had a fight, and she walked out, and they believed it.

Two weeks later, the cops came to my house and asked me if I knew who she was, and if I knew where she was. I told them exactly what I had told her parents. Then they told me she was dead. I cried for three days. That was all, I couldn't cry anymore.

Since then I use Sarah as my role model. I don't do dope or drink anymore. Sure, I drink at parties, but it's a soda or water or something. Thanks for listening and thanks for talking to my class. I'll be getting my license soon, so this is important to me.

Thanks,
Anjelika

Mr. Nelson,

Reading the letters you brought to class really got me thinking. I would like to thank you for sharing them.

I, like the others, have a story. My boyfriend and a girl who used to be my best friend got drunk one night together. While drunk they had sex with each other. My boyfriend regrets what happened, but it's too late now. My friend is pregnant and having the baby.

My boyfriend feels he is not the father, but I feel he says this only because he was drunk.

I really would like some more information about SADD, so please send it to me. And thanks for taking the time to read my letter.

Kathie

Mr. Nelson,

I'm concerned about a lot of my good friends. Most of them are alcoholics and addicted to drugs. One of my real good friends admits it but will not stop. I've tried everything to help him, but he won't listen. He also wants to die.

My father's an alcoholic also. He used to beat my mother in front of my brother and me. I don't talk to him much anymore. I'm too afraid that I might take the place of my mother.

This summer a group of my friends were at the river drinking, and a couple of them went into the water afterwards to swim. Then, when they were coming back to shore, the current got hold of one of them.

It doesn't seem like he's gone. He was very quiet and never did anything to hurt anyone. You may show people this, but don't include my name. Thanks for listening.

Colette

Mr. Nelson,

I'm writing this letter because there is no one else for me to talk to. There's this guy/boyfriend who I was together with. One night at a party (with me there) he got drunk and didn't remember what happened, so he did something he shouldn't have with someone else. He every once in a while does drugs.

The weird thing is he never does any of that with me around him. Ever since this happened, we haven't been back to normal. Some of my other friends drink every once in a while, but they don't drive. They stay where they are, but this guy always drives. What can I do to help him?

Confused and worried,
Jennifer

Dear Mr. Nelson,

I have a friend whose parents are alcoholics, and she doesn't know how to cope with the problem. At this point she thinks there's nothing for her to accomplish since her parents aren't really there for her. She tries to talk with them, but it seems to go in one ear and out the other.

I try to help her with the problem, but I don't know enough to actually tell her what to do. Now, since time has passed, she's really messing up in school. She is failing the 9th grade. She thinks there's nothing for her to live for, but there is.

I've known her for twelve years, and she's my best friend, and I care. If you can help me with this problem, will you please write? Thanks for caring!

Sincerely,
Jennifer

Mr. Nelson,

I have been going out with a guy who is about six years older than I am for a long time now. I love him so much. I couldn't bear to lose him. But since before I met him, he's been an alcoholic. For the three years that we've been together, he's gone out and gotten drunk at least every other weekend. I go out with him, and even though I don't drink, I know I'm in as much danger as he is the minute we both get into the car.

Since I just turned 16, I can't drive yet, and I have no other way to get home. My dad is a preacher, and he'd kill me if I called him to pick me up. I don't see any way out of it. Can you give me any suggestions?

Thank you,
Stani

Dear Mr. Nelson,

I'm a high school sophomore, and I'm worried about my friend. She is 16 years of age, and has been an alcoholic for over four years. She doesn't think she has a problem even though everyone has told her and has tried to help.

One night her mom and I found her in the houses being built across the street completely bombed. Later, after we got her home and cleaned her up, she came to. All of a sudden, she started crying and telling us what had happened.

Three or four high schoolers had found her while she was halfway through a six-pack of beer. They had more alcohol with them, so they kept giving it to her until she passed out. Then, while she was coming to, she found one of them on top of her and the other cheering him on. She was too weak to do anything.

Also, another time when I was at a party, I saw the couch moved away from the wall and didn't think anything of it until I saw a long line of guys going one at a time behind the couch. I was to find out that a girl had passed out and all the guys were raping her. Nothing came of it.

I don't plan to drink, but, if I do, I will find a sober ride home.

Melissa

Dear Mr. Nelson,

I have never liked the taste of alcohol. I've tried it before and even gotten drunk. I just don't see the point of getting drunk. I had a really close friend. We were at a party, and she got so drunk she passed out on the couch. When she woke up, she'd peed all over herself and the couch.

I called her stupid and told her to see where drinking so much had gotten her. She didn't answer and just thought I was putting her down. She started hating me from that point on.

I hate to think that I lost by best friend to alcohol. She has a lot of problems in her life, and I was always there to help her, but I guess she just doesn't need my help anymore. It hurts a lot. She won't see her alcohol problems. I just don't feel that I'm in a position to tell her what to do.

It makes me so mad to see how teenagers glamorize alcohol. Don't they see that it can kill? Even though I haven't lost anyone to alcohol, I wish I could prevent it.

Thank you so much for coming and talking. I really feel like you care. I wish there were more people in this world like you. Please write and tell me what you think about my situation.

Thanks again,
Kristin

Mr. Nelson,

I'd really like to learn more about SADD. This previous weekend, I was babysitting. At 12:30 A.M. five of my really good friends showed up at the door. Two were drunk and three were frying on acid. I let them in and let them sleep on the floor.

As a result, I'm grounded, and my parents no longer trust me. I did put the kids in danger, but I couldn't figure out any other alternatives. It makes me mad.

I probably prevented last weekend's deaths, but what about next weekend? They'll keep doing it. How can I stop them? I'm scared for them. It's so unfair.

Thank you for listening,
Jessi

Mr. Nelson,

I appreciate you coming to my driver education class. My best friend was the victim of an alcoholic. When we were in the 6th grade, my friend came to school with welts on the back of her knee. You must want to know what happened.

Well, my friend always had to wear corduroy pants every day. She finally got her stepmother to buy her a jean skirt. When she got home, her stepmother got drunk, took out a leather belt and started hitting her. We sat in the girls' bathroom and cried for a long time. I don't drink or do any other drugs. Neither do my friends. Please write back.

Thank you for caring,
Jaime

Mr. Nelson,

Someone who I'm very close to has an older brother who is an alcoholic/druggy. Whenever the guy gets drunk or stoned/high, he usually comes home and gets in an argument with his dad and brother (my friend). Most of the time my friend gets hurt, sometimes pretty bad, sometimes just emotionally.

I want to help, but I don't know what to do. I've told my friend that whenever he needs a place to stay, he can come to my house. He says he doesn't want to put his problems off on other people, but he needs someone to talk to and help him.

What else can I do to help him?

Love always,
Nicole

Dear Mr. Nelson,

Well, my story is sad but true. This happened when I was twelve. My sister and I snuck out of our home around 1:00 A.M. We took the car though neither of us had a driver's license. My sister and her boyfriend left me at his place with his friends, and they were drinking tequila. They asked me if I wanted to drink. I said, "sure."

We were playing a game called quarters, and they kept choosing me to drink. I honestly think that they had this planned. There were three guys, but it was only two of them who wanted it from a really young girl.

Well, I got drunk and passed out. They took advantage of me, in other words they raped me. I didn't tell my parents about this. They only ones who know are my cousin and sister.

The reason I'm writing this is to the other kids can read it and not let it happen to them.

Yours truly,
Renee

Dear Mr. Nelson,

I have a friend who drank and smoked and had sex at a party. Then that day she didn't feel good after the party. When her parents got home, they had a big talk about drinking and smoking and having sex.

Then we went to this other party. She had sex, but this time she got raped.

Your friend,
Charles

Dear Mr. Nelson,

Thank you for coming to my school. I have a story. I have this friend, and I love her like a sister. Her parents start drinking about 3:00 P.M. and drink to about 9:00 P.M. at night. After her parents are drunk, they hit her; they hit her a lot! I told her she should do something about it,'cause we can't keep coming and picking her up in the middle of the night because her mom and dad hit her.

She told me to shut up for a week and a half. She hasn't called me or anything. She's really mad. I don't understand. I can't help her if she doesn't want to be helped.

Thank you again,
Jessica

Dear Mr. Nelson,

I really appreciate the fact that somebody cares! I personally have never drank nor do I want to, but I have friends who drink. It's hard to go to school and know that one of your friends isn't ever going to be there because they're "gone." I don't understand why people drink. Drinking makes everything so hard!

I have one friend in class who drinks a lot and does other drugs, too. I try to help her but don't really believe that she wants me to help her. The thing that gets me mad is she doesn't know what she's doing.

I wonder what I could do? Just to help her before it's too late.

Trying to help,
Michelle

Mr. Nelson,

I have a friend who I know drinks, but I don't think her drinking is as bad as her other habits. She does drugs, smokes, and a lot of other things. She wasn't like this until recently, when she met her boyfriend. They have sex regularly, and she got pregnant once (she got an abortion).

She was kicked out of her house and is now living with her boyfriend. I'm afraid that she might go too far with her drinking and using drugs. She already has lost a lot of weight. I've talked with my counselor about her recently. Nothing has happened yet. I thought I would just tell you this. I believe you have already gotten a letter about her today.

Thank you for listening to what I have said.

Desiree

Hi Mr. Nelson,

I just want to tell you that I'm really concerned about a girl who used to be my best friend. We lived together in another town and ironically we ended up moving here together. Well, she got hooked up with her boyfriend, Tony, and started drinking. My friend, Desiree, and I went off to the office this morning to see if she'd been going to school. Well, not very much, and a couple of weeks ago, she got an abortion.

I don't know her anymore. She needs help. Her boyfriend drives drunk all the time. He's gotten stopped before and got into a little trouble. I don't want to see her hurt.

I'm confused why she turned her life around for the worse. When she called me the other night and sounded drunk, she asked me to get my mom to pick her up 'cause her boyfriend left her at a party. My mom picked her up, but I just hope you can help her.

Carly

Dear Mr. Nelson,

I have a friend who drinks all the time and smokes weed all the time, too. I really love my friend, and I'm afraid he'll kill himself or someone else, but I don't know what to do to help him. I've tried to talk to him and convince him to stop or even cut down, but he just won't listen. I've done everything I can to make him, but it just isn't working.

I've made a little headway with him. He's going to AA and NA meetings, too. But I love him so much, and I don't think he's being helped enough to be able to quit. I try to make sure he goes to all the meetings, but I can't always watch out for him.

Please tell me what else I can do to help him. I love him so much, and I don't want to lose him before it's his time. He's only 15 years old, but he drives drunk and he rides with people who are drunk. I'm so afraid that one day I'll go to school, and I'll hear that he's been killed. I love him more than anything in the world.

Brandy

Dear Mr. Nelson,

Hello! Well, I was reading your letters that you brought to our class. I don't drink, I can assure you, but I'm 17 years old, and my boyfriend is 21 years old. He doesn't have a drinking problem, but when someone offers him a beer he doesn't drink just one. His problem is he can't control his drinking.

I really care for him, and I don't want anything bad to happen to him. Please help me and him. I really do get embarrassed when he's around me and drinking and acting stupid.

Thank you for coming to talk with us kids. Thank you for caring!

Sincerely,
Isabel

Mr. Nelson,

I have a friend who is a guy, and he drinks all the time. Lately, he has been doing drugs. I have been his friend for about five years now. This is the worst I've seen him. His mother worries about him because she knows about his problem, but she can't help him. She even stopped working to help him, but he doesn't want her help.

The guy has dropped out of school because of his problem. He tells me that it helps solve the problem that he has. He is only 17 years old. He blames his drinking problem on his dad because, a couple of years ago, his dad was killed in a drunk driving accident. The accident wasn't his dad's fault. He wasn't driving. The other guy was.

Thanks a lot for coming and talking with my class. Thanks for giving me a chance to write you and read the letters that we wrote. But I have to go for now.

Please write back when you have time.

Thanks a lot,
Stacey

Mr. Nelson,

I have a friend who has a few problems in her life. Recently she was taken to the hospital for an alcohol overdose. I'm getting really worried about her. I think she's been doing drugs, too. She dropped out of school and doesn't seem to care or notice what she is doing to her life.

She doesn't care or notice because her mother is addicted to drugs and doesn't care what her daughter does. So if you would let me know how I can help her, I would appreciate it very much. We grew up together, sharing everything with each other. She's like my sister, and I wouldn't want to lose a part of my life over drugs and alcohol.

I don't want to take her to anyone, or tell anyone, because she and her mother belong together, not split up.

Thank you,
Sherri

Dear Mr. Nelson,

You seem like a pretty good guy, and I think I can tell you this. You see, I used to live in Rapid City, South Dakota, and I had a bad experience with two of my best friends. They were both killed because of alcohol, but it wasn't because of drinking and driving. It was in a car, though, and this is why I don't drink alcohol.

You see, my friends were on their way to school, and they each had a bottle of vodka, and when they got to school, they were both drunk. They got into a fight in the parking lot and one of them pulled out a gun and shot the other one, and then killed himself.

That's why people should not drink. Thanks for listening.

Your friend,
Cory

Dear Mr. Nelson,

My name is Daynah, and I'm almost 16 years old. Two years and almost six months ago my best friend died in a drinking and driving accident. He and two other friends were going to pick me up at my home, and the driver was drunk, and the others didn't know it. The driver was going on a busy street and didn't stop at a sign, and a car side-swiped them.

My best friend wasn't wearing his seat belt and flew through the windshield, hit a stop sign, then a fence and died instantly. The driver died, but one lived.

I made a promise I would never drink. That promise was broken a few years ago. Things got real hard and seven months ago at a party, I got really drunk and was taken advantage of. Since then I stopped, and I'm keeping the promise I made over Kain's grave.

I hope something like this never happens to anyone, but that's what I thought.

Thank you for coming,
Daynah

Dear Mr. Nelson,

Hi, how are you? I'm okay. I'm worried about my friend. I will not state her name out of respect.

One night she was drunk. It was the big homecoming game, and she decided to get drunk. I took a couple of sips and got a buzz. She took off her shirt and walked around in her bra. My friends and I made her put her shirt back on. After she did that, she decided to roll down the street.

I really love her, but she does this all the time. Her brother just got started, and I'm really scared she'll turn out like her mom, no job, seven kids by different fathers, and always getting in trouble. I don't want to find my friend's name in the paper under "Drinking and Driving Fatalities." Thank you for listening.

Love,
Valerie

Dear Mr. Nelson,

I have a friend who uses and abuses drugs and alcohol. Every time I try to help him, I get yelled at. I talked to his parents about him and they don't do a thing. By the way, his parents are both drunks.

I try to help, but all I get is lip from him. This was over three years ago. He's dead now. He died in a drunk driving accident. I felt guilty because I couldn't help him kick his habit.

Thanks for coming to talk to us about drunk driving. I really appreciate it.

Sincerely,
Jesse

Dear Mr. Nelson,

Over vacation time, my best friend when I was little came to see me. At first everything was going great, until one night he decided to drink a whole bottle of Jack Daniels. After a while he passed out. Then he got extremely sick. I didn't know what to do. I was afraid something bad was going to happen. I stayed up the whole night with him.

The next morning we had a talk. He told me his parents didn't care about him, and he could really care less about his life. He really scares me. I think that he would take his life it things got bad.

I love him, and I don't want to let him hurt himself. It's been about two years since I'd seen him, and when he was with me, I realized how much he had changed. He drinks all the time, and is into drugs. I want to help him, but I don't know what to do.

The really bad thing is, he lives in Colorado. The only way I can talk to him is on the phone, or if I write to him, but I don't think either would help. He doesn't even care about himself. I love him, and I don't want to lose him from his making a mistake, like killing himself or driving drunk, etc.

Please help me. He's a good person but just a little confused.

Love always,
Kelley

Mr. Nelson,

I really appreciate you coming out today. It made me think. I have a few problems in my life that involve alcohol.

Last summer, a senior who went to this school was involved in a drunk driving accident. It really hurt me a lot because I was close to him. I went to homecoming with him last year, and I had been in the car with him a few times while he was drinking. He's now mentally retarded.

One of my best friends, Nick, has had a real drinking problem for a long time. I've always made it clear to him that I don't like him to drink, but he won't stop. A month ago, he did something very crazy and very illegal, and I told him I didn't want to be friends with him anymore.

I guess I realize now that that was the wrong thing to do. I should have stuck by him and just tried to help him. I'm afraid now that it's too late.

I thank you for caring enough to listen. If you could, please send me some information about SADD.

Cristal

Dear Mr. Nelson,

There's this girl who's been a pretty good friend of mine for about three years. Last year she started smoking, and I know she's been drinking for longer than that. Last year I told her how I felt about it, and she said, "OK, man, I'll quit!"

For about a year and a half, she told me she quit everything, drinking, smoking, the whole bit. I found out via another friend that she hadn't. She was my friend, but she doesn't care anymore, and it hurts me a hell of a lot to care about someone who doesn't care about herself.

I listen to her tell me about her problems, and I really want to help her, but I can't. I've tried talking to her, but she only gets upset. I don't talk to her much anymore; we've really drifted apart. Her current friends have slipped LSD into her food, etc.

I don't think there's much I can do, but I need to get it out of my system.

Thanks,
Torreya

Dear Mr. Nelson,

I have a friend who is having a lot of problems in her life right now. Her mom is a straight out drunk. Her mom goes out every night. She goes out to bars and gets really drunk. She ends up bringing a man home and having sex with him and expects my friend to have sex with him, too.

She (my friend) is already pregnant and she's only 15 and doesn't even know whose it is. She's a straight A student at this school, and her life is going to be ruined because of her mom and alcohol.

I want to help her, but she is scared that if I tell, she'll be taken away from her mom. She loves her very much, but not the alcohol in her.

Please give me some advice to help her. Please!!! Thanks so much.

Sincerely,
Rosie

Dear Mr. Nelson,

I have a friend who has a drinking problem. I feel that he's also smoking pot. He's too embarrassed to tell you, so I though I would tell you because I care about him.

I think that he is getting worse instead of getting better. That's why I thought you should know. I would like to know how I can help him with his problem. Thanks for coming and talking with us. He doesn't want me to tell you his name, so I won't. So please help me help him. Write back.

Love,
Diane

Dear Mr. Nelson,
I have a really good friend who drinks 3-4 times a week. She's been my best friend since 2nd grade; now we're both in 10th. I think she's becoming an alcoholic. She does drugs, too, but not all the time. I'm really scared she's going to be like her aunt who is now in prison. Her aunt was an alcoholic and drug addict at age 14. I don't want her to end up that way.
I know some of the symptoms because my cousin is a drug addict and alcoholic, and her life is really messed up. I already lost one person to a drunk driver. I can't bear to think of losing another. What should I do to help her? Please send me some information about SADD. Thank you so very much.

Wendy

If you were a high school student, could you ask for a better friend than most of those whose letters you've just read? Almost all of the letters show a genuine love, and a tireless effort to change what the author sees as an awful direction their friend is taking.

At the time of writing, there seems to be close to a 100% failure in their effort to influence these friends. They conclude their letters with standard pleas of *"What can I do to help?"* or, *"Will you help me help my friend?"* Here are some of the awesome challenges these teenagers friends face:

"He drinks and his parents don't even care."

"He barely has anything going for him. He gets F's and his parents don't care, so now, he doesn't care."

"I've tried everything to help him, but he won't listen. He also wants to die."

"She's failing in the 9th grade. She thinks there's nothing for her to live for, but there is."

"She hasn't called me or anything. She's really mad. I can't help her if she doesn't want to be helped."

Yes, you've already read these quotes in the just-preceding chapter's letters. Many of my responses begin with the simple recognition of their concern about their friend's sad problem. *"Your friend is so fortunate in having a genuine friend like you who doesn't give up on them easily."*

To many writers, one of the hopefully-appropriate suggestions I make is that they somehow get their friend to accept help from a school counselor. I always assure the writer, as I've noted in an earlier chapter, that counselors can be confidential in most cases. Often, when the situation described seems almost hopeless, I ask the writer to contact the counselor themselves. I remind them that lives are at stake, and that they likely will not lose their friend's love. Some workable steps to fill a critical need have to be initiated by someone.

My role in actually helping to bring about a change would seem to be an empty one here. I'm loathe to suggest that the teenager go to their friend's parents. So often, the parents are already seen as indifferent or as part of the friend's problems.

A suggestion that they read part of my response to that friend, or to show him some of the literature I enclosed is sometimes considered, and usually dropped. Their friend has heard all of these facts. They don't apply to him!

Some of the situations described are so bizarre, my readers might well ask, "Can this be really true? Are you sure these teenagers aren't making up a lot of stuff just to get attention?" Although there's no certainty, my feeling is that most events related are factual. I don't give my young audiences a lot of time to dream up stories. They listen to my reading of the two selected letters about ten minutes into the program and receive those I circulate immediately afterwards. Any writing must be accomplished while continuing to listen to me or while the fifteen-minute video, 'A Call to Action,' is running. That isn't a lot of time.

It has always astounded me that some students can put together an articulate, two-page letter (a full page typed) in the time available. Spontaneity and limited time likely proved to be the keys to my getting those 3,500 letters. Over the period of fifteen years, more than 100 students approached me immediately after class with, "Mr. Nelson, I have something to tell you but didn't have time to write to you in class. May I have your address?"

My penned home address would be handed to them with a smile and an encouraging, "Here it is. That would be great! I'll look for your letter."

How many did I receive? There may have been one or two. There seems to be only that brief interval in their lives, stimulated perhaps by my approach, and certainly by the letters they heard me read, or read themselves during the program's continuation, that would result in their opening their hearts and putting their concerns into written words.

Giving those asking for my address a few hours or an overnight to compose their letters resulted in almost nothing. I regretted this because an opportunity was lost for me to respond to a teenager who obviously had a problem worthy of someone showing an interest. Why didn't they write? My best guess is that they mentioned the idea to friends, and were ridiculed. Maybe siblings or parents at home asked them what they were doing, and their writing became a wadded ball tossed into the wastebasket. My mailbox remained empty.

Another tactic to keep an open line of written communication has fared better. When a young writer asks for help but leaves too many questions unanswered in their initial letter, my first response includes a short list of questions along with the request, *"Will you write to me again, soon?"* followed by, *"I'm enclosing an addressed envelope so you won't have to hunt for one."* About half of the times this approach is successful, so my stamps are not all wasted.

CHAPTER TWELVE

"My sister (14) takes off at night without my mother
knowing, sneaks out and takes off with older guys
(the kind you wouldn't bring home) and drinks."
"He (my brother) has come home many times
after drinking, beaten up terribly."

Dear Mr. Nelson,

My older brother is an alcoholic. He goes out partying almost every night and absolutely every weekend. He is close to impossible to deal with when he is sober, but he's ten times as bad when he's drunk.

I'm sure my parents know about this problem, but they never say anything to my brother about it. I think they've given up on him. He used to stash beers in the back of our refrigerator where he hoped my parents wouldn't find them. I found them first and poured every one of them down the drain. When he found them missing, he yelled at me, threw things at me, and went out to drink. On the way home, he was in an accident, but he still drinks.

He has come home many times after drinking, beaten up terribly. One time, his eyes were so bloody, he couldn't see. I've seen so many terrible things happen to my brother that I'm definitely not going to drink and drive. My brother's mistakes have taught me that alcohol is not a toy and neither is a car.

Thank you for coming to talk to my class today.

Janet

Dear Mr. Nelson,

I really enjoyed your lecture today. It makes me feel good to know someone is trying to correct the problem of alcoholism.

My brother was in an accident last month because he was drinking and driving. He'd been at a party in Davis and was returning home. He either fell asleep or lost control and skidded off the road and into a tree. His accident put me through a lot and influenced me not to drink and drive.

The waiting for a whole week while he was in a coma, wondering if he'd live or die, really scared me. I met many families in the hospital who had relatives or friends who were injured by drunk drivers. I surely hope MADD can cure the problem. It's just not fair that so many people have to die or be injured by drunks. Thank you,

Kelly

Dear Mr. Nelson,

After reading the letters you brought to class, I thought I would tell you what happened to my brother. My brother and I are very close; we do a lot together. We're also popular and when we go out we're sort of expected to drink, and we did until about a month ago.

My brother was at a party, and he and two friends left in his car and followed a group of people in another car out to the river. They were out there maybe only ten minutes and decided to go back.

That night, we received a phone call at about three in the morning. It was a nightmare around my house for the next two weeks or so. My brother is fine but is emotionally scarred for life. He's not the same since the accident.

One of the other guys was in a coma for two weeks and is still in the hospital. The third guy had injuries and was in the hospital for a couple of days.

The hard part is that your friends who you think are friends are quick to sue you as soon as they get the chance. I'm out of time so I have to go.

Wayne

Dear Mr. Nelson,

I think what you're doing is great, and some day I want to be up in front of a class telling them how wrong and dangerous it is to drive drunk.

My brother was a real partier and always got drunk and would come home all messed up. Not only is drunk driving bad, but you put a lot of pain on your parents by doing it. My mom would cry all night thinking she had done something wrong! Not only are you tormenting yourself, but your family too. Please share this with people and help them realize this!

Heather

Mr. Nelson,

I have a brother who is doing some time in Juvenile Hall for his drinking. He has been arrested three times for driving under the influence, and also unlicensed, which really got him into trouble. He's only 17 and is an alcoholic, and has been for 2-3 years.

He's not a bad person so please don't think he is, but he has caused a lot of pain in the family. We all love him very much. My youngest brother and I will finally get to see him because he's being transferred to Sacramento and is to get out around July. I love my brother very much and really wish he could be with me and my family.

If there is anything I could ever do to help with the problem that students have, please feel free to ask me because I'm against driving drunk or drunk drivers. Thank you for visiting our school because it is really appreciated by me, and I'm sure a lot of others here.

Dayna

Mr. Nelson,

Your speech really made me stop and think. My brother was killed on a motorcycle by a friend who was drinking. His friend was going to kill himself so my brother tried to sober him up. His friend didn't succeed in killing himself but instead killed my brother.

After my brother was killed, my dad stopped drinking. My real dad was an alcoholic and beat on us. Then, my step-dad was an alcoholic. Finally, my step-dad quit.

I've lived in an alcoholic world! It kills me to know my brother was killed in an alcohol-related accident. I was 13 years old; my brother was 18.

Thanks for listening and reading. Please send me some information on SADD, please!

Melissa

Mr. Nelson,

I really think that your coming to our school is super. About two weeks ago, my brother got arrested for drunk driving. I guess my dad had a policeman following him for a couple of days because my brother has been getting in trouble lately. He only had his license for one week when he got arrested,

When I think about it, I feel that if it weren't for the policeman, my brother could have been killed. The officer said that he was caught driving erratically on the highway. Every time I think of that, I thank God that it was the police who stopped him instead of a tree or another car! I wish he went to this school, but he goes to continuation.

I don't mind going to the SADD meetings instead of him. I'll let him know everything that I learn, although he insists that he knows what he's doing. I'm not old enough to drive, but when I do go out, I always try to arrange transportation through a sober friend.

Thanx,
Gianna

Dear Mr. Nelson,

My sister used to drive drunk all the time, but about three years ago, she went into a rehab center. I was ten years old when she went in to AA. I used to lie in bed at times crying, wondering if she would ever make it home in one piece. She was one of the lucky people; she's now 22.

My brother is 18. He drinks, but I don't know if he drives when he's drunk, because he's seldom ever home. He signed a contract with my parents, saying if he drank, he would call or stay the night. I still lie in bed at night wondering where my brother is and if he will still be alive the next day.

I hope that someday my brother will make up his mind to stop drinking. I also don't understand why he might drive drunk when about three years ago, he lost about six friends in two years due to drunk driving. I'm really interested in SADD and would like to hear from you.

Karen

Mr. Nelson,

I think driving drunk is awful. I don't drink much. Every once in a while at a special occasion, my best friend and I will have a glass of champagne or so. I'm not worried about my best friend or me. Neither of us would ever drive drunk or let the other one go drive when they're drunk.

I'm worried about my sister. We used to get along real well until she started drinking a lot. She doesn't have the friends I have. They do let her drink and drive. I don't know what to do. We can never share anything anymore, and I'm worried. I would like to become involved in SADD. Please send me information on it. Thank you.

Kelly

Mr. Nelson,

Thank you for coming to our school. It shows that people really care. I have never drank, smoked or done drugs! I've never been interested in that sort of thing; plus it's kind of scary. People get killed or kill other people. Out of my dad's side of the family, a family of 8 kids, 4-5 were alcoholics, so I chose not to drink.

I'm kind of a ditzy blonde in some ways. I'm smart, but guys kind of get the wrong idea, I guess because of the way I dress and my body. I'm scared to go to parties because I've heard guys get forceful when they're drunk and could rape you or something. Plus, if I do drink something, or something gets spiked, my judgment could get messed up, and I could do something I normally wouldn't do. So, basically I'm scared.

My best friend was almost an alcoholic, and her dad was one. She got out before it was too late. I wish my sister would do that. She's 15 years old (my sister), and at her rebellious stage, it's going on forever. She takes off at night without my mom knowing, sneaks out, and takes off with older guys (the kind you wouldn't bring home), and drinks. She comes home at 8:00 in the morning with a hangover and smells. I wish I could help her. She does it only because her friends do it, and she won't get new ones.

My mom is just on the break of being burned out. My sister is just too much. Please send me some information so I can try to help her. I think she does this stuff because she wants attention.

Megan

Mr. Nelson,

Hi, I wasn't sure whether or not I should write, but I decided to. My parents got divorced 9 years ago because of my dad's drinking problem and his drug problem. He's 43 or 44 and ready to die. I haven't seen him for a year, but he's way too young to die. I tried my best to stop him, but it's too hard.

I'm graduating this year, and I wish he could come watch, but he can't. He's never even remembered my birthday, but I understand and still love him with all my heart.

My brother and his best friend were drinking once and Jerry, my brother, passed out, and about an hour later Don, his best friend, shot himself in the head. Jerry woke up and went nuts. Don had put his class ring on Jerry's thumb before he did it.

It's been about four years or maybe five, but it still hits him pretty hard. There's one thing I admire him for; he didn't let it take him down in the dumps. He's got his own family and a baby son. He's cute. And even with my father the way he is, Jerry still takes control. I love him and admire him very much.

Thanks for your time,
Janet

Dear Mr. Nelson,

This last weekend, my brother came down from college, and he brought a lot of alcohol with him, so we went and drank. It was I, my best friend and my brother. We had way too much to drink, and he wanted to finish the beer, so we were going to go to the park.

My brother is the only one who has his driver's license, and on our way to the park, we were caught by my best friend's parents. They took my brother and me over to my house, and we were in trouble. I don't think I'll ever do that again, but when we were driving, I was not thinking. I would like you to write me back.

Love Always,
Eric

Dear Mr. Nelson,

I very much agree with you about drunk driving. My mother has been an alcoholic since before I was born. I've been in my father's custody since I was about two because of this.

My sister, Mindy, was adopted into another family because my mother hit her a lot when she was drunk. My sister, Stacey, had a baby at 17 and now doesn't really have any place to go. She's also on pot. My little brother lives with his father because my mother couldn't care for him. And not only has it hurt others, it also hurt my mother a lot, too. She is sick a whole lot and many of her boyfriends beat her up a lot.

I'm not specifically talking about drunk driving, just on alcohol problems. Without this, we might (my family) have ended up living together, instead of this. I think that alcohol is not just a physical problem, but a mental one. My mother is a very different person when she drinks, a person I wish I did not know. She has tried, and although I want to help, I don't know how to help as I do not live with her. I wish that someday, she can get rid of this problem.

I hope that I can tell people that it's not cool to drink, and that if you do, look what can happen.

Sincerely,
Ina

Mr. Nelson,

I'm so glad you came to talk to our class. I'm very concerned about my brother, Augie. He's only 20 and has a baby one year old. I love him very much even though we fight often. I can see that he has a problem. Every weekend, he goes out to get drunk. His idea of fun is to go out and get drunk.

My mother doesn't help much because she gives him money to buy the alcohol. I don't think she sees that he has a problem. I would really hate to see his life go to waste. I would also hate for his daughter to think that all he ever was, was a drunk.

I want to talk to him about it, but every time I say "Augie, you're drinking too much. Why don't you stay home with us?," all he says to me is, "Shut up, you little brat!"

I live with my father because I feel if I lived with my mother, I would be the same as Augie. This weekend, I'm going to see Augie, and I want to have a serious talk with him, but I'm afraid he'll take it the wrong way.

I'm 15 and have only drank a couple of times. I don't like it. I never overdo it. One time I did, and I promised God I would never do it again. God has helped me a lot. I feel that I can repay him back by keeping my promise.

I love Augie. He needs help, but I don't know how to help him. Please respond.

Very concerned,
Brandi

Dear Mr. Nelson,

I'm 16 years old and have a very large family. Some of my brothers and sisters have drinking problems. My parents are too busy in their jobs to notice it. (My mother's a doctor, and my father's a lawyer). My parents think that our family has no problems, but we have lots of problems.

I'm the youngest girl, and I notice everything that goes on in my house. Many times, my brothers or sisters come home drunk days later. I always cover for them. I love my brothers and sisters; that's why I don't tell my parents.

But there are times I wish I would tell my parents because I don't want to lose any of my brothers or sisters. Then I think, my parents must have noticed by now that we have some alcoholics in our family.

Even though my parents may be very smart, they don't know a thing about their own family. They help others, but I don't think that they know how to help themselves. What can I do to help my family?

I hope you send me info on SADD because I really do need it. Thank you very much.

Sobia

Dear Mr. Nelson,

My dad used to drink, and he has finally quit. My brother drinks, also, and just because they do, they think that I will, too. I would like to tell my parents that they have nothing to worry about me drinking.

Sure, I've gotten drunk, but I didn't like it so I don't drink. I tell them this, and they say, "Sure, just like your brother!"

Maybe you understand my situation, but I think that if I joined SADD, they might change their minds. Thanks for coming to our class and talking.

Thanks for your time,
Mike

Mr. Nelson,

My brother is an alcoholic and a drug abuser. When I was 12, I used to think that drinking was real cool. Now that I've grown up and realize what a problem alcohol can be, I try very hard to stay away from it. My brother now has a son, and I'm worried that my nephew will grow up to be an alcoholic and drug abuser. What should I do?

Sincerely,
Carrie Ray

Mr. Nelson,

My dad was a drunk driver and got into big trouble. He took a pill to stop his drinking, but that's not what I want to talk about.

My sister is drinking, and she is 18 years old. I'm scared for her. My dad got into a lot of car crashes, and I don't want my sister to do the same. I told her I don't want her to become like my dad. Can you help me?

Casey

Dear Mr. Nelson,

Hi, my name is Stephanie, and I have nothing to do with drugs, alcohol, or anything like that. I was always the outgoing type and have many friends. My sister, on the other hand, is the complete opposite. Ever since about the 8th grade, she started hanging around with the wrong crowd. I always tried taking the cigarettes, weed or beer I found of hers, and threw it away.

She would get very mad, but I didn't think much of it. As she got into high school, I thought things were getting better. I thought she'd quit and was doing great. I was real proud. Boy, was I wrong!

She confronted my dad and said he was the reason why she started doing these things. She had slit her wrists and told me she wanted to die.

She seems to be doing a little better and is now going to counseling, but she still comes home drunk every weekend. And, she drives herself home. She told me the other day that she didn't want to look like a loser, so she drank shots of tequila. She needs help, and I don't know what to do but listen.

Thank you,
Stephanie

Sisters write about their brother's or a sister's problems with alcohol or other drugs. Brothers tell about their concerns over another brother's drinking, but nowhere does there seem to be a letter where a brother opens up about his sister's problem.

Do they not see it? Are boys too embarrassed to talk about it? Or maybe, they're just not willing to expose their sister's actions to outsiders?

Siblings express love and deep feelings. They lose sleep. There are often the questions, *"Should I tell my parents what I see going on? Or would that lead to loss of trust if I squeal? That would be worse!"* Across the board, there is always a statement of great concern about the damage being done to parents and the family generally.

This often opened the door for my suggestions that the writer choose the time carefully to share their feelings with their 'ailing' brother or sister.

"There will be times when your brother is completely sober and seems to want to talk about himself. You can be certain that for all his spoken indifference, he has periods of awful worry. He doesn't want to do bad things. Your brother's just in too deep. Tell him that if he doesn't care much about himself, to please consider your parents' lives, and how much his actions are hurting them, and that they deserve better."

Most parents do deserve better, lots better! Even teens, as self-centered as they naturally are, acknowledge that. After the shock of learning that their son (or daughter) has become deeply involved with alcohol or other drugs, the first reaction has to be, *"Where did we go wrong? We've tried to provide love and a good, solid home life. We gave him the freedom to choose his friends, and made our home open to them. He's been such a good, obedient son and never hinted anything was wrong. Why didn't he tell us?"*

As parents we regret and don't understand our son's suddenly defiant reaction, *"Well, you guys drink and have a lot of fun, why shouldn't I? Drinking can't be all that bad or you wouldn't do it?"*

Why not, indeed?! I've watched the flow of letters to see if there's a significant correlation to parents' drinking, 'social' or 'alcoholic', and the resultant habits of their children. Your conclusion, like mine, will probably be that there's a much less likelihood of teenagers drinking if they come from homes where alcohol is not a regular part of parents' daily routine. If fun activities go on without alcohol, maybe it isn't a needed party accessory.

Parents' 'social' drinking is obviously carefully observed by growing children. Most don't tell us how they view it, but they hear the laughter, the fun, and the noisy chit-chat. Is it not logical that their thoughts follow, 'It can't be really bad, so why not try it with friends in the next party situation, especially if parents are not home, or if supervision is lax?' Too, children know that there's a stock of alcohol in their parents' liquor cabinet. 'No one would miss it if I tried a few sips'. Most of us wouldn't miss a quarter bottle.

Teenager letters from families with enormous alcohol problems all sound the same alarm and a determined commitment, "I sure don't plan to be like my alcoholic mother (or father)!" But half acknowledge that they already are headed that way. They are concerned about it, but see it as an unavoidable happening, another tragedy in the making.

The earlier group can turn to their parents as one option for help, if they choose, once the alcohol or other drug usage is out in the open. The latter group faces an even more difficult route, and many acknowledge this fact. Often, they ask, "Is this a hereditary thing in families as I've heard?"

Yes, despite their desire for complete independence, many teenage writers wish their parents would become part of the solution to the fix they're in.

Although I often suggest that the writer ask a school counselor to intervene (assuming both they and their brother or sister attend the same school), I have no data to support how many have taken that step.

My final plea is that they not give up on their sibling, that somehow help will surface and positive changes will occur.

Am I only indulging in wishful thinking?

CHAPTER THIRTEEN

*"I want to be invited to all the best parties and have
all the best boyfriends, but I'm not sure this will happen."*

Mr. Nelson,

*I'm in the 10th grade and right now, my family is going through a great lot.
I think it's mainly because my mom and my stepfather drink a lot. They go to
a lot of parties in Stockton, and we live in Sacramento.*

*About three weeks ago, my parents told me that we were moving to Stockton.
I got mad because my girlfriend and I are finally really in love, and my mom is
going to ruin it, so I drank a beer, and then I drank another. Now I drink even
if I don't want to. I'm trying to stop. I know I can do it because I can stop for
three or four days, but yesterday, I started again.*

*I really want some information about SADD. I think I'm really going to
need something/someone when I move to Stockton.*

Well, that's my problem.

Thanks a lot,
Oscar

Mr. Nelson,

*I have had an experience with alcohol that has changed my life forever. It
happened when I was eleven years old. See, I trusted my friends, and they fed
me drinks. I had no idea what it was or how it would affect me.*

*Well, the next think I knew, I was on a 19 years old's bed with my
blood on the sheets. At that point, I realized that I had lost all of my pride,
childhood, and instincts. I can never get that back, and it has changed me a
lot.*

I have never told or written of this 'till now. I ask of you to let others know that you can never trust friends. They turn on you. I sill have so much pain that I know will never go away. Sex means nothing to me anymore because my virginity is lost.

Erika

Dear Mr. Nelson,

My father has always had a drinking problem. I know a part of being an alcoholic is claiming that you don't have a problem with it. That's exactly what he does. He will have about eight beers or more when he comes home. Then, he'll have glasses of wine until he goes to bed.

I was refusing to believe that he was an alcoholic until one year ago. I've been told that alcoholism is hereditary. That scares me because, as it is, I already do drink. My parents, however, do not know, and I don't want them to know.

I don't want to become an alcoholic. I know what it does to people. But, what can I do? Please, if you can, give me advice to help stop the drinking. My sister is in Peer Resource and SADD. I want to be in those groups next year. Hopefully, that will help.

Thank you,
Lorie

Dear Mr. Nelson,

Hello, my name is Diana, and I'm 15 ½ years old. Two years ago, I took my first drink of alcohol, and on that same day, I lost my virginity.

I was with a real good friend of mine (a boy), and he asked if I wanted to drink with him and some more friends. I said, "O.K.!" That was the biggest mistake I've ever made in my whole life. We were driving around in a small Honda Civic when suddenly we crashed into a pick-up truck. We were out on a country road.

Well, when we hit, I was kind of knocked out and my head was busted open. The man in the pick-up truck was thrown out of his truck and was unconscious. That was when the boy I was with took advantage of me. I never thought anything like that would happen to me, but it did. I consider myself a lucky person because I am not injured for life physically, just mentally!

Ever since then, I've not gotten into a car with anyone who has been drinking or doing drugs. I listened to the speech you gave, and I took it to heart.

Sincerely,
Diana

Mr. Nelson,

I am what you call a'stoner.' I go out every weekend, get not only drunk but do many drugs. I've been in a car with drunk drivers, drivers who were strung out on speed, and drivers who were on acid.

I've never really thought about what could happen to me. I guess I could get hurt, but I'm going to die some way. I might as well go happy. I've been drinking since I was about 12 years old. I will be seventeen in three months.

I will grow out of it some day, or I will die in a car wreck. If I don't drink, the guy in the car behind me will be drunk. Why should I drive sober when a drunk will eventually hit me?

Jeromy

Mr. Nelson,

Hello, I'm not a girl with too many problems, but I sometimes drink, not often, but not by myself, either. My friend drinks with me. We just want to have some fun. I almost want a hangover at times, just so I can tell some of my friends that I got drunk over the weekend.

I want to be invited to all the best parties and have all the best boyfriends, but I'm not sure it's true that this will happen.

But, mainly I'm writing to you so that I can join SADD and get some information about it.

Thank you for caring. Most people don't give a damn.

Lee Ann

Mr. Nelson,

Society today says, "Just say no!" Society today says, "Friends Don't Let Friends Drive Drunk." But when the bottle begins to beckon, when your friends wait for you to take that drink, it doesn't matter any more.

I'm left with a hollow feeling reaching deep within myself, only to find nothing. This frightens me and makes me wonder if life is really that important. After all, we all must die.

Leah

Mr. Ken Nelson,

My mom and dad have been alcoholics at one time, and their parents, and it goes on and on. This runs in our family. Everyone in my family is either having a problem with alcohol or has had one.

I feel that I'm becoming an alcoholic, but I can't stop it. I will say to myself that when next weekend comes, I won't drink at all or will have only one. But it never works out that way.

What should I do? I can't tell my family. Please write back to me!

Kim

Dear Sir,

I've read some letters that were hard to keep reading because it brought back old memories that I don't like to remember. I was taken away from my father because he and I drank and got stoned all the time.

I never went to school much. I stopped, but I'm doing it again, just not as often. I'm scared! I need help but can't get it. My aunt and uncle don't know I do this stuff, and I don't want them to. I live with them.

I can't go into the rest right now. Please try to help me before it costs me my life. What shall I do?

I would really like to have all the information on SADD and become a member.

Thanks,
Tonya

Dear Mr. Nelson,

While I was reading the letters from the other students, a not so good memory I have came back.

It was last March, and one of my good friends was having a party. I was always one to try and catch at least two parties a night. Well, I got to the party, and everyone was there, drinking, smoking pot, and doing cocaine. I wasn't one to do cocaine, but I was one for drinking.

As the night passed, I eventually got smashed. Three different guys I didn't know tried to get me to go into a bedroom with them or out to a car.

Later that night, I saw a guy who was a senior. He was in the popular group. I was only a freshman. We had met up a couple of times, and he knew I was interested. He always set out the ideal, nice-guy image. I thought he'd be perfect for a boyfriend; so we got to talking and later ended up in the bedroom. By the end of the night, I'd slept with him three times, only once using protection.

During the whole time, I remember him telling me he wanted to have a relationship, and he really liked me. The next day, I felt terrible, but I figured on Monday, I'd have a boyfriend, and he really liked me.

But after I got there, he didn't even care. It resulted in my being pregnant. I told a friend and then him. He told me, "There's no way you can prove this." I hated him and had an abortion after four months of trying to get him.

I still have nightmares of the abortion, and it has affected my life greatly. I never told my parents. My dad was an abusive alcoholic and beat me while I was pregnant. I couldn't have brought another human being into this sinful world.

Thank you,
Emily

Dear Mr. Nelson,

I'm 14 years old and a freshman at this school. I've been drinking for about a year. I drink kind of a lot, but not really, so I think. My friends tell me that I drink way too much.

When I get drunk, I do way stupid stuff and stuff I regret badly. How can I stop myself? My parents really don't know that I drink, and I don't want them to find out.

Maybe I do have an alcohol problem. I really don't know. Could you please write back. I would really appreciate it.

Thank you,
Danielle

Mr. Nelson,

My father and his father, my mother and her parents are all alcoholics. I should say were; her father died two years ago. My mother is recovering and planning to remarry.

My father has remarried and is ruining his new family. I live with my paternal grandparents, and luckily, my grandmother doesn't drink.

I drink, too, sometimes a lot. This has gone on for four years, and I have no idea why I do this to myself!

Few people care enough about this ongoing and prevalent problem to try to help. Thank you for coming to speak to us. Some day, I want to make a difference, too.

Lori

Dear Mr. Nelson,

I really don't know what to say. When I was fourteen years old, I began to drink because my good friend drank. I feel alcohol is a person's choice, but it is wrong. You see, at that time when my friend drank, she did other things, too. She was a year younger than I.

I never thought the things she did would affect me until I went to a party with her around Christmas time. The kind of people she used to drink with were mostly guys. That night, after most of the people left, I was forced to have sex with a guy who was there. I was not drunk, but he was, and he forced me to do something I really hated myself for.

I have learned to forgive myself and to see it was not my fault. I despise alcohol to this day and will not drink. My friends do not drink now. I'm not around alcohol anymore and learned to like myself. I do regret to say the friend I used to drink with now has a two year old son. She was drunk when she got pregnant.

I just wanted to show and tell you I understand how dangerous alcohol is.

Your 17-year-old friend,
Vicki

Hi, Ken,

This is real weird. Just this last weekend, I was pulled over for drinking and driving. I was just lucky I didn't kill myself or someone. When you read that first letter, it really got to me. That boy had a lot in common with me, like when he goes to parties, he's like expected to drink.

But, I'm not going to end up a drunk. I think I'm going to do something about it. I'll get help. I think it's cool to see you going to different schools and talking to people.

Eddie

Dear Mr. Nelson,

I'm a 10th grade girl here at this school. When I go to parties, everybody expects me to drink because I'm like the person who knows everybody. I drink just to prove to my friends that I can do everything they can. I really try to stop, but I can't. I never thought that me drinking now will lead me to drink for the rest of my life.

I'm only 16 years old and 16 is too young to die. Two weeks ago, my mom let me drive her car to go to a party. I got so drunk that I tried to drive home but couldn't do it, so I called my mom and told her I was staying the night.

I'm really going to try to stop, but I can't do it alone. Thanks for speaking to us. And, Hey-thanks for caring.

Nikki

Dear Mr. Nelson,

Hi. This is really nothing big, but I'll write you anyway. I started drinking when I was thirteen, but now that I'm 15, I've been getting a craving for liquor (beer). I went to a party Saturday and drank a lot! If I don't drink, I feel like I'm nothing. When I don't have anything to drink, I kind of go crazy, not violent or anything, but I crave it a lot lately!

When I was at that party, I was so scared because my ex-boyfriend, Dave, was s-o-o-o-o messed up. I worry about him because he could have died. Now, he's in juvenile hall. The fault on his part was taking someone else's car and other stuff.

I felt like it was my fault because we got in a fight and then he started drinking a lot, and so did I. Can anything happen to me in the future with drinking because I really can't stop drinking when there is alcohol around me? I'm sort of afraid. Thanks a lot. Please write back.

Staci

Dear Mr. Nelson,

I read one of the letters; it was written by Jenni. Reading that letter brought back a bad memory of what happened to me. I was 13 years old.

It was Halloween night. My parents are really strict so I was not allowed to go to parties. I snuck out and went to my best friend's house. His 22-year-old cousin was there. He had my friend drinking, and eventually, I did.

I completely passed out and can't recall what happened except that when I woke up, he was lying on me with his pants down and most of my clothes off. I pushed him off and ran home. I stayed sheltered for at least a week.

Three weeks later, I found out I was pregnant. I had an abortion and never said anything to anybody, not even my best friend. I thought I tucked it all away, but the letters brought it all back.

I have drank since, but I never get so drunk to the point where I don't know what I'm doing. Thank you for your time. I had to get it out.

Thanks,
Melodie

Mr. Nelson,

Hi, I have a problem with drinking. I'm very ashamed of it. It started when I was nine years old. I wasn't doing it that much, but gradually, I got to doing it every weekend. I've been in a car accident, but it wasn't that serious. The person driving was drunk.

I'm scared that my drinking will end up taking my life. I'm trying to quit, but it's hard when there's peer pressure. Also, whenever I go to a party, I will do my best not to drink, but I need support. I'm very interested in the SADD club. I'm also very thankful you came to our school and talked. I've known many people who have lost their lives from drinking and driving.

Oh, my mother doesn't know, and I'm scared she'll find out before I quit. Well, that's about all I have to say.

Love always,
Debbie

Mr. Nelson,

My boyfriend drinks, and I hate it when he gets really drunk. I hate having sex with him when he gets drunk, but I do it anyway because I don't want him to maybe get mad.

Because he's 20 years old, and I'm only 14, I can't really tell him how I feel about his drinking. I don't know what to do. I wish he wouldn't drink. It really scares me when he drives drunk.

I love my boyfriend a lot so I don't want him to leave. Please write me and give me some advice.

Kim

Mr. Nelson,

Well, I think you're a wise and good man. I think drinking and partying is lots of fun. Although my friends and schoolmates and I like to get really smashed at parties, I never get in a car with a drunk driver! I think that driving drunk is the most stupid thing anyone can possibly do.

Although I cannot stop people from drinking and driving, I still try to. I'm not trying to say that I'm some angel or anything; I mean I'm 15 years old, and I've had one sober weekend in three years. But, no matter what, I will never get drunk and go driving.

Thanks,
John

Mr. Nelson,

My mom's husband has a drinking problem and has hit my mom twice. When I was 12 years old, he would call me bad, very bad names. He would tell me to pack my stuff an get out, and he would overrule my mom because she had a weight problem. She is scared she is going to lose him and not get anybody else.

I'm not living with him now because he got drunk and started to fight with me and kicked me out. I've been looking for a steady place ever since I've been 13 years old.

Thanks for coming in,
Kelly

Dear Ken,

My name is Jarod. I'm turning sixteen later this month. My dad left when I was two. The divorce was final when I was seven.

My 29-year-old brother got me started on drugs and alcohol when I was in fourth grade. I'm now in tenth grade, and I have a drug problem. I'd like to stop, but I feel the high puts me away from everyone who bugs me. I'd like to have some info on how to quit. Please write back.

Sincerely,
Jarod

Dear Mr. Nelson,

My step-dad has a serious drinking problem. He gets drunk almost all the time during the week. When he's drunk, he starts fighting with my mother. Once in a while, he'll take his problems out on me.

He's a big influence on my older brother, and now my brother gets drunk at parties and comes home at 3:00 in the morning. When he's drunk, he'll throw things around.

Thank you for reading this letter and for coming into our class and talking to us about SADD.

Love always,
Emily

Dear Mr. Nelson,

I drink but don't drive because my older sister, Brenda, was hit and died by a drunk driver. I was only five, but I remember her, and I loved her very much.

Even after admitting he had a couple of beers (drunk), they let him go; he didn't get any sentence. I'm so angry because she was a bright person. She had an A average and was a well-rounded person, just plain perfect almost.

I just want to hit him so hard.

David

Dear Mr. Nelson,

I'm 14 and in the 10th grade. I don't have a problem with drinking. My mom does however drink occasionally and lets me drink also. She doesn't let me drink enough to get drunk. Most of my friends drink to get drunk. I drink with them sometimes but not a lot. They make fun and say I'm a baby because I don't get drunk.

I have been in three drunk driving accidents. In the second one, my shoulders were knocked out of place, so now, I walk with my neck bent over. I'm just afraid that one day, I'll get too much to drink with my friends, and my mom won't mind. I'm trying to look out for myself. I don't have anyone to stop me from drinking.

Thanks for listening,
Elane

Dear Mr. Nelson,

I don't know that much English, but I'm going to write a letter. Well, Mr. Nelson, I don't know if I have a problem with alcohol, but I think yes. I drink when I'm in my house sometimes, but mostly, I drink at parties and sometimes I drive.

But my problem is not with alcohol only. I do some other kind of drugs, and sometimes when I'm with my friend, I smoke marijuana, and I have to drive back home because my parents don't know I do all that. But, I'm scared that someday, I'll get hurt or something like that.

I tried to quit smoking and all of those things, but I'm really addicted to it. I tried not smoking for one week and felt that I didn't have any energy.

Well, Mr. Nelson, I trust that you're not going to tell anybody, and please write back. Thank you.

Sincerely, your friend,
Nancy

Dear Mr. Nelson,

I come from a long line of alcoholics in my family. My grandmother, aunts, and uncles, even my younger cousins all drink now or did for a long time. My very own mother chose alcohol over me. Because she did that, I had no father and no life. I used to get beat and moved around a lot because my mother would gain a reputation in that area where we were living.

My mother had gotten two younger brothers taken away from her by the time I was seven; I'm almost 16 now. When I was nine, she abandoned me for alcohol, and I ended up living in another alcoholic house with my aunt and uncle. I got beat a lot more.

Finally, I ended up in a foster home with an alcohol problem. I have overcome that problem now, and I thank you because my grandmother has given up alcohol because of the MADD program. Rehabilitation centers couldn't help her, but MADD did, and she's been clean for two years.

Can I please get some advice on how to deal with my other family members' problems?

Thank you,
Carol

So many teenagers wrote that their parents weren't aware of how deeply they were involved with alcohol or other drugs that I had to conclude this to be a common situation.

It does prompt several questions. Are parents too occupied with their own activities to notice? Are their children just too clever in their ability to keep the use of illegal substances from being detected? Do some parents think they see but don't want to accept that a problem is developing?

Equally of concern, although a few students indicated a desire for their parents to learn of their situation and thus be able to help, most often the writer concluded with, *"My parents don't know, and I don't want them to find out."*

That position narrowed the likelihood of these young people going to counselors on their own. I'm sure that in their minds, the writers were certain that their parents would get the first call from the school. That was the last thing they wanted to have happen. It reduced my enthusiasm for revealing such problem letters to counselors, although I usually did take that step. I was tempted each time to ask the counselor to respect a student's statement that he didn't want his parents to know, but seldom did that. Counselors read the letters and took a copy. They were the experts. I was merely bringing the information to them. Eventually, parents had to become advised. If they were solid parents, their involvement would prove to be the most helpful of all.

Teenagers who wrote of parents who had severe alcohol/drug problems of their own represented the least hopeful group. They had seen and had long-experienced the personal damage caused by their own alcohol and drug-abusing parents. Many said they had made an early commitment that they never wanted to become like their own father or mother. But as one wrote, "I have no idea why I do this to myself."

In about half of these cases where a brutal parental environment had been outlined by a child, counselors thanked me for bringing the letter to their attention, but acknowledged that they were already aware of the family problems. It's likely that teachers and counselors are on top of these situations involving parents of their students, especially if police actions related to drugs or impaired driving have shown up in print. I'm confident that the letters gave the counselors an added tool to help these teens escape an environment where they might end up like their parents despite their expressed desire not to.

The spontaneous letters provide the greatest stimulus for me to continue my volunteer speaking at high schools. I'm often asked if many students continued writing after an exchange or two of letters. There were several dozen who did choose to continue corresponding, far beyond the initial letters. A few kept writing on into their college years, or following engagements or even marriages. My policy then became one of delaying my answers for longer and longer periods, but always responding. Eventually all letters from them would stop. It had become apparent the once-13-16-year-olds didn't need my advice anymore.

CHAPTER FOURTEEN

"I want to stand up for myself and say "No," but I always find myself giving in. I've had a lot of trouble (in the past) with alcohol, but I don't see myself as an alcoholic."

Mr. Nelson,

I'm an alcoholic and 14 ½ years old. I have been drinking since I was 12. I don't drink to fit in or be "cool," I do it to get away from everything. I drink nightly. I drink by myself or with my friends, even after my 18-year-old brother got caught drunk driving. Nothing will stop me. When I get stressed, I find myself saying, "I need some brandy," or, "Boy, do I need a cigarette!"

My dad has a small shot of brandy every day when he gets home from work. Both of my parents love me very much, but we don't get along at all. When we fight, I go outside and have a drink.

I should also say my parents have no idea I drink. They've told me that if I'm ever caught drinking, they'll kick me out to live with my grandma.

I'm afraid I'll turn out like my brother. I'm too young to drive, so I've never drank and driven, but I know I'll end up doing it sometime. I'm scared for my future.

Thank you for caring about us. Please write back, but send it through my teacher.

Thanks,
Megan

Dear Mr. Nelson,

Hello, my name is Laura. I'm not an alcoholic or a drinker, but I am concerned with the amount of my friends who make the choice to drink and drive. I know what the consequences are. I've been there with my 17-year-old cousin when she's gone to rehab centers numerous amounts of times, not by choice but because the law gave her the easy way out. She chose to drink and drive, and she ran off the road and killed her 16-year-old boyfriend. That's something she'll have to live with all her life

My uncle killed himself by overdosing on drugs and alcohol mixed, and he was my best friend.

All this loss is hurting me, mainly because students who make that choice are not seeing all of the others who are caring for them. I hate to see my friends drink and drive. I'm only 15 ½ years old, and I've had to be the designated driver for many who have been smart enough to keep their lives.

I respect you 'cause you give children a way out, and they feel comfortable about talking to you. Something good will come to you for being so dedicated to use your time to convince others of the right choice. Please write.

Thank you,
Laura

Mr. Nelson,

I personally don't have a drinking problem, but my boyfriend does. I can't say I've never drank before, but I don't need alcohol to get through the day. My boyfriend, Ryan, drinks a lot. Right when he gets up, he drinks. Yeah, he's over 21, he's 25. I would think that his party days were over, but they're not.

The first day I met him, he was drunk. That night we partied together, and he got me drunk. Now that we're together, he hates for me to drink. He says that if I drink, he'll break up with me. Why doesn't he take his own advice?

Just a week ago, I told him how I felt about his drinking. He listened to me and has been sober for a week. I don't know if it will last. Will it? Now I find myself calling his house to make sure he didn't go out and drink. Am I stupid or just overprotective?

Thanks for listening,
Natalie

Mr. Nelson,

Two months ago, I was over at a friend's house to stay with her because her parents were out of town. We got really drunk that night. I drank over one pint of Southern Comfort in 15 minutes, not to mention that I hadn't eaten all day. My parents called to say they had gotten home. When my friend couldn't wake me up, my mom and dad came into town to pick me up.

They found me on the floor in the bathroom, passed out. By the time they got me to the emergency room, it was barely in time. My blood alcohol level was .231, my veins collapsed. I had hypothermia from lying on the floor in the bathroom. I had quit breathing, and my heart stopped.

My parents were out in the waiting room and heard the call for a "crash car." They freaked out. I was the only one in the emergency room, and their 15-year-old little girl might be dead for all they knew.

Needless to day, I learned my lesson. The hard thing is my parents are recovering alcoholics. So it was really hard. I sit and think about what happened that night, and if my parents had not called, I would be dead. My dad had asked my mom to call, and she said, "No, she is fine," but my dad insisted that she call. I thank them so much for that one little phone call. My friends who were with me were going to put me to bed and let me sober up. I would not have sobered up or woken up.

Thanks,
Auldeen

Mr. Ken Nelson,

For a while, I was an alcoholic and sometimes still have a drink. I still sometimes get high and am now addicted to my medication. I continue to smoke and drink because I figure, if my medication kills my brain cells, why not help it along?

My boyfriend is still a heavy drug user, although he's trying to stop. He used to go to school with a 5-inch curved needle in his arm filled with morphine and would slowly inject it into his body throughout the whole day. He once bought an ounce vial of acid, poured it on his arm, and he fried for six weeks straight.

I don't know why I'm writing you this, but I need some sort of adult to know. I've seen my dear friends jump off bridges, thinking they could fly, but they didn't hit water. That sobered me up quickly. I wish I could stop my addictions, but I can't; there is just too much pain.

I get angry when my friends get high, even though I still do it. When I was in an institution, this one girl who was on crank for three days pretended to "love" one of my friends there. He went to her room to wake her up, and she told him to get the—out of his face. He then tried to die by tying a belt around his neck. I can't tell my parents about my problem. I feel that if I try to quit, I will die.

Thank you for having an open heart. You are one of a kind.

Love,
Deborah

Mr. Nelson,

I'm Tiffany, and I live with my aunt and uncle. I moved here because less than one month from now, a year ago, I drank almost a full bottle of vodka, and tried to o.d. on ibuprofen. I was passed out for a while, and I also puked off and on for about 24 hours.

My mom was afraid I'd do it again, so she sent me here. She says it's to help me! But my step-dad is a true drunken loser. He drinks every day from about 4:00 p.m. on. He's been jobless for nine months because of it.

He broke a table in our house. He tried to stab himself and my mom, and he gets kind of abusive with my siblings. I yelled at him for it, and he won't dare try anything with me now. Why won't my mom help him?

Pray for me 'n care for me always,
Tiffany

Dear Mr. Nelson,

Hello, well I love to drink and smoke. I don't do it all the time, but when I do, I get messed up. My parents don't know, but my friends do. Do you think I need help? No, I don't because it's under control.

Always,
Lil

Dear Mr. Nelson,

I don't think I have an alcohol problem, but I absolutely love to drink. If it's alcohol, I'm the one who will want some.

I don't drink on a regular basis, or even on a weekly basis, but when I do drink, I get drunk, real drunk. Should I get some type of help, or do you even see this as a problem?

My friends also drink just the same way I do. I say I don't believe it's a problem, but it is a problem. I don't do any drugs, and I do pretty good at school, so should I stop drinking or what? I've tried many times, but temptation gets to me. Write back if you feel the need to.

Sincerely,
Myreka

Dear Mr. Nelson,

Lately, I've been experiencing a problem with substance abuse, not alcohol, but speed. I don't know why I do it. I guess just because I like the way it makes me feel. I've been doing it recreationally for the last year, and then almost every day for the last month.

I've been trying to quit, but how can you say "No" to something you love? I can't quite remember as well as I could before, but I really don't think it matters. I haven't done any drugs since yesterday, and I feel like dying. What can I do?

Thanks,
Roger,
A dwindled sophomore

Mr. Nelson,

I am a drinker. I have been for a few years. It started when I was in 7th grade; I am now in 11th.

A long time ago (about 4 years), I went through a terrible experience. My mother was shot in the head by her boyfriend. I didn't know how to deal with my feelings and turned to liquor. Now, it seems anytime I'm bothered in any way, I turn to alcohol.

Sometimes, I wonder if I need help. I haven't drank in a long time, to be honest, for about a month. I think alcohol is the only way for me to deal with my feelings. I don't understand.

Sincerely,
Salina

P.S. My mom didn't die. She's okay, but she's blind.

Mr. Nelson,

As I sit here listening to you talk, I think back to my not so happy holidays.

When I moved to my dad and Renee's house about 1 ½ years ago, I knew my father was an alcoholic. It didn't bother me then. During the holidays, he took my life and many other lives in his own hands when he drove drunk on numerous occasions. We would be at my grandparents. He would pass out. Then, he would wake up, have a drink, and then drive me, Renee, and my two brothers home. My stepmother was also too drunk to drive. She passed out in the car.

I get so mad at them being alcoholics; I get drunk at lunch and on weekends. It's affected my GPA. I was on the Honor Roll. My teachers now get mad at me because I sleep in class. But, that is the only time I can honestly have good, peaceful sleep.

When my friends party on weekends, one person, the driver, doesn't drink. When I drink, I usually pass out. That scares me because one year, I was raped on New Year's Eve, and the next year, my boyfriend got me pregnant. The scary part is, I can't remember half of those nights.

I hate thinking that just one drunk person can kill me or my friends and wake up and not remember what happened. Please write back.

Thanks for listening,
Dannie

Dear Mr. Nelson,

I wrote you last semester concerning my drug problem. You can see I'm taking the class over. I stopped doing speed after two rehabs and about 1½ months of Narcotics Anonymous meetings twice a week.

Well, now my friends have started snorting cocaine, and I have, too. I don't know if I can handle it. I started doing it about a week and a half after the second time I went to rehab.

I don't know what's wrong with me. I just wig too hard. Who could imagine a Redneck using coke? I just can't quit doing drugs.

Roger,
The Dwindled Sophomore

Mr. Ken Nelson,

A lot of my friends and I go to parties on the weekends. There's always alcohol, and I usually drink. I'm not saying I have an alcohol problem, but I am saying that I notice how easily influenced my friend and I can be.

Sometimes it scares me (the drinking), but I try to use good judgment. Your visiting our class made me realize how easy it is to lose a friend or loved one.

Thanks for waking me up to reality, and for listening to a complete stranger.

Alicia

Mr. Nelson,

As I sit here listening to you read letters which you have received from other students, I feel guilt and embarrassment. I feel this way because I want to become a member of SADD, yet I know it would be very hard for me to live up to the name I would be representing.

After all, how much control would you have over your friends if you, yourself, were drunk? Yet, everyone does it, and you're just not 'cool' unless you party.

I want to stand up for myself and say "No," but I always find myself giving in. I've had a lot of trouble (in the past) with alcohol, but I don't see myself as an alcoholic.

Most of my friends drink, and they make it sound like it's so great! I really don't think that it is but I do it too. I'm confused for myself. I don't want my parents to know that I drink because I don't want to let them down . . . AGAIN!

The contract you and your parents sign may say that they will come pick you up if you drunk, yet they will still blow up and threaten you and make you feel worthless. "Do as I say, not as I do," that is getting old, and I think parents shouldn't be so judgmental!

Thank you,
Stephanie

Mr. Nelson,

I read most of the letters today. Some sounded like me, but with me, my problem is that people in my family, from grandmother to cousins, all have a drinking problem. All my life I've had to fight this. It's been hard because when I was little I used to drink with them. It's been like that for all the little kids in our family. Some have tried to stop. Others just don't want to.

Myself, the basic reason I don't drink is because, if something happens to me, that person is drunk. From people being drunk, I've been in car wrecks, raped, and molested by my father when I was only ten.

Your discussion today I know will help other people a lot to open up and discuss their feelings. I know it's helped me.

Thanks for listening,
Corinno

Mr. Nelson,

I think what you do is really great! My grandfather was a serious drunk and used to come over and go crazy on my mom and our family. I have also had problems with my stepfather. He's also a drunk and drinks about a case of beer (24-pack) every day. Sometimes when he goes out and comes home, he's really drunk and goes crazy on my mom and then comes after me and my sister. One time he hung my sister from the balcony by her feet and told her he was going to drop her.

Lately, I've noticed I have been drinking a lot. I can't help it. It's just that when I start drinking, I can't quit. I just finished reading one of the letters you passed around the room. It was about a young girl who was taken advantage of at a party. Something similar happened to me.

We were at a party. My cousin and I got really drunk. There was a guy I liked a lot. Well, we started to kiss and mess around and then he took me to the bedroom. I woke up the next morning lying next to him without my clothes on. I felt so ashamed. I didn't know what to do but cry.

That was two years ago, and I was a virgin, and I wanted to save myself for someone I really loved.

Well, I just wanted to thank you for coming to our class and talking to us. You're a really great guy.

Amber

Dear Mr. Nelson,

There are a lot of things bothering me. I usually get rid of these problems by going out with friends and drinking. I could go for a drink now.

Nothing bad has really happened when I drink. If I'm drinking with things on my mind, I will take shots of hard liquor, but if I'm just drinking, I will drink anything from beer to whiskey and even wine coolers.

I have a lot of problems I don't talk about, but even though I have problems, my drinking isn't one of them. Put it this way, I'm not an alcoholic.

John

Have you thought about how many times you've read letters where the writer first listed his or her sizable alcohol-related difficulties, then at the end denied having a problem?

"No, I don't, because it's under control."

"I say, I don't believe I have a problem."

"But even though I have problems, my drinking isn't one of them."

Responses to these teenagers aren't as easy as when a student acknowledges that the problem has become acute and asks for help. I still compliment the writer on their straightforwardness and honesty. Not much would be gained if I then said I thought they were dead wrong and that a big alcohol problem did exist. On the other hand, agreeing with them that they probably didn't have a serious dependency on alcohol would be doing them a serious disservice.

At least they had opened the door to possibly re-thinking their situation, and I could encourage that. I could suggest that they review their use of alcohol, how often, under what pressures, and how they reacted if they drank nothing for a few days or weeks. I would remind them that from what they wrote, I could see that some problems might develop really soon if regular dinking continued. I often made a suggestion that they ask some recovering alcoholic, an older friend or relative, if they went through this period of thinking they could quit drinking if they chose to, and had felt that no problem existed.

I always ended my letter asking that the writer please not allow the alcohol to take control of his or her life. My plea was that they do take steps to get help if they found that quitting drinking turned out to be too difficult, and to write to me again and let me know how they were doing.

Over time I felt comfortable in showing letters to quite a few of the teachers involved. I felt it reasonable to ask that they not indicate they had read letters handed personally to me, even if asked. I suggested they even use a little white lie, "Mr. Nelson tells me he doesn't make it a practice of showing you students' letters to their teachers." Many teachers soon became my strongest boosters. It was sometimes embarrassing to listen as they extolled my virtues as part of their introduction to the class. I'm sure my student audiences often said to themselves, "what's that old guy got to say that's so great?"

One teacher told me on the side, following several years of regular visits, "You can't believe how you affect my students. It often lasts a month after you're here. They actually treat each other differently. They like each other more. They're even more considerate and respectful of my feelings."

Another teacher confided, "I don't know what you wrote to one of my girls. She'd been a jerk all year and had always disrupted the class. Now, she's completely changed and has been one of my best students. Her other teachers say they're amazed, too. I knew you must have written back to her because I saw her hand you a letter the last time you were here."

Another teacher told me that I just mesmerized her students, that they sat leaning forward and couldn't take their eyes off of me, and that how amazed she was that her normally somewhat restless class remained starkly quiet during my talks. My joking response was that I was maybe hugely effective in putting them to sleep.

The flow of spontaneous letters and the wonderful level of attentiveness provided the greatest stimulus for continuing the volunteer speaking at high schools. I didn't want to miss a single opportunity to respond to those students who wrote.

As each teenager handed a letter to me, I asked a question: "Did you put your name on the letter?"

If the answer was a nod or a "Yes," I followed with, "look for a note from me." A "No" answer prompted, "Will you please do that for me? I surely don't want to miss writing to you," as I handed their letter back. I only recall one student refusing, with "It really wasn't important."

Occasionally, I was overwhelmed with letters being handed to me. The few seconds available while these young people rushed from the room left no time to quickly examine their notes or to ask questions. I only had time for a quick smile and "Thank you" as I folded and tucked each letter into my bulging shirt pocket.

CHAPTER FIFTEEN

"I don't think my mother's an alcoholic,
but I do know that I hate her when she's drinking."
"My father has a drinking problem, and every time
my mom and dad get into a fight (when he's drunk)
it tears me apart. I don't want to take sides,
and I don't want to feel alone."

Mr. Nelson,

Hello. I have this problem with my dad. He likes to drink a lot, and sometimes I don't even know my dad.

What do I do? When he doesn't drink, I love him so much, but I don't know what to do. I'm so scared for him because sometimes he's so drunk, he doesn't even know who I am.

Please give me some information to help my dad. Thanks for your time.

Karla

Dear Mr. Nelson,

I'm a 10th grader here at this school. I don't have a problem 'cause I don't drink, but my dad does. He drinks a lot. Every time I go visit him (Mom and Dad are divorced), he always has a beer or other drink in his hand. His fridge always has beer in it.

My father's a cop. You have to realize that cops don't think they can do anything wrong. I know, I've tried to talk to him. One night I wouldn't get into the car with him 'cause he had been drinking. He got very defensive and said he wasn't, and if I didn't, he would hit me.

He's never hit me before, and I was very scared 'cause he's a very large man. We (he) ran a red light and almost hit a car. Now I'm afraid of him. No one should be afraid of their dad. How could I talk to him?

Thanks for caring,
Buffie

Dear Mr. Nelson,

I want to thank you for coming to talk to us. In April 1988, my father was drinking heavily. I was very scared of him that night, so I left. When I came back that night, my father started to punch, slap, and kick me.

I'm not sure how long this went on, maybe about an hour or two. I had black eyes, bruises, and cuts everywhere, in my eyes, mouth, and all over my body. I couldn't go to sleep that night; my nerves were shattered.

After finally falling asleep, my father busted in, telling me to go to school or he would hit me some more. I got ready as fast as I could. As I was walking to school, I met up with some of my friends. I went to the school nurse and told her what had happened.

The whole ordeal was awful. I'm not sure I can only blame alcohol or my father, but I can't blame myself.

I still see my father but not by choice. My brother still sees him. I don't know why I love my brother so much. When my father was hitting me, my brother didn't try to stop him. He didn't do anything. He just left the room.

Thank you very much,
Monica

My name is Anthony. I'm having a problem, too, but I just don't know how to tell you this.

First, I'll start with my mom. She was a heavy drinker, but she stopped drinking. Then she got into that church stuff real bad. I have nothing wrong with that, but she expected too much, so I left.

Now I live with my dad, step-mom, and my three little brothers. Now, here's the problem. He drinks and drives a lot. A couple of times, he crashed, but he got lucky. I want to tell him to stop, but I'm scared because I just met him when I was fourteen, so I don't really talk too much to him.

Drinking for him is a big problem because he doesn't hardly pay for the food for the kids. I'm not really concerned about the money. I'm worried about his life because one day, he's not going to get so lucky.

Thanks for trying to help,
Anthony

Mr. Nelson,

Listening to another girl's letter, I decided to tell you my situation. I'm very much against alcohol of any kind because of what it has done to my mother, my father, and now my older sister. I don't think my mother's an alcoholic, but I do know that I hate her when she's drinking or has been drinking.

She thinks of me as her favorite little girl. She's even told my older sister that she likes me better, when she was drinking. She expects me to be perfect, and recently I received a D+ in Geometry.

I'm a good student, but I just don't understand it. My mother didn't blame me. She blamed by teacher for my D+, but it was my fault. She kicked my dad in his ribs and hit him in the arm. She hurt him, and she hurt me. She didn't hit me. She's never hit me when she was drinking, but she hurts me internally with words.

When we go over to friends' houses, both of my parents drink, and then they drive home, and I tell them about it, but they get upset. They don't realize what it does to them, and that's what hurts because I can't do anything about it.

Hopefully, I won't fall into their same situation.

Thank you,
Tiffany

Dear Mr. Nelson,

Thank you for coming to talk to our class about alcohol, and drinking and driving. I don't have a problem with alcohol, but someone in my family does.

My father has this problem. He gets drunk almost every day. He gets mad and starts screaming and yelling at us. Last Saturday he went to a friend's house with my mother and younger sister. He got drunk and on the way home he started yelling at my mother. He told her that he hates all of us, and that he doesn't care if we leave him because he doesn't need us.

This all hurts me because what all this ended up to is that he kicked us out of our house. I love my father very much. I just wish he would stop drinking, and he could be the same loving father he used to be before he started drinking like he does now. Write back.

Thank you,
Marisela

Dear Mr. Nelson,

I am not a drinker anymore. I already learned my lesson. I got drunk, and I got real sick the next day.

My dad drinks a lot! When he drinks he's totally different than when he's sober. When he's drunk he starts yelling at me for just anything. He gets mean and likes to argue when he's drunk. I don't like being around him when he's drunk.

One thing that scares me is that when he's drunk, he will still drive. He's gotten pulled over for drunk driving. He's even gotten in an accident. Thank God he wasn't hurt. But, maybe next time he will be hurt or maybe dead.

My dad won't admit to being an alcoholic, but he drinks three for four times a week. On almost every weekend his favorite words are, "I don't drink much, just with someone or by myself." He thinks it's a joke, but to me it's not.

Thank you for caring, but I just don't know what to do. I don't want to have to ride with him when he's drinking. I also want to join SADD.

Thank you,
Gina

Dear Mr. Nelson,

I've been suffering from the effects of alcohol for 15 years. My father has been an alcoholic for those 15 years, and I predict he will be one for the rest of his life. And, I promise you this, alcohol will be the death of my dad.

It's hard to tell you the way I feel inside. The anger that I feel is probably the easiest. My dad gets pissed off all the time. It's hard to deal with it. Alcohol was the death of my uncle. One would think that that would be some incentive to quit drinking. As it looks right now, nothing will stop him.

If this letter can help somebody think twice about drinking, then I've done my job as a friend to all. I appreciate your talking to this class and to the school.

Please, if you write back, don't mention anything I've said.

Sincerely,
Daniel

Mr. Nelson,

I don't have a drinking problem, but my dad does drink. I don't think he's an alcoholic, but it scares me. I think he needs to talk to somebody, but he probably won't listen.

Right now I'm mad at my dad. He is mad at me, too. My dad gets drunk almost every weekend. When he's drunk he gets into fights with my mother. My big brother tries to calm him down, but my dad hits him, so my brother beats him up . . . not really, but something like that.

I know that my dad doesn't like me at all. I can't tell you the reason right now, but I know my mother doesn't, either. I've really thought about drinking. I'm really scared about getting into the car with my dad. I need help fast!!

Olga

Dear Mr. Nelson,

I guess I don't really have a problem, but, see, my dad drinks, not a lot but just enough. When he drinks all he wants to do is fight. He doesn't listen, but when he does he takes it wrong, and gets it all backwards. I really get upset.

Lately, I think it's getting worse. See, he doesn't drink at home. He does it after work and then drives home. I'm just waiting for him to get into an accident and hurt himself or someone else, and I'm getting worried.

I really don't think it's a big problem, but I would like someone to talk to or write about it. You are the only one I have really opened up to. I really don't want you to tell anybody about it. But please write.

Thank you,
Tanya

Mr. Nelson,

My father has a drinking problem, and every time my mom and dad get into a fight (when he's drunk) it tears me apart. I don't want to take sides, and I don't want to feel alone.

I can't go to my dad for advice, as I don't want to get advice from a loser. My mom is thinking of divorce. I don't think that's the way out! I'm confused and feeling alone. Do you have any advice?

Thanks,
Michelle

Dearest Mr. Nelson,

I'm a child of an alcoholic. My dad is an alcoholic and will always be one. I've lived through so much depression caused by him. He'd beat my mother up so badly she'd end up in the hospital.

This was five years ago. They would fight like cats and dogs, bloody fights, clean fights, this was sad. All this happened since I was little, five years at least. I'm 16 now.

My mother has been married with him for 18 to 19 years now, and all those years she spent with him were painful for her. She still stays with him.

Not so long ago I tried killing myself. I overdosed and ended up in a psychiatric home for a while. It was all because of my dad. He's strict, mean, and he's always putting my mom and me down all the time.

When it was time for me to go out, my dad promised me, my doctor, my mom, sisters and brothers, that he'd stop drinking. It's now a year from the same day since he said that. He still sits at home, drinking constantly.

I love him so much, but what am I going to do with him?

Sincerely,
Melanie
"The girl with the messed-up life"

Dear Mr. Nelson,

I don't have a drinking problem at all. I've only been drunk about two or three times, and I realize it can do a lot of damage to you because my father is an alcoholic. He got taken away from us because he wanted me to kill him with a gun. I would always get hit and beat, and my mom would always say, "One day it will change."

About a year ago, it all changed. He came really close to dying, but he didn't. He said, "Melissa, this is all your fault. I could have been out of your hair if you would have done what I told you to do!"

So, I feel bad because he really doesn't care to see me, only my mom and brother and sister. He blames everything on me, but I realize that I did nothing wrong. It wasn't my fault. We still get in fights, and he still blames me for all of it.

In a way I think it is my fault, though. Is it my fault? Why does he do this to me? Why? I don't like for people to drink, but it's their body, and if that's what they want to do, then they can go right on and do it!

Teenagers don't like it when parents say, "Don't drink, it's bad for you," but when a friend says it, they may consider it.

Write me back and let me know what you think.

Thanks for caring,
Melissa

Dear Mr. Nelson,

I was adopted by my grandparents when I was three years old. My mother and father were alcoholics and druggies. I'm fourteen now. When I was little, before I was adopted, they would keep me in my crib all day and close the door. They wouldn't feed me or change me, or anything.

My grandparents would come and my parents would be sitting at the kitchen table drinking and doing drugs. Sometimes they would put beer in my bottle and make me drink it. They thought it was funny.

They don't live together anymore, and my father doesn't even want to know me. He hasn't written or anything on my birthday or Christmas for eleven years. My mother still talks to him. She told me he's still drinking and that he got in an accident last July. He almost lost his foot.

My mother still drinks, too. She wants to stop because she wants to see me. My grandparents won't let her take me anywhere without them being there. Please write back.

Silvia

Dear Mr. Nelson,

Hello. Well, you have just read to my class two of the letters that you brought with you. They really got to me! My entire family is just a bunch of heavy drinkers, and sometimes I start to wonder if this will ever happen to me.

I live with my mother, my grandmother, and my two-year-old baby sister. I will be able to get out of that hellhole in 2½ more years (I'm 15½ now), but my sister still has the rest of her life to go!

When I was about 12, I was into drinking. My mom gave me a little beer once in a while to calm me down, but that was only when she was really drunk.

Since then I drank off and on, but my family doesn't know this. My mother and I are always fighting, and if I say anything about her drinking, she just gets more pissed off at me! I would like to try the "Contract for Life" with my mom, but I'm afraid of what she would say.

Well, I guess I've said enough. Thanks for listening to my problems. My boyfriend also drinks and smokes weed once in a while. Please respond to this letter! I need help.

Yours truly,
Elizabeth

Mr. Nelson,

Hi! How are you? I'm doing okay. I'm more or less a typical teenager. I don't drink or anything else but my parents do. I'm so scared to be around them when they're drinking. They treat me like they don't care.

I've tried everything to keep them from drinking, but nothing has worked. I've poured out their bottles of booze, but they just go out and buy more. There are times when I feel like coming home drunk so they can see how they act. They don't realize how badly they hurt me.

I wish I could get them help, but they've got to get it themselves. It wouldn't bug me if it were only one or two drinks a day, but it's usually nine or ten.

What really scares me is that they come and pick me up from places, and I'm always scared I'm not going to make it home.

Could you please give me some advice for getting help?

Love,
Tammie

Dear Mr. Nelson,

My parents are divorced, and I live with my mom. I only get to see my dad every weekend. I haven't been over there for one month because he has a drinking problem.

He is constantly getting drunk and always trying to get me drunk while I'm there. He will put alcohol in my soda or will try and get me to drink. I can't tell anybody about it. I've tried to talk to him, but nothing does any good.

I don't know what to do, and it seems like you are a very understanding and helpful person.

Thanks a lot,
Mikell

Dear Mr. Nelson,

I'm a victim of alcohol. I have been for most of my life. It started when I was only about seven.

My dad was an alcoholic. He came home drunk every day. I remember times when he would come home really mad and start throwing things and start hurting us for no reason. There would be times when he would be passed out in the back yard, or anywhere.

Now I'm 15 years old and don't have a dad.

Thank you for your time,
Lorraine

Mr. Nelson,

My dad has a drinking problem. He's not an alcoholic or anything like that, but sometimes he drinks too much. He comes home and is violent with my mother and sometimes us kids. He yells and screams and sometimes even hits my mom for no reason. My mom gets mad and kicks him out, but when he gets sober, he apologizes, and my mom forgives him.

How can someone I used to look up to, do something like this to himself and other people. I just don't understand!!

Thank you for your time,
Adrienne

Dear Mr. Nelson,

My mom has been an alcoholic for a long time now. I try to help her out, but she won't listen to me. I guess she can help herself, but it seems like she doesn't want to.

I've always been against alcohol ever since I learned how bad it was. One day one of my mom's boyfriends came over drunk, and he brought more alcohol. When my mom was passed out on the bed, her boyfriend touched my breast and my vagina. I was so scared! CPS won't do anything. I also had a drunk dad who did the same thing, except he French-kissed me. My dad lives in Idaho, and I never want to see him again!

My mom also hits me a lot and leaves a lot of bruises. Until she gets sober, I want you to pray that I get to live in a Christian foster home.

Thanks,
Frances

Dear Mr. Nelson,

Hi! I'm very concerned about my mother. She has a very serious drinking problem. She drinks at least a pint of peppermint schnapps a day up to a lot more. I've told her how I feel, but she only gets mad, and often hits me. I've also asked her if there's anything I could do to help, but that just gets her mad, and she tells me to get out of her face. Another thing I mention to her is, what might happen to her one day? She only gets mad.

I love my mom very much, and I want to help her, and she doesn't think her drinking is a problem, but I'm concerned. She already got a DUI and crashed once. Luckily she only got a flat tire and the sides of the car smashed. My grades are dropping, and I'm not eating properly. Thanks for caring. Please help! Write back soon, before it's too late!

Sincerely,
Stephani

Mr. Nelson,

I just don't know what to do anymore. My mom is a drunk, and my dad and I try to help her, but she just won't listen. She's the greatest person in the world when she's sober, but when she's drunk I can't stand to be with her.

I love her so much, and I want to see her get better, but she just won't try. I wish she would try, and that she would also see what the alcohol is doing to her . . .

I ask that you give me some information on what do.

A worried son,
Joe

Dear Mr. Nelson,

My mom drinks. She doesn't think it's a big deal because she gets drunk off of beer and wine. It's not in the daytime, it's at night. I know she drives drunk. I worry about her. I told her she has a problem, and she agrees. Then she promises she won't anymore, but in the next couple of days, she's drinking again.

I've only been drunk two times, but I don't even like it, and I was at home both times. I have never driven drunk. I don't know what to do anymore about my mother. I need more suggestions or help.

Thanks for being there,
Jessica

Dear Mr. Nelson,

Thank you for coming. I was wondering if you could send me information on how to help my mom. She is a heavy alcoholic. I love my mom so much, and it hurts me to see her the way she is. It's also very hard on my brother and me.

Two Novembers ago, on her birthday, my mom wrecked her car driving drunk. She flipped the car seven times. They had to start her heart with machines. I was so mad at her for that. She scared me.

My dad left when we were young, and she's been with me all my life. Even though she's not a very good mother, I don't know what I'd do without her. My mom has threatened to commit suicide many times. That's very hard for me to accept.

The last time she threatened to kill herself was last night. I'm scared that I'll come home from school one of these days and find her dead. In the last year my mom has had two surgeries, and she was on heavy painkillers. Even then she drank. The first time I had to stay up all night just to make sure she would be

OK and then go to school the next day. The second time she made me remove stitches from her stomach with a razor blade. I was crying. I didn't want her to do it, but she made me.

I don't know what to do about her anymore. I've tried to help her, but I can't. My dad is also an alcoholic, but he lives in New York, so I don't see him. I hope that my mom will be OK, but I worry about her a lot. I really do love her.

We might be moving soon, so will you please write me at my friend's house. Her address is enclosed. Thank you.

Love always,
Diane

Dear Mr. Nelson,

My mother is a drunk, too, but I don't live with her and I probably never will. I love her very much. She is a hard-core drinker. I love her but not what she does. She's such an understanding person when she's all together, but when she's drunk, I don't know my mother at all.

I wish I could help her, but there's no way I can. She just can't quit drinking. I've tried a lot of different ways to help. When I found out she really didn't want to quit, then I knew there was no hope, but I just have to love my mother when she's sober. She has a lot of feelings, but she has a very serious problem with drinking. One thing I know is that I'll always love my real mother. I hope you know how I feel.

I don't drink and don't plan on it ever!!

Love,
Jenny

Dear Mr. Nelson,

My name is Sandra, and I'm a 15-year-old sophomore. I live in a foster home, and I feel that my mother's addiction led me to this home. Ever since I was very little, she drank and did drugs. I was offered drinks when I was a baby. It's in my baby pictures. All my life, I've been raised around drunks. My mother is an alcoholic, but she denies it.

Personally, I don't like the taste of beer, but a few times I have drank. I've never gotten drunk, though. Well, yes I did. I acted hella stupid and laughed the whole time! I felt like such an ass.

But, anyway, I wish I could help my mom because she moved to Texas. Her new husband was drunk, and they got into an accident. Her hips and ribs were all bruised. She wears her seatbelt over her shoulder now. She never told me until a while after because she didn't want me to worry. I'm so scared she's going to die.

Well, I want to listen to your speech on SADD now.

Love,
Your friend forever,
Sandra

Dear Mr. Nelson,

I feel really stupid writing you this letter, but I'm in a really weird situation. My step dad drinks very heavily. He gets drunk or buzzed almost every day. He even drives with a beer in his lap, even if I'm in the car, maybe if my friends were in the car.

He's been caught drinking and driving, but that doesn't make him learn. I don't know what will. My mom threatens him, but I don't really think he cares. He is really embarrassing. He goes to bed early, and at night my mom drinks. She says it's all right because her little ones are asleep. She gets drunk and also kind of violent.

I hate both of them when they do it. I'm the oldest, so I feel like I have to do something. Please help me. I don't know what to do.

Sincerely,
Nicole

Dear Mr. Nelson,

Hi. I've been around an alcoholic for a while; my mom is an alcoholic. I was worried for my mom. Every day when she would get home from work, she would grab a drink, usually wine. She would talk on the phone and drink her wine. She would usually make me get another bottle out of the refrigerator while she was on the phone.

I moved out here with my father. After I moved out, I felt extremely guilty. What if she slips and falls, and she has no help? What if she gets into an accident? She would have no help because I'm out here. I've decided to live with my dad for two years now.

Last Christmas, I asked her if my brother and I could come to her house. She said that we could. Two days before Christmas, I called her just to remind her about seeing us. She told me that she didn't want to see me. Anyway, her alcohol problem had gone to her head. I tried to help, but I can't do much anymore. I'm old enough to care for myself.

I used to have to take care of my mom, instead of her taking care of me. But, I guess she has to live on her own now. But, I'm worried for her, and scared. Sometimes I wonder if it was a big mistake to live with my dad.

My mom calls me every now and then, but she makes me depressed. When we talk on the phone, she says how she is, and how much she misses me. She gives a major guilt trip, and that makes me depressed.

Thanks,
Shae

Dear Mr. Nelson,

My name is Jenn, and I'm 15 years old. My mom and dad got a divorce when I was 4, almost 5 years old. My mom and dad both drink. I don't see my dad anymore 'cause he moved away. I live with my mom and step-dad. My mom is a chronic drinker. She drinks every night, and every night is worse. My mom screams and yells for no reason at all. She's never hit me, but she has hurt me inside. Things she calls me, it hurts so bad.

I will cry myself to sleep, and the next morning she pretends that nothing happened at all. I always tell my mom to quit drinking, but she won't listen, or she gets mad. I want to help my mom and so does my step-dad, but we don't know how. She won't listen.

So can you please write back and give me some advice?

Jennifer

When you are certain you've heard it all, along comes another letter detailing a brand new situation of parental abuse of alcohol, and with it, severe and ongoing abuse of their family members.

Teenage writers clearly express their hurt from physical beatings. Many of their stories lay out years of these continuing tragedies. They escaped only when the child was separated from the abusive parent(s) via a family break-up, the teenager running away, or intervention by other relatives or the courts.

The larger question is why so many children endured these beatings for so long, often for many years, without the information leaking out. If someone was aware of a dog being mistreated, the entire community would know and be up in arms. Why weren't these children entitled to the same publicity, and why weren't the abusers exposed? If you extrapolate the number of serious abuse cases outlined in this chapter alone, representing a limited number of classes at a few high schools, to a state or national level, the magnitude is obvious.

For many of the writers, the need to keep this abuse a family secret appears to have been compelling. Was it an unquestioning love for the parent, a fear of the consequences if outsiders were told, or was it simply embarrassment that prevented the teen from divulging what was going on in their homes? Many of these letters that told of continued physical abuse ended up in a counselor's hands after I went through the routine of advising the writer that this had been my route of action.

The number of letters recounting bodily abuse dropped off dramatically in my later years of speaking. Teenagers have always shared intimate secrets with close friends. Now, though, it seems much more acceptable to alert someone outside the family that these abuses exist. I had happened to be that interim outsider during the change.

Yes, some writers talk of having 'jumped from the frying pan into the fire.' Their foster home parent or a group home adult was an abuser. This is a problem that fortunately is getting wide attention.

Yet, tales of emotional abuse continue to be numerous. I still read letters with revelations such as these:

"She's never hit me when she's drinking, but she hurts me internally with words."

"It's hard to tell you the way I feel inside. The anger that I feel is probably the easiest."

"I know that my dad doesn't like me at all. I can't tell you the reason right now, but I know my mother doesn't either."

"I'm so scared to be around them when they're drinking. They treat me like they don't care."

My readers may question why a significant number of student writers cite numerous DUI's or crashes on the part of an alcoholic parent, then add that they themselves were continuing to drink and drive. It seems nonsensical. It is important to note that most of these statements came from earlier letters, in the 1980's, before our lawmakers, law enforcement people, and courts were fully responding to Candy Lightner and her MADD organization's pressure to remove such irresponsible drivers from the roads.

In recent years, if my program ends a few minutes early, I've sometimes asked my young audiences how they feel about impounding vehicles being driven by repeat offender drinking drivers, regardless of the car's owner, even if it is the driver's employer, a friend, or a relative. I note that this impounding of cars is already being tried in some communities. My question is preceded by the observation that research shows that the majority of 'social drinkers' today use a Designated Driver system, where someone stays fully sober to handle the driving, but that is not the case with so-called "problem drinkers." I remind the teenagers that these problem drinkers are mostly alcoholics and are almost impossible to keep from driving unless someone physically stops them.

To build a consciousness of the serious problem that still needs correcting, I point out that although alcohol-related vehicle deaths are substantially down from the 26,000 in 1980, the year MADD was started, or in 1981, SADD's beginning year, the 2001 number of such needless deaths still totaled 17,400, over five times the number of lives lost in the 9/11/01 terrorist tragedy.

Some teenagers are quick to remind me that an employer, a relative, or a friend isn't responsible for the drunk guy's actions, that it's his problem. They're probably thinking how difficult it would be for their mother if she lost her ability to drive her car to work because their father had drank too much again, driven it, got caught and the car impounded.

I have to acknowledge that impounding vehicles is a debatable approach for reducing the number of repeat DUI offenders, but then ask that my teenage audiences consider another thought:

"Here I'm asking you students to act as true friends, and to do what you need to do to prevent your friend from getting behind the wheel if you're aware that he's been drinking.

Wouldn't an employer, a relative, or a neighbor be also acting as a true friend if they refused to loan their car to a guy who kept on being picked up for driving drunk? Wouldn't the threat of having their car impounded make the owner more cautious? They might even insist on giving the guy a ride somewhere, or picking him up at a bar."

If this approach struck a chord with subsequent writers, it never showed up in their letters. Neither have comments about legal drinking ages. Those students wanting to express themselves continued to focus on the very personal sides of their lives.

CHAPTER SIXTEEN

"I live with my father, and when he gets drunk, he gets violent.
I've learned how to deal with it, the beatings and everything,
but it still hurts."

Dear Mr. Nelson,

The letter from the girl in Ukiah inspired me to write to you. Her situation is remarkably like mine, except I want attention from my mom. My dad works nights and sleeps days, so I don't see him much.

My mom says she loves me, but it's hard to believe her. She turns right around and says hurtful things a minute later. The last thing out of her mouth this morning was "Damn kids, I hate you."

I don't know what to do. I talk to my friends, who know how depressed I am, but they don't seem to care. My parents have seen and asked about scars and cuts on my wrists and hand, but they don't believe the problem is really bad

Thanks for listening. You don't have to write, but if you do, here's my mom's address.

Thanks,
Abby

Dear Mr. Nelson,

The other day in our class we had a discussion about drinking, and a friend of mine said her parents let her drink at home but nowhere else. And, if she was to have a party, her mother would call all of the kids' parents and let them know.

Our teacher said that if our parents did that then they were stupid, and that really made me angry because my mom is the same way. I don't drink unless I'm at home, and I'm not going to leave my house. I only drink about once a month anyway.

Do you think that means my mom is stupid because I would rather be safe than sorry?

Sincerely,
Kristy

Mr. Nelson,

I have really strong feelings about people drinking because my mom drinks. When she drinks, sometimes she's nice, but sometimes, she's really mean. By her drinking, she tried to kill herself.

I've asked her to stop, but she gets upset and tells me that she's a big girl and knows when to stop. She was a very good mother. I had to move in with my dad because she was already drinking when I lived with her. It hurts to see my mom doing that to herself. It made me get knives and put them to my wrist because I was scared that I wouldn't have my mom anymore. It was always a scary feeling and still is.

Thank you,
Dusty

Mr. Nelson,

All my life alcohol has been there. When I was little, my dad drank a lot. That was the reason my parents split up. He would take over weekends, and the only thing I remember is him drinking.

When I was about 11, I moved to my dad's. At the time, he didn't drink that much, but when he lost his job and times got tough, he started drinking heavily again, and we started fighting more. I love my dad, but when he drinks, I hate him.

I wish he could understand that he's not only hurting himself, he's hurting me, too.

Always and forever,
Malysa

Dear Mr. Nelson,

I have a very big problem. It's not me, it's my dad, and he's been drinking all my life. It dragged me to it, but then at the same time I was doing drugs. In September of '95 I got some help, and I quit it all. But when I quit, my 12-year-old sister started.

Yes, I do still get some feelings that I want more, but I sit back and look at my dad and sister, saying to myself, "You don't want to end up like that again."

I would really like to find a way to help them. My mom and I will sit up all night wondering what's going to happen when my dad comes home from the bars.

I sit in my bed with my little brother, crying because my mom and dad argue all night long, but I don't know of him hitting her. My sister just stays out all night. I wonder when she's coming home. Sometimes she doesn't come home for about two days. I really need some help for them. Help us, please. Please help me.

Thank you,
Joanne

Dear Mr. Nelson,

I thought I might write you because my dad is an alcoholic, and when he gets drunk, he gets abusive. He and my mom used to fight a lot, and my dad almost killed my mom by choking her and by slamming her back into the tub, sink, and refrigerator. He also grabbed my two sisters and me by the arms and hair, and has left bruises.

When my dad got drunk, he disowned my sisters and me because we tried to stop him from beating on my mom. He said that his kids would not do that to him, so we must not be his kids.

But that's all over now because my mom got a divorce from him. So, I know we don't have to worry about anything. I don't have to be afraid for my life and my family's life.

Thanks for everything,
Kimberly

Dear Mr. Nelson,

Hi, my name is Valerie, and I'm 15 years old. My mother happens to be the person I worry about. She has a drug and alcohol problem. She seems to lie about it all the time. She also seems to do it all the time.

I used to live with my mother until I was about 12 or 13 years old. I left my house when I figured out how serious her problem was. When my mother got drunk, she would get mad and hit me. It went through this kind of abuse for up to 12 years until I figured out there was something better.

I live with my aunt now, but I talk with my mom once in a while. My mom tells me that she no longer has a problem, but isn't denial the first sign of a problem?

I will never be like her.

Thank you for listening,
Valerie

Dear Mr. Nelson,

Hi, I'm writing because I thought you should know. My best friend's dad is someone who drinks a lot. Last summer he was so drunk he came home and got mad and threw the phone at her mom. So, he went to jail and still goes to jail on the weekends. The only time he doesn't drink is on Wednesdays and the weekends, weekends because he goes to jail and Wednesdays because he has to go and get a test done.

Well, my best friend, who is 16 years old, her little brother, who is 5 years old, and her mother still live with her dad. Things are okay as long as her dad doesn't drink. She stays at her boyfriend's until 8:00 P.M. almost every day to avoid her dad, and to be with her boyfriend.

Thanks for taking the time to read this and coming to our class. I don't drink, but my best friend has started to drink and asked me to.

Thank you,
Susan

Mr. Nelson,

I'm 15 and have been away from my parents since I was nine years old because of alcohol in my life. I won't be able to go back to them. My mom and dad are in jail for trying to run over a cop. My brother just got out of juvenile hall. He is eighteen. Now my cousins and my aunts are involved in alcohol, except me. I guess I'm the lucky one.

I just hope that my baby brothers and sisters don't turn out bad. My dad is writing from jail and he tells me, "Don't drink." My mom is so messed up from drugs that she doesn't make sense at all. I don't even want to write her back. My dad wants to divorce her and wants to know what I think. It makes me cry when I think about how my mom almost committed suicide right in front of me. I've got more to write.

Louie

Dear Mr. Nelson,

Hi! I've had a very bad experience with my mom. She is a really bad alcoholic. I've tried to tell her how I feel, but she just seems to think I'm trying to run her life.

We now don't talk. It's like I don't have a mom. I don't live with her anymore. I live with my dad. I just wish there was some way for me to get through to her. I really miss having a mom. She is so involved with her beer that she doesn't want to have anything to do with me.

Thanks for listening,
Julie

Dear Mr. Nelson,

My father drinks and does drugs really heavily. I don't live with him, but my older sister used to, and he almost raped her. When I found out, I was afraid to go and see my dad. I also have a little brother who doesn't know any of this. It scares me to know that he may try to hurt my little brother.

He never hit us, but when I was younger, he used to hit my step-mom. Now they are divorced. My younger brother is only five years old, and I love him so much and want to know if there's any way to help my dad. I've sat down with him, but it doesn't seem to help at all. I don't know what to do anymore.

I enjoyed having you here. I would like info on SADD.

Thanks a lot,
Diana

Dear Ken,

My family has a long history of drinking. My grandfather, my father, and my brother are all alcoholics. My mom thinks she is. My father has tried to go into recovery, but he started up again after five months of being sober.

I love my father but . . . sometimes I wish he were dead. It's because he drinks so much. He doesn't drink just a beer or two, he drinks all day long. He drinks beer, and then goes to brandy.

My counselor says that I have to take care of myself, and if I have to stay away from home, I have to stay away. The real reason I am writing to you is because I know there are a lot of people (kids) going through the same thing.

I think I may become an alcoholic, and I don't want to end up like my father, but I do enjoy the taste of alcohol.

Thank you for talking to our class.

Roxanne

Dear Mr. Nelson,

Within the last year my mother was diagnosed with cancer and I became pregnant at 14. This caused my father to drink more than usual.

Because I was pregnant and putting my baby up for adoption, I was living at a maternity home. While I was there I got a letter from my mother saying that my father had admitted he was an alcoholic.

My father and I aren't very close, but I love him a lot. Sometimes he's really hard to talk to. Would you please send me some information to help me along, and some advice to help me give it to him? Thank you for being here.

Thanks,
Jessica

Dear Mr. Nelson,

I am a happy 15-year-old girl. I have a wonderful family, and we are very close. For you and anyone who might be reading this letter, let me tell you what it's like to have an alcoholic father.

He comes home drunk and tells you he just got in a fight. He's 45 years old. He's all scraped up and injured. He comes home drunk and tells you he is going to kill your boyfriend because you had a little disagreement.

He comes home drunk and tells your mother he's going to get a separation because he can't handle it anymore. He doesn't come home, or get in touch for a week. He doesn't come home drunk. He's in jail.

When an alcoholic drinks, he's not only hurting himself, he's hurting anyone who loves him, or anyone who might accidentally come in his path.

> *Love,*
> *Heather*

Dear Mr. Nelson,

I don't really know how to start this letter. I have so many things that are relevant to the drinking topic. I guess first I'd like to say that lately I've seen and heard a lot of speeches, commercials, and TV shows on drinking, so I've been thinking a lot about alcohol abuse. I know some of the things I say will be hypocritical.

Ever since I can remember, my mother has been an alcoholic. She often would go out to bars and parties and leave my four-year-old younger brother with my sister and me. My sister is only a year older.

When my mom came home, she would be very drunk and would puke her guts out and pass out. She never was a very responsible mom, but I loved her.

Well, anyway, my mother left me, my brother, and my sister to live with my grandmother. She always told us she would always love us and be with us, but she's gone.

Now that I'm in high school, I often to go parties and drink, sometimes a little and sometimes a lot. I'm worried that I may become an alcoholic, too. I don't want to hurt my family like my mother hurt me. I hope people see from this letter how alcohol hurt me and tore apart my family.

I have forgiven my mother and speak to her. She's still an alcoholic and even offers alcohol to me. Sometimes we party together. I feel like I have to make her love me again. Alcohol is all we have in common.

I would like for you to write me back.

> *Emotionally affected by alcohol abuse,*
> *Holly*

Dear Mr. Nelson,

I really appreciate your coming to our school and talking to us about drinking and driving. Almost every weekend, a bunch of my friends and I usually go out and drink. I really don't like it, but it's really hard not to do.

My mom drinks a lot. When I get mad at her, I tell her bad things, and one of those things is I tell her all she is, is a drunk and an alcoholic, and I don't like her for it.

After I do that, I feel rally bad. I know that it's not my fault, but sometime I feel that it is. My mother doesn't know that I drink unless I tell her. I love my mom a whole lot. I don't ever want anything to happen to her. I'm really afraid that she will never come home one day. I tell her I think she should get help, because she is an alcoholic, but she denies it. I am really scared.

She doesn't really drink hard alcohol, it's just beer. I hope that she will get help, and I don't turn out like her. I do drink, but I don't really get that drunk when my friends and I go out.

Well, anyway, I really would like more information on SADD. Once again, I thank you for coming and talking to us.

Nicole

Dear Mr. Nelson,

Hi! I was wondering how I can help my dad to get him to stop drinking, because when I was little, whenever we got money he would spend all of it on beer, and he would beat my mom when he came home from the bar.

One time he hit us when my brother and I were sticking up for my mom. Now he doesn't want anything to do with my brother and me because we want him to stop drinking so we can have a dad when we need one, but not a dead one from drinking and driving. Thank you,

Forever friend,
Jared

Mr. Nelson,

Hi, how are you doing? I really enjoyed your talk. It did me a lot of good. I don't drink, neither does any member of my family, except my dad. He doesn't get violent, thank goodness, but he's so dependent on it my mom had to give him a choice, either beer or us. He plainly said, "I'm not gonna quit drinking."

My mom was ready to leave, but for some reason she didn't. I really don't know why, she hates his drinking, and so do I. I tell him how bad it is. He knows it's bad, too, he just won't quit. Don't get me wrong, my dad's a great guy.

I love him so much. If there's anything you could possibly tell me to tell my dad to hopefully get him to stop, I'd be very grateful.

I'd love to share information about SADD for you, and join.

Thanks for caring,
Lara

Dear Ken,

Not to be rude, but when you said our parents care a lot about us, I do not believe that. I know my father loves me, but my mother left us when I was one. My father at the time was in the Air Force. When he was at the base, my mother left my brother and me in the house alone to go drink. Then two weeks after that, she gave me up to a person I did not know. Now I live in a group home. I'm trying to get back to my grandparents.

I'm against drinking in general. I'm not trying to say that parents don't care, I'm just saying that sometimes they just choose not to. Please write back.

Thanks you,
Justin

Dear Mr. Nelson,

My dad is a drunk, and he uses drugs. He doesn't live with us anymore. He would go out and get drunk and come home and beat up my mom, and he would beat me up, too.

When my mom kicked him out, I felt so much safer that I finally told my mom that when he sometimes came home drunk, he did things a dad wasn't supposed to do. He raped me, and he was supposed to be my dad. The reason I didn't tell my mom was because he told me he would hurt my mom and my two sisters if I told.

So, I didn't tell, but when he left, well, got kicked out, I told my mom everything. She was mad. At first I thought she was mad at me. Then she told me she wasn't mad at me, but at my dad. Please write back.

Thanks for listening,
Sarah

Mr. Nelson,

My mom's boyfriend has a drinking problem, and he is having a hard time stopping. He stopped for a few months a while ago. Then he got transferred to a different town, and he met some new people and now he has started drinking again. My mother talked to him about it, but all he said was, "If they're buying, then I'll drink it."

Every Friday he goes out with his boss, and they both smoke weed real bad. So, almost every Friday he and my mom get into a pretty big fight. They scare me because he grabs her, pushes her, and hits her. My mom always fights back, but he is very big, and she says he could grab her lower arm and crush it. He doesn't want to hurt her, but he doesn't know his own strength. He really gets drunk.

Twice my mom tried to hurt him back. Like one time she grabbed a knife and almost stabbed him, and I was in the same room. Last Friday she tried to strangle him, but my brother stopped her. I don't know if I could help, and if I could, how?

Thanks,
Robin

Mr. Nelson,

I have a lot of drinking situations in my life, but fortunately for me, I have a clear head and a perfect vision of the future.

The first incident was when I was 10½ years old. My mother had a lot of stress in her life and a high blood pressure, so she had to take sleeping pills to go to sleep. My father died three months before I was born, and my mother was lonely, so she went from boyfriend to boyfriend. This particular boyfriend had been drinking and taking drugs.

One night, as I half slept, he came in and molested me, not rape, but molest. I told my mother, but she denied it, and I was spanked by her boyfriend.

Ever since then I've hated her. Two years ago when I was fourteen, I watched my mother slowly slip away into drinking. We began to fight, and I ran away from home to my Godparents' home.

My mother finally realized that the family she had was slipping away. I told her again about being molested. We cried and cried together. She kicked him out.

Now we have a new home, and my mother is engaged. A few months ago, I noticed my almost stepfather sneak away to a bar down the street a few times. What do I do? I don't want anything else to ruin my family.

Sincerely,
Smiley

Dear Mr. Nelson,

My mom is an alcoholic. When she's drunk she hits my little brother and she yells at me. Sometimes she punches my little brother in the face. When my mom is drinking, she denies she even has kids. My little brother is three years old.

She drank the entire time she was pregnant with my sister and me. We are twins. Dawne hates my mom. Dawne says mom doesn't love us.

I believe she does but she has a funny way of showing it.

Thank you for listening,
DeAna

Dear Mr. Nelson,

My father, mother, and my brothers are all alcoholics. I live with my father, and when he gets drunk, he gets violent. I've learned how to deal with it, the beatings and everything, but it still hurts.

I get drunk often. I stay somewhat conscious, but I know it's not good for me. My father is also a drug addict, which is hard to deal with. I would like to see something done about drinking and drugs, but I don't know if there's anything that can be done for my father. He's already over the edge.

I wish I could help, but I know I can't. I miss my old father; he used to be really cool. We used to go places and travel, but we don't anymore'cause all out money went up his nose. My friends drink and drive, but I try to not get involved in that.

I would like to have a response from you, and I would like to keep in touch. I hope something can be done.

Sincerely,
Jennifer

Dear Mr. Nelson,

My friend's mom has a drinking problem. She gets drunk quite a bit, and my friend cries a lot. Her mom even hits her sometimes. She drinks when I'm there, too, but she's never done anything to me.

The sad thing is that her mom always offers us alcohol to drink. It's like she doesn't want to be alone and the only one who is drinking. One of my friend's other friends tried to talk to her about her problem, and the mom just got mad.

The mom is a really great person when she's not drunk. My friend is scared to talk to her about it. She's scared of her mom because I know I am.

My parents don't know about what my friend's mom does, though. Whenever the mom offers us alcohol, we tell her, "No."

Help!

Love,
Kelli

Dear Mr. Nelson,

I play Pop Warner football. Usually after away games, my family and other families go to dinner. Some of the parents get drunk. I know it's not funny, but sometimes the kids can't help laughing at them. Sometimes it's just embarrassing.

My mom and I have talked about it and realized that it can be really unhealthy. What should we do to help them? Please write back.

Sincerely,
Spencer

Dear Mr. Nelson,

Hi. I just want to say that my dad has been drinking, and he wants me to try it, so I sometimes take a little swig, but I don't drink that much. I don't know what to do. He never drinks and drives or hits me. All he does is yell at me.

I'm just letting you know why I might become an alcoholic. My family, all the men, have a drinking problem, and I need help with this because I don't want to become an alcoholic. I once got drunk before, but I was only in my room, so it didn't hurt anybody else.

Thanks for letting me write to you. I think I want to join SADD.

Thanks,
Jesse

Dear Mr. Nelson,

I'm 14 years old. Alcohol abuse is a very sensitive subject for me. My biological father was an alcoholic. My mother divorced him when I was five.

I remember him not coming home until early the following morning; sometimes he didn't come home until mid-afternoon. The reason my mom divorced him was because he was a drunk, and he had done some stupid things while he was drunk.

Since my mom divorced him when I was five, I have only seen him twice, but not within the last six and a half years. I miss him, and I love him. I'm thankful that my mother realized staying around him could affect my little sister and me.

Thank you,
Sasha

Dear Mr. Nelson,

I'm 14. I had a very bad childhood. My parents divorced when I was five. The court ordered me to live with my mom and my brother to live with my dad.

After six months living with my mom, she gave me to my grandma (Dad's mom). The court gave temporary guardianship to my grandma for six months (so my mom could get back on her feet), but then my grandma requested full guardianship. The court granted it. I ended up living with my grandma five years, but my dad finally got full guardianship of me 2 years ago, and I live with my dad and brother, and now I'm very happy.

All of this happened to me because of my mom's problems with drugs. I haven't seen her for two years now, and that was only for four hours. Before that it was two more years.

My mother has a problem, and it makes me sad. When people ask, "Where's your mom?" I just shrug.

I tasted beer. It is the nastiest stuff I ever tasted. It looks like pee! I don't know how people drink that stuff. Thanks.

Love,
Danae

Dear Mr. Nelson,

Just to get straight to the point, my mother is a heavy drinker, as well as her whole side of the family. When I was eleven, I made a bet with my family that I would never even try alcohol or drugs, because of what I see it do to my mother.

To inform you, when my mother gets drunk, which is regularly, she becomes angry and violent and will usually come after me and pick on me verbally and physically. Sometimes it just makes me so mad. I really don't understand why I have to respect someone who is supposed to be an adult, but actually acts like a child.

At one time it became so bad I just left and stayed with a friend. When I went home I explained to my father why I had done this. When my mother found out I was home, she attacked me and told me if I didn't like living at home, I should leave, and go with what I was born with, nothing. My dad stepped in and made her stop, but this goes on way too much and sometimes I get to the point where I don't understand why I'm living.

Then I think of all my friends, basketball team, and my dad, and I remember how much I actually love them all.

The really sick part is that even though with all the pain my mom puts me through, I still love her so very much. I try to get her to stop, but she doesn't feel she has a problem, so what can I do? I don't want anything to happen to her or to my little brother.

Thank you for caring. If you have any tips on how I can help myself and my brother, please write back.

Yours truly,
Kristin

Dear Mr. Nelson,

Hello! My name is Kalani. I don't have any problem with alcohol or drugs, but my step-dad does. I tend to worry about him because when he does drugs or drinks, then when people don't do what he wants, he gets mad, starts beating on people, and throws stuff around the house. I don't understand or like it when he does this.

Now, because he does drugs and/or drinks, he's in jail for having illegal drugs on him. I don't know what to do. I just want to completely give up. Thanks for caring about us.

Sincerely,
Kalani

You've observed lots of fodder for a counselor's attention among the prior two chapters of letters, as I did when I initially read them. I would have liked to have known what steps were taken by the counselors because having such information would have helped me to make more sure-footed suggestions when future responses were made to similarly troubled teenagers. However, I never asked to be informed, and only two ever called or wrote.

When I pulled open the door to the counselor's office with a letter or letters involving abuse in my hand, I always worried that the child might be yanked from their already dysfunctional home, and maybe assigned to an equally bad environment with foster parents or a group home.

You can understand my concern, too, that the offending parent might well have been sober when contacted by the police or social workers. How many times have student writers commented that their parent was a totally different person, in many ways a nice person, when they weren't drinking? Supposing the questioner was assured that everything was fine, or they could be confident that it would be so, and left the teenager in custody of the parent.

Imagine the extreme danger the teen writer would be in when this parent again went on a drinking binge and took their ire out on their child. This scenario very likely has caused many young people to endure long term atrocities.

You might ask, as I ask myself, how can these young students possibly be functioning today after the two years, five years, or even ten years of extreme emotional stress from being the targets of alcohol or other drug-abusing parents?

As mentioned earlier, once I memorized the current speech I was delivering, my concentration could be on the expressions shown on these young faces. Occasionally, a tear would be wiped away, but otherwise I saw little hint of the pain and fear that each of this group of letter writers were experiencing through most of their waking hours. Yes, there was an intensity in their expressions, but always they returned my smile when they handed me their letters on the way out.

A few included a sentence stating that they had learned how to handle a problem-drinking or drug-abusing parent. Is that just wishful thinking? They try to put on a front of strength, but they are still hurting teenagers whose pleas come across so clearly: *"I wish I could have a real mom again."*

I'm relieved to find that many schools now have peer counseling groups. Our young people in trouble with parents who aren't acting like parents should, do need an outlet where they feel reasonably comfortable when revealing confidences.

CHAPTER SEVENTEEN

"I feel like I should quit, but I don't want to look like a dork in front of all my friends. And lately, I haven't really felt like living."

Dear Mr. Nelson,

I've been drinking since the age of twelve. I'm now fifteen. Drinking has been in my family long before I was born. I was born on drugs and alcohol, weighing 3 lbs, 2 oz. When I was younger, my dad, uncles, and grandpa would always give me sips of their beer or whatever. Nobody ever thought anything of it except for the fact it was funny to watch me stumble around. But now look at me, I'm ruined.

Every time I have a problem, I turn to drinking or smoking weed. You would think I would learn from others' mistakes, having been taken from my parents from them constantly drinking and on drugs.

I don't know how to help myself, though I wish I could. I've tried to stop, but all it does is cause me to become moody and hurt people mentally who are around me. They are completely innocent. I hope you can help me understand what I'm going through, and why.

Your friend,
Angie

P.S. By doing what you're doing, you have become one of my idols. I appreciate you much.

Dear Mr. Nelson,

I don't think I have a drinking problem, but if it keeps going on, it could get bad. I don't want that to happen. I'm only 16 years of age, and the problem isn't drinking, but I do a lot of drugs, not a lot, but almost every day. When I do drugs, that is when I drink.

There are a lot of people in my family who do have a problem with drinking, and I don't want to turn out like them. I've seen what they've done, what they have, and what they do in their lives. They have done nothing, they have nothing, only their drinks in their hands, and I don't want to be like them.

I know what's right, and I know what's wrong. I also know when to stop and when to go on with what I'm doing. I smoke a lot of weed every day, but when I drink, it's mostly on the weekends. When I drink, I drink hard stuff. I'm not happy about any of that, and I wish that I never would drink at all. I don't know if I'm asking for help because I think I could stop on my own. I would love to keep writing to you. I know that there are a lot of people like me, and I would like to try and help, so if you can write back to me, I would love to have your feedback. Thank you for coming.

Adam

Mr. Nelson,

I am 15 years old. I just made 15 in July. I'm not writing to you for sympathy or anything else, I just wanted to share my alcohol and drug experience with you.

When I was 12 I was kicked out of school for fighting, and I was sent to a special school for problem kids. Everyone there was either drunk or high when they got to school. Before going to that school, I had smoked weed, but not as much or as heavily.

I started going to school high every day and not caring about where my life was going. My aunt would let me smoke and drink as well as anything else I wanted to do. I soon got worse than that. My sister used to go out driving and getting in the car with drunk friends, and all kinds of things they shouldn't have been doing. My oldest sister almost dropped out of school because she smoked so much. At the time, I was only 12 or 13 years old.

I recently stopped smoking and drinking because my father was a smoker, and he ended up being a crack head, but what really made me stop doing it was seeing what it was doing to my sister, and how my sister hurt my mother by doing it.

Almost everyone on my father's side of the family is either drunk or a crack head, and they all started as young as I did, and began with weed and beer. They ended up with crack and strong alcohol.

I now play a starting position on the basketball team and haven't had a drink or smoke in two years.

Sincerely,
A young girl,
Talecia

Dear Mr. Nelson,

I understand fully what you are saying. However, being in the position of being drunk, or around people who are drunk, it is not as easy as it sounds.

Many speakers who I've heard all seem to say the same things, "Don't get in the car of a drunk driver," "Don't let your friends drive drunk," and "Always say No." I've been out many times, and I cannot recall any time when someone says those words to another.

The only time when those words are said is when mocked. Teenagers tend to love and use those words as a joke. Even when those words are said seriously by a person, that person gets to be made fun of. No one looks at that person as "smart," but instead they think to themselves, "We come out to have fun, not to have a lecture from you."

What are we, as teenagers, supposed to do? Teenagers hang out as a group. It's not guaranteed that everyone will know everyone in the group, at least not well enough. If the driver all of a sudden takes out a beer, what can we do? Get out of the car? Silly. That may be what we learn in school, but not something we would do.

Love,
Phoeng

Dear Mr. Nelson,

Fortunately for myself, I've never had any problems with drinking, but I have and do drink. The difference with me is that I've always been allowed to. My parents always told me they would rather me drink with them, and know what I was doing, than me going out and partying. What they saw a lot when they were my age was kids going wild and rebelling, drinking too much.

The reason I'm writing is because I know other kids will be reading this as you travel around. For those who do drink (you're not supposed to, but I understand), please do so responsibly and especially don't drink if you know you have to drive. And for those who don't drink, that's good. And for those who are thinking about whether or not to drink (maybe you've been pressured lately), whatever you do, DON'T GET DRUNK.

I got drunk once and I HATED it. I can never see why people want to do that. I couldn't think, my head was spinning, everything made me cry, and it was terrible! And don't drink just because your parents tell you not to. They really are looking out for your best interests. Your friends, if they're pressuring you to drink, obviously don't care as much as your parents.

OK? Okay! Well, Mr. Nelson, thanks for giving me an opportunity to kinda put my opinion and advice out there.

Always,
Bernadette

Dear Mr. Nelson,

My name is Brooke, and I'm a sophomore in high school. Lately, I've been getting into 'going to parties,' and kind of wanting to experiment with alcohol. I know that's not good at all, and the more and more I hear about it, the scarier it seems! I know alcohol is not something to get into, but I'm overwhelmed with curiosity.

One reason I feel like I want to drink is that I feel very excluded from everything these days. I just broke up with a boy who was my first 'true love.' We're still friends, but I have to watch him date all these other girls and show him I don't care. It's s-o-o-o hard!

I know drinking is not the answer, and I don't want it to become my scapegoat. After all, it's my dad's scapegoat.

Well, if you can help me any, write me. Thanks for letting me talk.

Brooke

Dear Mr. Nelson,

I really appreciate you coming to our school and taking the time to speak to us. As for myself, I, too, drink, smoke, and do a variety of drugs. I don't like it, but it's all I can think of what to do when things go wrong.

I'm 15 years old and hoping to see my 16 in August. I have had, and still do have, suicidal thoughts. Most everything I do in my life is bad, wrong, or stupid. I, too, have driven when I was drunk, even though I don't have my license yet. I'm not a good student, but I am smart. I cannot get my life straight to do good in life.

Another reason for my depression is, well . . . I'm bisexual. I have to deal with all those rude comments every day at school, home, and in public (even though people don't know I'm bisexual). Just to make it go away, I think that drinking, drugs, or suicide is the answer for all those problems I'm having. Even though I know that those are not the answers, they seem like an easy way out of this horrible world.

Thank you so much for your time of listening, and talking to us, especially me. Please do not let my parents or family know about this letter. Thank you.

Love always,
Scott

Dear Mr. Nelson,

Thank you so much for coming. I have an ex-boyfriend who has a pretty bad past life. He almost lost both his sister and brother in drinking overdoses. His older sister is now 17, and she's an alcoholic. She's so mean when she drinks. She yells and cusses. She even beats my ex-boyfriend. I don't know what to do, and I care about him so much. He's always unhappy because of it, and I'm afraid he might take the same path. He's totally against drinking, but we broke up just recently, and he got drunk Friday. I don't want to lose him. I need help. Thanks for caring.

Love always,
Melanie

Mr. Nelson,

Hi, my name is Nina, and I have a father who does drink a lot, and when he does, he fights with all of us. Like my dad, my brother who is 17, gets drunk often and fights with us, also.

I really want to help because I feel like it is my fault for their drinking, because every time my older brother hits me and I tell my dad, my mom yells at me and says I just want to get him into trouble. Please help! Thank you for coming to our school.

Sincerely,
Nina

Dear Mr. Nelson,

I don't normally drink to get drunk. I do drink some of the time, but I don't know why it all started to happen. My dad drinks, and he gets drunk. My mom gets mad, but for some reason I stick up for him all the time.

I've started to drink when I go out with friends. They expect it from me. I even drink when I'm alone. My parents don't know, and if they ever did, I don't know what I'd do.

I'm very much into horses, and I barrel race. Most of the people I hang out with are cowboys. They drink all the time, and I'm usually always around them on weekends. I don't know why I drink, but I can't help it. I have to. Thanks.

Sincerely,
Justine

Mr. Nelson,

My boyfriend drinks quite a bit. Yes, I drink ever so often. Even so, I will not give up my life to be "cool."

My boyfriend says he will never drive himself or with anyone who is drunk. I trust him very much, but I feel that this is a lie. His older brother is an alcoholic. One night they will get drunk and have to get home. My boyfriend's brother will drive. He will not say "No" to his brother.

Sure, he's been lucky so far. I feel that his luck, driving drunk, is running out, and I'm terrified that my boyfriend will be with him when it does.

It's not our fault if we drink, but it is our fault if we drive. I would very much like to be associated with SADD. Thank you for your time and caring about us. Please write back and so will I.

Yours truly,
Cristen

Dear Mr. Nelson,

It's really a nice thing that you're doing for all those kids, and I'm one of those kids who drinks. I just started this year. It's probably from so much depression. My closest friend just passed away and my brother did, too. My brother died in a wreck from a drunk driver.

I know that's a really stupid thing for me to do, but now that I've started with my older friends, I feel like I can't quit, and my mom or dad doesn't know.

I feel like I should quit, but I don't want to look like a dork in front of all my friends. And lately, I haven't really felt like living. Thanks for caring.

Love,
Patricia

Dear Mr. Nelson,

I wasn't going to write to you, but after listening to that letter from Melanie, I decided to. My mom, dad, aunts, uncles, just my whole family drinks. It really hurts me when they drink, especially my mom. Whenever she drinks, it's like she doesn't care about anything I feel. She always thinks that she is the queen and everything should go her way.

After drinking, it always seems to me that everyone fights or disagrees. I'm so worried about my mom and family. They do drink and drive, but they always think that they are able to, and that they aren't that drunk. Every time they drink I get so scared that one of these days we are going to get into an accident and die.

My worst fear in life is to become an alcoholic and end up like my parents and the rest of my family. How do you think that would make you feel? I don't want my kids to end up feeling like I feel about my parents, if I become an alcoholic.

What can I do? Please give me some advice on what to do and how to handle these problems I have.

Thank you for your time,
Veronica

Dear Mr. Nelson,

My family is one big drinking problem. The only two who don't drink are my mom and my sister. Yes, I have a problem, but my life is over. Sometimes I can go a couple of days without a drink, but that is it.

I'm an alcoholic, and I'm saying it. Being that I've said that, I feel I can start to recover. Do you think I'm in the right direction? I hate drinking and someday I want to quit! Do you think I can quit?

Jason

Dear Mr. Nelson,

I'm a drinker, not an alcoholic. Every weekend I will go to my cabin and drink some 90 proof. I mix it with Kool-Aid or my soda pop so my parents will not smell it so badly.

Ever since I've been in football I have been sober, almost. I have to drink before class so I can get my work finished and not fall asleep in class. I've not been caught at it in school yet, but that is luck. I do not go to parties and get drunk on purpose

James

Dear Mr. Nelson,

Howdy! Right now we're watching your film. I'm the little cowgirl in the third seat, third row. I've been drinking for about 3-4 years (I'm almost 16). I've never driven drunk.

I'm not an alcoholic, but I depend on alcohol sometimes because it helps me relax. Just recently, I have also started taking pills, nothing illegal. Sometimes it would be 4-5 aspirin to give me energy, 7 allergy pills to make my ex-boyfriend mad another time, and sometimes I take stuff to help me sleep, because I get insomnia and nightmares sometimes.

I've backed off the pills quite a bit, and today I'm going to stop drinking and taking pills altogether. I'm really glad you came to talk to our class. I will never drink illegally or take pills for bad reasons again.

Thanks for listening. Please write back.

Sincerely,
Melinda

Dear Mr. Nelson,

I have somewhat of a problem. I drink, smoke, and smoke pot. It's nice that you can come to talk to us. I know it's bad to do these things, but I can't help it. I even smoke at school. Today I took a dip before school. Please help and don't tell anyone.

Thanks,
Dave

Dear Mr. Nelson,

I know drinking is wrong, but I can't control myself. I've never told anyone. It's hard to hide to your friends that you drink, but I have. My friends are good friends, but they're naïve.

I don't use alcohol in an abusive sense. I do it because I'm depressed. My parents are pressuring me to be the best. I am a 4.0 student, but I can't seem to make my parents happy. I hope that someday I will be up to my parents' standards, but if I don't, my life has no meaning. I'm scared because I can't control my feelings and problems.

Thanks for listening,
Trishelle

Mr. Nelson,

I am an alcoholic. I'll be 15½ on Saturday. I'm not a social drinker. I didn't start to drink to be popular or "cool." I drink as an escape from life. I drink quite a bit. One time two of my friends and I drank almost a half-gallon of vodka. I passed out. One friend puked for hours and the other got her stomach pumped. This didn't faze me.

I do drink with my friends, but if they aren't available to drink, I'll drink by myself. I drink every Friday and Saturday night. I would drink every night, but it's not in my budget. I'm not a loser. I get very good grades (3.92 is my cumulative GPA). My friends respect me, and I can say "No" to drugs I don't want.

I quit smoking cigarettes, but I can't imagine life without alcohol. Right now my life is in balance. I'm sure a lot of alcoholics have said that before.

I would really appreciate it if SADD would send me some stuff. I don't want to ruin my life. I want some help. Car accidents, death, etc., associated with alcohol don't scare me. I'm not afraid of death.

Thank you for coming today,
Michele

Dear Mr. Nelson,

I've been drinking since I was in 8th grade. My mom doesn't know, and I intend to keep it from her 'cause I would get in so much trouble. Once in a while she'll give me my own drink, but they're really small. When my parents aren't home I go to the liquor cabinet, and I drink vodka, and sometimes too much. I came to school one time drunk, for a bet, and at the end of the day I passed out.

My great grandmother was a heavy drinker. She drank a whole bottle of whiskey. I'm afraid if I keep it up, I'll be like that. It's hard to quit, but maybe I can. My friends tell me not to drink, but they smoke so I never listen to them.

If you could, or if you ever come back, maybe you can help me. Thank you for taking the time to hear me.

Chantele

Dear Mr. Nelson,

When I wrote you last semester, I was in a freshman health class. You helped me a lot on those days when I was sad and read you letter over. You also changed my life. You gave me a lot of self confidence in myself. I just wanted to say thanks to you.

I changed and grew up a lot. Sometimes I cry because my family is troubled. They always drink, then drive. I would love to drive them around, but I'm just too young. I'm almost 16 years old and act like a 19 or 20 year old. You changed me and made me grow up. Thank you sooooo much.

I am a member of SADD.

Love always,
Kelli Annie

Dear Ken,

Hi. My name is Orlando. My mom is a really bad drinker. She doesn't know when to stop. I've tried to get her to stop. She doesn't listen to me and my little brother. She likes her alcohol more than her children. She's been in and out of rehabilitation centers.

My brother and I were taken away from her when we were little. I was 4½; my brother was 3. We have never been steadily with her since. She still drinks to this day.

I drink almost every weekend. I can stop if I wanted to. I just want to fit in with my friends. Sometimes I don't drink, but I do the rest of the time.

Peace out,
Orlando

Dear Mr. Nelson,

I'm a 15 year old girl who has a number of problems. I have a step-dad who was an alcoholic. He drank all of the time. He beat my mother and me up. They got a divorce now, but he still scares me.

During the last two years, I've had problems with drinking. When I'm with my friends I drink sometimes. I'm not an alcoholic or anything. I have been in two drunk driving wrecks. I have a friend who is now paralyzed. Just recently I was in a car crash with my ex-boyfriend. He had been drinking and so had I. I never told my parents. The police never came either because it was out in the country.

I didn't want to get in the car, but he made me. I had been drinking so I was a little buzzed. I don't want to go through the rest of my life living like that. One of these days I could be killed by a drunk driver and with my luck I would end up being in the car. My life is really difficult for me right now. I just moved in with my dad, and I have a lot of problems. They are building up inside. I'm trying so hard not to drink. I feel it doesn't do anything good for me.

Well, I really appreciate your coming to our class. I learned a lot from your talk. I would like to get some information from you about being a SADD member.

Thanks,
Michelle

Mr. Nelson,

After reading some of the letters I guess I won't feel so embarrassed to ask for your help.

A lot of my friends drink and, of course, so do I. Yet, we just don't drink, we do drugs. I've had a few friends either die when intoxicated or killed by other drunks. It never stopped me or any of us, actually. I guess none of us ever thought of the consequences of drinking. We don't just get drunk on weekends or at parties, some of us just sit around the house, either alone or with someone else, and drink.

I started drinking when I was 12. My oldest sister who is 14½ years older than I, and my brother who is now 28, would sit around the house and drink either beer or hard liquor. I would join them and later I acquired a taste for it. Often (very often) I will go over to a friend's house where there is alcohol (My mom doesn't allow alcohol in the house anymore). I will get totally blitzed out of my mind. Sometimes I will drink so much I will puke for two days.

What I'm actually trying to say is, my friends and I need help!

Thanks,
Andrea

Teenagers are very observant when viewing the consequences of family members' long struggle with alcohol abuse. How could any of us miss seeing the obvious, even if we weren't victims. Children hate what's going on in their lives. They are absolutely positive that they don't want to turn out the same way as those people in their lives with these problems. One girl writer summed up her feelings. *"I've seen what they've done, what they have, and what they do in their lives. They have done nothing, they have nothing, only the drinks in their hands, and I don't want to be like them."*

Letters come not only from the poor-achieving students. Some wrote of strong GPA's and active participation in sports and other school activities. They're smart enough to see evidence of the ultimate downfall from the regular use of alcohol or other drugs. They express worry about their use of these illegal substances, but then their letters show a reluctance to change, even confidence that they can get free at any time.

Parents, even those who are great role models, teachers, counselors, drug abuse experts, and medical professionals face a difficult challenge. As illustrated by hundreds of these letters, the situation is very complex.

The teens with developing problems have to be identified and contacted. They have to be convinced of the need for some counseling. They must want to take charge of their lives, and ignore the pressures of friends who may shun them if they change.

Once begun, ongoing treatment must be consistent and taken seriously by the teen. Family situations cannot be permitted to conflict with the therapy, or to detour the progress that may appear slow. Relapses may occur but must not be allowed to derail the whole process. The target of saving young lives from their own destructive decisions is all important.

Yes, a few among the thousands of letter writers claimed that they had accomplished the change in their lives before becoming fully addicted, or, if addicted, had the willpower to suppress their yearning for the alcohol or drugs and return to a happy, productive life. Our congratulations certainly have to go out to them.

My role, as the first person to examine each letter, has been the easy one. I have had to make a decision as to the severity of the situation described, write a response, and alert a school counselor where I was certain this would be helpful. Beyond that I have had no contact with any student, except to continue with encouragement and suggestions if the writer chose to keep the dialogue open with further letters.

True, I have spent thousands of hours with the lecturing sessions and another several thousand hours hand-writing two-page responses to each of those who had shown confidence in me, and had shared their personal concerns. But this has never become a chore.

CHAPTER EIGHTEEN

"Yes, I have a problem, but my life is over. Sometimes
I can go a couple of days without a drink, but that's it."

Dear Mr. Nelson,

*I used to drink once in a while, but I was and still am hooked on drugs.
Last summer I got so hooked on cocaine that I never came home. I sold my
$400 CD player for it. Well, anyway, I got so hooked on it I got put in a
psychiatric hospital.*

*I was so unhappy with my life that I tried to kill myself and hurt myself a
couple of times. When I was in there I broke out. I got caught two hours later.
The police found me in a crack house.*

*Well, ever since I got out I've been doing better, but then on Halloween I
relapsed and did it again. I went three months straight without any cocaine,
but I picked up the habit of drinking.*

*I'm trying so hard to stop all of this and so are the courts and probation. I'm
really scared. What's going to become of me? I do as best I can to stop, but I just
can't. Living day after day wanting some cocaine is so hard to deal with.*

Regina

Dear Mr. Nelson,

*Thank you for coming to talk to us. I do drink alcohol. I drink it a lot more
than I should. I need to go to AA, people tell me, but I don't know if I should
or not.*

*I've had one of my really good friends killed in an accident because of
alcohol. You really made me think today. Thank you very much! I'd like to
know more about SADD and what I should do.*

Those student's letters were very good to make people think. They made me think. I want to stop drinking, but I don't know how.

Thank you very much,
Terry

Dear Mr. Nelson,

I'm 16 years old. I am not a drinker, though. I am always pressured by my friends to drink and have sex while intoxicated. I tell them I can't or I have something else to do. They tell me, "You're no fun," or, "You're a traitor."

I don't mean to be that way, but I know what's best for me. I know peer pressure is hard and sometimes I won't be able to say "No." It will be hard for me.

I'd like to be a part of SADD. If you could send me some information about joining, I'd appreciate it.

Helpless,
Beckie

Dear Mr. Nelson,

Hi. After reading all those letters about alcoholics, I got very emotional. They brought back memories. About three summers ago my brother and I went back to Alabama to visit our family. About a year before that, our uncle was in a construction accident and since then has become an alcoholic.

My grandfather said some things about my aunt and my Uncle Johnny got mad, got drunk, and got madder. He decided to go to my grandparent's house and teach Grandpa a lesson. He beat him with a 2x4 and left him on the ground to die.

When I woke up in the morning my brother explained to me what had happened. I was very upset with my uncle, but have forgiven him.

I have alcoholics on both sides of my family. Both my brother and I drink, and my mom constantly warns us to be careful, that it can be hereditary. Is this true? Before I go to a party I promise myself not to drink, but always end up doing it. I just get really depressed and it takes my worries away. Maybe not for very long, but for that short period I'm a happy person. I know it's wrong, but I just can't seem to keep myself from doing it.

Thank you for listening. You're a neat person. Please write me back and send information about SADD.

Sincerely,
Stephanie

Dear Mr. Nelson,

Hi, my name is Gina. I'm 16 years old, and I'm totally against drinking. My mom and dad have problems drinking. Ever since I was a little girl, they've drank. I do not like alcohol, it's bad.

Yes, I have drank before. It was in October, 1991, at my best friend's 16th birthday, and over 100 people were there. My ex-boyfriend kept saying, "Come on, just drink one beer," so I drank one beer. That one beer turned into four, then six. At my sixth one I stopped because I was silly, sloppy drunk. My head was spinning and my stomach felt like it was bloated out.

After I stopped, some friends and I went out to the store to get more for them, not me. I had too much. When we got back I fell asleep and woke up three hours later and everything was still going on. Everyone kept telling me to drink more, but I didn't.

The next day my mom asked me if I had a good time, and I told her what I'd done. She told me, "I figured that." I got in trouble and I made a decision that day, I would never drink again. That was my first and my very last time I'll ever drink.

Another time my dad was drunk off his butt, and he came home with some friends. My dad is a very violent man when he drinks. He grabbed me by the neck and slammed my sister. From then till now I don't talk to my dad. He also raped his own daughter(my half-sister). I could never trust him, ever.

I told my mom how I felt about drinking, but she won't listen. I am a Born Again Christian and was one when I drank for my first time. I felt bad about drinking. I asked Jesus to forgive me, and I feel he has.

Thank you for coming to our school.

With all respect,
Gina

Dear Mr. Nelson,

Hi. I'm 17 years old and feel I have many problems. Both my mom and sister are heavy drinkers. My mom says she needs it for sleeping. My sister does it for a good time.

Well, I started for a good time, too! Now, after it killed my cousin, I want to stop, but I can't. My sister and I were in an accident, and we were drunk, but we had an air bag and that's what saved our lives. I'm glad my parents are very supportive. I just need my sis to stop, and me, so we can grow old and have kids.

Mr. Nelson, my sister is my big sis. She is the only one I have, and if I lost her because she drinks, I would die. We're so close. She is my best friend. I just can't lose her 'cause of drinking. I only get drunk when I want to.

I would like to know more about SADD. Thanks for your time. This might not make much sense.

Love,
Cynthia

Dear Mr. Nelson,

I'm 15 and a freshman. I'm not a drunk or anything (I think), but I do drink sometimes on weekends. I want to stop but it's hard when everyone else is drinking and they always ask me if I want something to drink. I try to say "No" sometimes, but most of the time I say "Yes."

While I was growing up my mom was an alcoholic, and I would tell myself I didn't want to turn out like that, but it's hard for them because they like to drink.

I would really like to know a lot more about SADD to help me understand. I'm really glad you came to my class. Well, thank you for listening.

Jennifer

Mr. Nelson,

Thank you for coming to our high school. My name is Nick. I'm 15 years of age, and I am a light drinker. My real dad was killed by drinking. My step-dad, whom I love, doesn't drink beer, but he drinks medium on brandy.

My mom was involved in a car accident when her friend was drinking. My mom went through the front windshield and had to have extensive surgery done on her face. Now my mom drinks heavily with brandy and beer, and takes pills with the beer. When she drives me in the car, it doesn't make me feel good.

Please send me the big information packet with the bumper sticker included. Thank you for your time.

Nick

Dear Mr. Nelson,

Thank you for coming to our school. What you do, going from school to school, is great.

My boyfriend has a drinking problem. He drinks every day although he doesn't do it around me. I tried to talk to him about it, but he doesn't want to listen. But one time we were talking and his drinking did come up. I told him he needed help and he agreed. He admits he has a problem, but he says he doesn't want help. He likes his life the way it is.

I think that's really sad. I love him and we've even talked about marriage, but his drinking is driving me away. It's even gotten to the point where he pressures me to drink, too. I drink every once in a while, but that's it.

My boyfriend needs help, and he knows it! What can I do to make him want to get help? Please write back. I need some help!

Thanks,
Malissa

Dear Mr. Nelson,

I do not know what to do. My girlfriend and I are having problems. I love her so much, but I don't know what to do about her drinking problem. She goes to another high school in this area so I can't see her every day like most couples. I'm going to be 15 in a month, and she's 15½, so we can't drive yet.

Back to my problem, though. She gets drunk every time she goes to one of her friends' houses. One night, after I left her friend's house, she got very drunk. A couple of guys, my friends, went up there. My girlfriend cheated on me, not sex, just fooling around with this other guy. I was very angry. I don't think I can trust her ever again.

I've asked her repeatedly not to drink. I don't want to break up with her because I love her dearly. Please help me. Write back if you have time, please!

Thank you,
Jeff

Dear Mr. Ken Nelson,

I like to drink with my friends on the weekends. We don't only drink, we smoke pot, too. Lots of people around here smoke pot and drink together. They mix them. People older say not to drink and do drugs together, but nothing bad happens so we don't care. Everybody smokes pot. It's not a big deal since we live in this county.

My friends really don't know, but I have lots of problems with other drugs, too. I'm really afraid when I do speed and then drink. My friends want me to drink with them when they don't know I had just done a line. I need to say "No" because I don't want to die.

I don't drive yet, but when I do, I don't want to drink before I drive. But I can't say I won't do any of the other drugs I do when I drive. I'm only 15, but I've been around a lot and have grown up fast. I've done lots of things I regret, and I'm glad right now that I'm not dead or pregnant.

The first time I ever drank was in 5th grade. Drugs started in 6th grade. But I wish all of this would have started later, because now I'm not in very good shape, physically or mentally.

Thanks for reading this,
Jessie

Dear Mr. Nelson,

I'm 15 years old and attending high school regularly. But age aside, I had one of the heaviest drinking and pot smoking problems out of all of my friends. I started drinking when I was in the 4th grade! It was because I was very curious. By the time I was in junior high, I had started drinking every weekend. I used to get A's and B's in all my classes. Then my grades slipped down to C's and D's.

My parents never knew what I was doing. I noticed that I was being really cruel and mean to my parents, but I always thought that it was their fault, and I wasn't mean to them, they were mean to me. I knew that wasn't true. I just needed another excuse for my actions, other than drinking. Since I blamed them for my drinking problems, I though I should get back at them. So the only way I could think of that would work was defiance, so I tried pot.

I really thought I liked it. It became a daily process. I gave up drinking for pot. After a while, I missed getting drunk and going to parties, so I started drinking again. Then I started mixing drugs and drinking.

I've completely stopped using drugs. I haven't stopped drinking, but I do drink a lot less. The true reason I wrote you is because if a situation comes up when a student has a problem like I did, maybe they can read this letter and see that they can find help. But help won't come from meetings, or friends, and sometimes your parents won't help. You are one of the only people who will help yourself.

Mr. Nelson, I would really like for you to give my mailing address to anyone who has this problem, or one similar. I'd really like to hear from them.

Thanks for your time,
Lisa

Mr. Nelson,

I have a problem. I drink almost every weekend. It seems like that's all I think about. I've been drinking since seventh grade and now I'm in ninth. My parents don't know and if I told them it would break their hearts. I think about it a lot and sometimes I cry because I know I have a problem, but when I drink it takes all my problems away.

I hope you understand and thank you for taking the time to read this letter. I also smoke marijuana. It's like I'm a fiend. I always gotta have it. Thanks for your time.

Donna

Dear Mr. Nelson,

We can't really say that teenagers who drink are completely at fault because we teenagers get our drinks through adults. Also, alcoholic beverages are easily accessible.

The few times that I've drank alcohol, I got it through adults who were actually willing to get it (alcoholic beverage) for me. These people weren't even friends. The first time I did it, I was only 13 years old, along with several of my friends. We managed to get wine coolers, beer, and rum through an adult who bought it for us.

The adult doesn't even have to be willing to purchase alcoholic beverages for a minor. Alcoholic beverages can be found in our own refrigerator, purchased by our parents.

Yes, the teen is at fault for "deciding" to drink, but it shouldn't be so easily accessible. If you can also see, the media has a great part to do with all of this.

Sheila

Dear Mr. Nelson,

Reading the letters all of the other teenagers wrote to you really got me thinking. Every weekend I'm around people who drive drunk. I know it's wrong, but we all go along with it.

I drink practically every weekend, sometimes during the week. It just depends on where I go and who I'm around. Most of the people I hang out with are older than 18 and younger than 23. They all drink and do other drugs like it's a natural thing. Sometimes I think I have a problem, but then I think, no, I couldn't. When I drink I get very vulnerable and do things I always regret.

Alcoholism runs in my family. My father and my aunt are both alcoholics, but my father is doing well. He's been going to rehabilitation. I don't live with him so I'm not exactly sure how he's doing now.

I think what you've been doing for the past eleven years is great. The fact that you respond to letters like this one gives teenagers someone to share their thoughts with.

Thank you for taking time to read my letter.

Sarah

Dear Mr. Nelson,

Hi! I'm a junior here. I'm glad you came to talk to us. I am also glad that you care enough to come out to talk to people.

I had a bad family experience with alcohol a few years ago. My mother's boyfriend was a drunk. He smoked, drank, and did drugs every day. He was so much of an alcoholic that beer was all he drank. He didn't drink water, milk, nothing but alcohol.

Now, I'm in a foster home due to him, because he physically, mentally and sexually abused my sister, my mother and me. Also, I have to rebuild my relationship with my mother just because of alcohol.

I hope the presentations you make are listened to. I have listened. I hope I can make a difference like you.

Thanks,
Erica

Dear Mr. Nelson,

I want to thank you for coming in and talking. I'm out of my home and in a foster home due to abuse. My parents would drink and beat on us. I'm very stressed because of this. Listening to you has encouraged me.

I have been hanging around my boyfriend who drinks. I don't drink, so I drive. I'm so afraid that someday he will have an accident. Due to stress, I have been tempted to drink, to get my mind off my situation. I have given in a couple of times and regret it. I'm afraid to become just like my parents. I'm so afraid.

I want to get information on the SADD program. I need all the help I can get. Thanks so much for reading this. I have to talk to someone, someone who understands. I hope I can be an influence on my boyfriend and my other friends. I want to help. You're great. Keep up the good work. Thanks, again.

Sincerely,
Kristi

Mr. Nelson,

I don't think I have a drinking problem, but everyone says I do. My parents wanted me to go to "Charter," but I lied at my evaluation, and said I only drank once. I've been drinking a lot since 8th grade. I'm in 10th now, and I don't think I'm an alcoholic. Everyone says I drink too much.

When I drink, I can't stop. I always want more. Once I was almost raped (molested) when I got drunk. Do you think I have a problem? Should

I get help? I can't help it that I love to drink and get drunk, or sometimes stoned.

Thanks for listening. Please write back.

Sincerely,
Becky

Dear Mr. Nelson,

Hi, my name is Amie and I'm a 10th grader here at this school. I drink a lot, and now I'm trying to stop. But, it's a lot harder to stop than I thought. I tell myself just one drink and then I take one more, and so, on and on, until I'm drunk.

My friend says guys take advantage of me, but I don't remember and just get mad at her. I'm glad you came today because you really helped me think. I hope I succeed with my plan to stop. Thank you for your time.

Amie

Mr. Nelson,

At all of the parties I go to, I've been pressured to drink and drive. They tell me it's okay and everyone is doing it, and that I didn't need to call home for a ride.

One day I was at a party, and I was drinking and so was everyone else. I don't think I should have been drinking, but it was hard to say "No" because of peer pressure. It is hard to be a teenager now-a-days, very hard!

I'm not a heavy drinker, but when I drink now, it takes longer and more to get me drunk. At first I would drink every now and then, but now I drink every time. It's way easy for a teen to get alcohol now. It's hard for me not to drink and it's getting harder and harder.

It hurts me to know that I might end up hurting myself or someone else, or even worse, killing me or someone. I have been thinking about getting help. Now, thanks to you, I will go and get help. I'm only 16 and I think it's time to get my life straight and start getting better grades at school. A 0.7 GPA isn't how I wanted to spend my first year in high school.

Thanks for helping me.

Jennifer

Dear Mr. Nelson,

How are you? I'm fine except for the fact I sometimes get drunk. At my friend's fifteenth birthday party I drank almost a quart of vodka. I was feeling really good until I passed out on her parents' couch. They had to hose me down and make coffee. I knew that coffee wouldn't help, but they made it anyway.

I think it was a good thing her parents weren't home. Ever since then I've drank. I really need help. Please send me some information about SADD. I'm totally against drunk driving. Thank you so much!

Love,
Glenda

Dear Ken,

I'm an 18 year old senior, and my parents have been alcoholics in the past. My parents were the first people to turn me onto alcohol. At first I thought I could control it. I just have to have a drink.

My parents don't even know that I have this problem. I don't have a reputation as a party animal, but my friends supply me with alcohol all the time. They steal it from their parents, bring it to school, and I end up getting drunk by lunch.

I'm not an alcoholic, and I'm not a drunk, but I would like to receive some information on some places to go help me stop drinking. Please help me and feel free to use this letter as an example.

Sincerely, and thanks for caring,
John

Dear Mr. Nelson,

I'm a ninth grader at this high school. I listened to you speaking about drunk driving and stuff. I've started getting high with my friends. I didn't think I ever would, but now I can't stop. Every day before and after school I like to shoot up. I have a younger brother who is 19 months old, and I don't want to set a bad example for him, but sometimes the cravings for a drag are so great.

Because of doing pot, my asthma is worse. I can't remember things, and I can't run track or ride my horse. Every day I get so mad at myself for being high that I've tried slitting my wrists and once hanging myself. My mom has given up on me and my dad disowned me. I'm sorry to do this but I need someone to talk to. Sorry it was you.

Azure

Dear Mr. Nelson,

I used to drink a lot. Every day I would go home and drink. I decided to cut down and try to quit. It's been two years since then. I'm still trying to quit.

I haven't had a drink in three months. Once in a while I want a drink, but I stop myself.

Then I take it out on my little brother. I hit him and slap him and get in trouble. Then I tell my parents it's my hormones. I need to know how I can stop beating my brother without drinking. My parents can't help me because I haven't told them. Please help me.

Justin

Mr. Nelson,

Well, I really don't know where to start. I'm fifteen years old, and I'm only a sophomore. I started drinking with a lot of friends about last Halloween and kind of couldn't stop. It really gets scary sometimes. My dad is no longer around, and my mom is wrapped up in her own life, so I really don't have anyone to talk to about my problems.

I have tried everything to get my life together, such as drugs, suicide, therapy, and alcohol. I stuck with alcohol because it worked and was the easiest to get. I've had many boyfriends who have tried to help me, but I seem to just push them away and get really abusive towards them.

I don't know whether this is normal for a teenager's life, and I really need to get some answers. So, I decided to write to you and see if maybe you can help me. Nobody has ever told me I have a problem, and I hide my feelings really well.

Please write me back and help me figure out my life.

Thank you,
Kristen

Dear Mr. Nelson,

Hi, my name is Jamila. I'm listening to you talk to us about drunk driving. Well, I drink. I don't drink often, but when I do drink, I drink a lot. I also do drugs and am having sex. My parents don't know about anything that I do.

All of this started when my grandpa died from drinking too much. His heart and liver failed him. He was my best friend. I could talk to him about anything. I know that drinking and having sex and doing drugs is wrong, but when I get around my friends and we are partying or just having fun drinking and doing other things, I just don't know how to say "No."

I get so depressed sometimes that I try to kill myself. My parents know that I think about it, but they don't know that I've tried to do it. If I'm not trying to kill myself, I'm doing stuff like drugs and drinking. I don't know what to do.

If you could send me some information on what to do, I would appreciate it. Thank you for coming to our class to talk about it. Please don't think I'm crazy or stupid.

Sincerely yours,
Jamila

Mr. Nelson,

    Who in the hell do you think you are to tell me how to live? My mom does not even tell me not to drink. That is, she did not say it was okay to drink and drive, but that is stupid to start with. I have been drinking a long, long time. That does not mean I'm a drunk.

From,
A Drinker

My young writers divulge a multitude of reasons for their drinking. They do it to be like their friends. They don't want to be left out! They drink to temporarily push aside emotional hurts. They feel depressed and find that alcohol blurs reality. Drinking overcomes shyness. They are curious about alcohol's effects.

Far too many letters outline family drinking problems by grandparents, uncles/aunts, parents, and older siblings. Most writers are adamant about not wanting to follow in their relatives' destructive footsteps. Yet, a few sentences later we read, *"I don't want to be like them, but find myself doing the same thing."* This gives credence to the widely held view that many alcohol and drug abusers do come from family situations where the damage can be viewed daily. Why would an observant young person knowingly allow himself to be drawn into an identical trap? It is apparent from the letters that many have.

Many acknowledge that they drink or do drugs on some regular basis and are considering quitting, but then follow with . . . . *"but I don't think I have a problem or anything like that."* As one student wrote, *"Teenagers are very smart, but . . . ."* He's right. Their improved judgment will come only with time and experience. The one thing we don't want is that they have to experience a serious dependency on alcohol or other drugs before they move to a more healthy lifestyle. They are prime candidates for counseling, and in many cases I took that step.

I sometimes suggested the concerned teenager talk with an older relative who now has, or has had, a bad drinking problem. *"Ask them when they first began drinking. Was it fun? Did the stress or personal problems they had go away for awhile? Did they feel it wouldn't become a problem for them? When did they realize they had become addicted?"*

Only letters indicating a strong plea for help were delivered to counselors. I detoured only one time from this approach, with predictable consequences. A counselor asked if she could read the balance of the letters I'd received that day, about six beyond the two I'd shared with her. Understandably, perhaps, she saw a strong reason for intervention in five of these six situations, and apparently all were called in for counseling.

My worst fears were confirmed. Here I had been able to pry open this marvelous door to get these spontaneous revelations from troubled teenagers. Now, the word spread across the campus quickly that I couldn't be trusted with confidentiality, and letters from that school almost dried up for the following two years. Then, the wonderful letters flowed again, and I conferred regularly with the counselors but only when the need was clearly apparent.

CHAPTER NINETEEN

"I just wanted to share a not-so-terrible story with a not-so-terrible ending with you."

Mr. Nelson,

I'm writing you, not in grief, but in happiness. You see, my step-father used to drink an awful lot. My mother and he got into fights every time he would drink. We were all very much afraid of him at one time because, when he drank, the alcohol took over his actions and feelings. He would break things, hurt my mother and say terrible things to my brother and me.

Over a period of time my hatred for him grew very intense. I hated him for what he did.

But, over the past years he has stopped drinking as much as before. He drinks once in a while, but he never drinks so much as to do something totally out of character, like before.

Since then we have grown much closer. I still can't say I love him, because the memories of that period of time will always remain in my deepest thoughts.

I just wanted to share a not-so-terrible story, with a not-so-terrible ending, with you. Thank you for you presentation. I enjoyed it very much.

Sincerely,
Denise

Dear Mr. Nelson,

I have had a lot of problems in my life concerning alcohol. Two years ago my aunt was in an accident. She had been drinking and she died. This hit my family and me very hard.

After my aunt died I didn't care what happened to me or anyone else. I went out and drank, got drunk, and got into a lot of trouble. I just kept on drinking. I think I drank to get my aunt's death off my mind.

I kept on threatening my family that I was going to run away and it even got so extreme that I tried to commit suicide. Now I'm doing pretty good. I stopped drinking. I learned that drinking wasn't going to bring my aunt back. I got counseling to help me through this tough time.

When my friends ask if I want to go out and drink, I simply say" No." I am proud that I have come this far. Thank you for coming to our health class. I like to learn as much as I can about how dangerous drinking can be.

Alison

Dear Ken,

Thank you for your support. I had almost given up on myself as well as my brother.

I know you probably don't remember who I am, but the knowledge that one person could care so much about so many people made me think. I was in a class you spoke to during the spring semester, but failed the course, so I'm here in summer school.

I've already given up on my brother. He's a drug abuser and a raver, so he's around it all the time. As for myself, I've been clean of everything for two months, well, almost. I've had one beer, but I'm almost all the way clean. I'm trying to turn my life around.

One good thing that has happened is at the end of the year, instead of having straight F's like I thought I would, I only had two. I got two D's, one C, and a B. Right now in summer school I have the second highest grade in the class.

I hope by the time I become entirely clean, I can have the highest grade, because I now know I really do have potential. Even though you don't really know me, the fact that someone believed in me helped me realize how far in life I can go. I'm back in water polo, and I have new friends. I hope to never return to the life I had. Thank you again for all the support.

Always,
Allison

Dear Mr. Nelson,

My name is Stephanie, and I'm a sophomore at this school. I'm real glad you've come today. I hope it helps some of our students. My mother is a recovering alcoholic. She stopped using alcohol about five or six years ago. I'm very proud of her because it took a lot of courage for her.

She used alcohol for a long time and it was getting old. When we moved out here she became a licensed babysitter and was still drinking. Finally, about two years later, my father gave her a choice, him or the alcohol.

She took my sister and me by train to her brother's house in Oregon. She admitted herself the following night to a rehab center, and cured her problem.

Now she gets sick to her stomach with just a sniff of alcohol. I'm really proud of her, as I said. She's since gone to college and is now a certified medical assistant, and is still with my father. It just goes to show a little courage can bring you a far way.

Stephanie

Mr. Nelson,

I think you're doing a cool thing. Well, three years ago my brother and his friends did drugs and alcohol. My brother didn't have SADD, so he had to quit the hard way. His girlfriend wouldn't talk to him and my mom threatened to kick him out of the house.

Well, now his girlfriend, who wouldn't talk to him, is his wife. He's in the army and stationed in Germany. The year after he quit, he became the best pitcher for his school's baseball team.

Peace,
Duane

Mr. Nelson,

I used to be involved completely with people who drank and used. It got so bad that I would get mad at the littlest things and soon it affected my personal life.

I got tired of how screwed up my life was so my mother introduced me to Alcoholics Anonymous. Now my life has straightened up within four months, but I will always have a problem and never be able to drink again.

I'm still very scared because of my drinking and using. My dreams may not come true, but I keep hoping and praying. At least my life has been cleared up and unfogged.

Please write me about SADD. I want to get involved. Please let others know their lives can change. My mother is in AA, too.

Kris

Dear Mr. Nelson,

Hi! My name is Billie Jo. I want to thank you for speaking to my class about mixing alcohol and driving. I'm 16 years old and a junior in high school. I've only been drunk one time and ever since then I have had only one drink about a year ago. Now I can't stand the taste of alcohol.

My mother, sometimes after work, would come home and drink because she said it calms her nerves. She would say she was going to take the car and go to the store. I would tell her that I didn't want her to drive, even though she didn't drink a lot. I was surprised when she listened to me.

Now, I live in a foster home, and my foster mom told me that if I ever drank, she didn't want me coming home drunk. I am also proud to say I have the" guts" to tell people (my friends) that I don't drink, and I don't need to get a thrill by drinking.

I would also like to thank you for making me feel even more proud for not drinking and making me more courageous to say" No" when people ask me to drink. THANKS! You're a great man, and you'll always remain in my mind when someone wants to drink and drive. Thanks for caring!

Sincerely,
Billie Jo

Dear Sir,

When I was six, my mom got remarried. I was in a house with an alcoholic. For six years I was molested and raped. In 7ʰ grade I became an alcoholic. Every day, before, during, and after school, I was drunk.

We moved to Sacramento, and I didn't have many friends. I drank alone. I got so scared I stopped. I was shaky and edgy for about six months. Sometimes it got so bad I had to have a drink.

Well, I'm 17 now. I'm going to court at the end of May to testify against my old step-dad. My life is starting to come back together after three attempts to kill myself, and finally telling my parents about my old step-dad. My friends love me and know I don't drink anymore.

Thank you so much for caring. I did it. I helped my girlfriend stop, and I just had a long talk with one of my guy friends last night, and he promised to stop. I told him I believed him, and he needs to let me help, but first he needs to help himself. He said," I know."

I haven't explained a lot, but I did the main points. I thank you, and if more people cared and showed it but didn't preach, merely listened, it would solve so many of these young alcoholic's problems.

Thank you! I can't thank you enough! We need more people like you to make us feel needed.

Love,
Jolene

Mr. Nelson,

A lot of people I used to hang out with got drunk a lot. I had, I don't like to say, a drinking problem, but I did drink a lot at parties. When people get drunk, they do things they regret. I was with someone I really liked for a long, long time. I thought I could trust him, and I thought he was sober, but he wasn't. He took advantage of me. He didn't rape me, but I still felt so used.

I'm still a virgin, and I plan on waiting for a long time. I'm only a freshman and the guy was a really popular sophomore. Only my very best friends know what happened. I'm so ashamed.

My mom and dad found out I had been at parties. My parents and I have always had the best relationship. I'm so glad. I don't drink anymore. I lost some friends, but I have regained the respect of my parents and old friends. In fact I think my parents and I are better friends now. Thank you so much!

Love,
Rosie

Dear Mr. Nelson,

It has been about a year since I last saw you. I had told you about my 15 year old friend who is now 16 years old. He had been drinking and going in a car with a person who had been drinking. Like I said, this was last year.

This year my friend sobered up and does not go with people who drink and drive. He is a very special friend, and so are you. If he drinks he will call me or stay the night at his brother's house. I thank you for your letter and for saving our friendship. I thank you from the bottom of my heart.

Your very thankful friend,
Nancy

Dear Mr. Nelson,

I'm a recovering drug addict/alcoholic. It's really hard for me to stay away from it, especially when I go to parties with my friends. I was clean for one year, then I blew it.

I just want other teenagers to realize that if you're clean, stay that way. Drugs or alcohol don't solve anything or make you a better person. I've pressured friends into drinking, and now I regret it. I was a heavy cocaine addict and if I didn't have it, I would drink.

My parents put me in a drug rehab for 2½ months. I went through a lot of hard times. I used to sit up and cry in my room because I couldn't believe I did this to myself. I stole from my parents, lied, and did anything to get what I wanted.

To this day I'm trying to gain my parents' trust back. It's hard but I know I can do it. I'd better end this letter, but I want other teenagers to ask themselves," Is it worth it?"

A recovering drug addict/alcoholic,
Tina

Dear Mr. Nelson,

I'd like to share with you my painful experiences with drugs and alcohol. My father used drugs and alcohol during the nine years I lived with him in Oregon. He was very abusive to my mom, sister, and me for as long as I could remember.

I was molested by my father, and he would make me use drugs and alcohol to cover up the abuse. I grew up already addicted to numerous drugs from the age of two, until it almost killed me when I was eight years old. My father tried to kill me numerous times under the influence, and it was a nightmare having to face him day after day, not knowing if I was going to live or die.

My mom didn't know about the abuse until she caught him. She immediately turned him in, but there wasn't much she could do to help me. Luckily, my mom was loving enough to get some help, so I was very lucky. I was able to kick my habits after a lot of work and after almost dying after many overdoses.

Since then, I have never picked up any drug or alcoholic beverage. I intend not to. I know the effects of drinking, and I've seen it kill so many people. I've lost many family members to drinking, so I support what you are doing. I thank you for coming and talking because I know how true everything you share with so many kids is. I understand how difficult it is to get someone to listen to you and not drink.

Thank you again for coming. I enjoyed listening to you.

Sincerely,
Kerri

Mr. Nelson,

I myself have had problems with drinking and major drug abuse, but now that is in the past, and I'm a much happier person. A lot of people ask me how

I made the decision to quit, but for me it was easy. I just totally made up my mind that I would never do it again. It was easy for me because I am really strong-minded, and I knew that this was something that I wanted.

I am so much happier and life is a lot easier and more productive. I feel so much better about myself, and I actually enjoy living for once. I would never go back to my old way of life.

As a matter of fact, I'm actually glad I went through hell because now I know how easy and good life really is. Now, it hurts me to see friends I care about drink because I know the hell they are going through, and know that no one deserves that.

Thank you,
Amanda

Mr. Nelson,
I want to thank you for coming to our Peer Resource class. I'm a junior here. My sophomore year I started going to parties a lot, and I thought if I drank people would accept me more. I hated the taste of beer and hard liquor, but I did it to be accepted.

I was drinking every weekend and on some weekdays when I could get away with it. All through my sophomore year and some of my junior year I drank heavily.

Almost halfway through my junior year my uncle passed away because of drinking. He got so drunk he jumped off a very high bridge and died instantly.

This really hurt me. My favorite uncle dead because of drinking. This really opened my eyes. It's funny how a tragic accident with drinking could change your life. Now, at parties, I'm always the designated driver. I don't drink and if my friends only have one drink, I still drive.

I've lost one person from drinking who I loved very much. I'm not about to lose another one from drinking.

Thanks for everything,
Sara

Dear Mr. Nelson,
My life has been pretty hard, and a lot of it had to do with alcohol and drugs. My father was killed in an alcohol-drug related scene. All my friends did it, and I had a parent for an example. I thought it was okay.

I never realized that it was a problem, but when I did it was really hard to quit. I did quit and now I won't touch any type of alcohol or drugs. I know that both of them kill, and I'm not going to throw away my life.

Thanks for coming and talking to us. You can count on me that I'll always be against drunk driving.

Thanks,
Frances

Dear Ken,

I was in this class when you came last semester. Thank you for writing me back and for sending all of the information on SADD. Once I received the info, I showed some of it to my father (what applied to him), and I noticed an immediate change in him. He has been wearing a seat belt, and he has my sister or a friend drive us home from any barbecues or get-togethers. He still has a nightly drink, but not three or four. I think that the" packet" had a good impact on him.

As for me, I don't drink heavily, and I don't think that I'm in as big a danger of it anymore. I do, however, still drink occasionally, but only in the presence of an adult (usually my mom), and at home.

Things are going much better at home alcohol-wise, and I want to thank you for it. So, thank you!

Sincerely,
Christina

Dear Mr. Nelson,

I'm 17 years old and a junior. My mom passed away last year. The cause of her death was alcohol. She was 49 years old. She was a heavy drinker; my father is also a heavy drinker. I've lived with my sister since I was 14 years old. She's my legal guardian, and I'm very proud.

When I lived with my parents, I could never be calm because they were always fighting. They used to get very violent, especially when they drank. They didn't drink beer or wine coolers, they drank hard liquor (vodka). During the week they drank up to 15 bottles or more, and over the weekend they drank more. I was so scared because I never knew when one of them would get killed during their fights. I wanted to do something about it, but they were so addicted already.

I'm still very upset because I don't know if my father is still alive, and because I can't see my mother anymore. I loved her so much. I'm also scared because I might get involved in drinking. I used to drink when I was 13 because there was no one to control me.

Then when I came up with my sister, I stopped. I changed my whole life! From being a gang wanna-be, drinker, and C or D student to a mature, well-dressed young lady and an honor roll student . . . . And thinking of joining the Army or becoming a police officer.

I would like more information on SADD. Thank you for listening.

Patricia

Dear Mr. Nelson,

While you were speaking I started to understand what happened in my life. My mother used to get drunk all day, every day. She used to pick on me and my sister and brother. She hit me once. I used to hate coming home at night to see my mother drunk, so instead, I would drink as much as I could, non-stop. I thought that would help me. I started at the age of 13, now I'm 16.

I understand my mistake, and I'm glad I stopped while I'm ahead. Now my mom has stopped because I told her how it affects me, and the family told her what I did. I told her she has my little sister to look after now.

Please don't show my real name. It's not common. Thanks for coming.

Yours truly,
Lucky

As a reader, I can't help but choke up when I sense the relief felt by these teenagers as they write about their lives becoming worth living again.

Every letter of this grouping is significantly different from any other. Some acknowledged help along the way to a better life. A few pulled themselves out of the quicksand. It all happened by the time they were sixteen or seventeen. They've experienced the ugliness of life at such an early age. The common threads of these stories' endings are appreciation and relief, and resolve to move forward in their new lives, all this before seventeen!

You and I fervently wish this chapter could be filled with many more such letters, but what appears represents most of those I could find among the 3500 received.

We can realistically hope that many more have benefited and have significantly turned their lives around since I spoke with their classes and they responded with letters.

Many students in my audiences indicated approval of the concepts of SADD by filling out membership applications and (hopefully) carrying their SADD I.D. cards that I prepared. Most who wrote follow-up letters said they did so, though some questioned in a side note, their right to be considered a good member, worthy of the club's standards.

Further evidence of the rather immediate value of the students' ability to listen and react to my appeal that they use their unique power to change this drunk driving fatality problem came from one of a San Francisco Bay area school's driver education teachers. His school, located in an acknowledged problem area, was on a quarter system, enabling me to visit fifteen to eighteen sophomore classes each school year. Letters were handed to me frequently.

His observation in later years was that after my first year or two as a guest speaker, the school had experienced no deaths due to alcohol-related driving on the part of their students for a period of five years.

Prior to that time, this teacher said that between one and three such deaths of their students had occurred each year for as long as he could remember.

My notes recording student sign-ups in SADD, indicated that after three years of lecturing, with now all of the sophomores in my first year's classes at that school being seniors, there were consistently six or seven hundred students on their campus carrying SADD I.D. Cards. As I recall their student body numbered something over two thousand. That school also provided over three hundred letters from students during the fifteen years that I was a regular visitor, many now showing up in print in this book.

CHAPTER TWENTY

"Please tell everyone that if someone cool says you have to drink to hang around with them, maybe they're not so cool, or not going to be such good friends as you'd like."

Dear Mr. Nelson,

I think what you are doing is awesome. It's nice to know that there are people out there who care about changing things for kids for the better.

I fully agree with the SADD program. I think it is ridiculous for kids to think they have to drink to be accepted. I don't believe that people can blame their drinking problems on their parents. My dad drinks a lot but rarely gets drunk. Because of his drinking habit I have learned that I don't want to be involved in that. I am interested in becoming part of the SADD group. Thank you for coming.

Kayla

Mr. Nelson,

Both of my parents are alcoholics, and so is my sister. I have an uncle in jail for drunk driving. My grandfather eventually died of alcoholism. I lost my best friend to drug addiction, and another died very recently in a fatal car accident. I am familiar with the effect substances can have on our lives.

However, it never gets easier. Every time someone's life is affected or even ruined by alcohol, I'm angry at just how helpless I feel. Thank you for telling students what they can do, which is to take care of themselves and avoid alcohol.

I cannot force help on my parents, but I can be careful about what I do. People need to hear that. You can't blame yourselves for your parents' actions, but you can blame yourself for your own!

As soon as we start taking care of ourselves, we will start making changes. That is all we can do, and it's time we started doing it.

Melissa

Mr. Nelson,

I would like to tell you that I love the idea of SADD. I am very much against alcohol. My parents got divorced when I was three years old because my father was an alcoholic. I never spent much time with him because drinking was his first priority.

Three years ago my dad's girlfriend almost died from drinking too much. That finally convinced him that if he didn't stop drinking the same thing could be happening to him real soon. They are now happily married and have an alcohol-free life. I am very proud of both of them, and I'm very close to both of them.

I think that is why I have such a strong feeling of not wanting to drink. I've never been drunk and don't plan on ever getting drunk. I'm very proud of myself. With alcoholism being hereditary I don't want to take a chance. Most of the men on my father's side of the family are alcoholics.

People ask me if I've ever been drunk, and are amazed when I say "No." I know that if I were at a party with alcohol, I wouldn't drink or let my friends drive home drunk.

I think this is a great idea. I would like to join. Keep up the good work.

Wendy

Dear Mr. Nelson,

I think that SADD is a great idea. I also think it's great what you are doing and hope it will save lives. I agree with the message, *"Friends Don't Let Friends Drive Drunk."*

My mom rarely drinks, but sometimes my dad drinks too much. He is a jerk when he's drunk. I am embarrassed to be around him when he's like that (if we're at a party or in public). I think that's why I will not drink. I cannot lie to you, I'm sure I'll try it when I'm older, but I occasionally will have one drink and that's it!

I'm a good student and have big plans for my future, and alcohol is only going to ruin that future. You are doing a great job. Keep it up! Please write back.

Brandon

Dear Mr. Nelson,

I think it's really neat how you come and talk to students. It may seem as though some of the people don't listen, and it's really strange because the ones *who don't listen are usually the ones who drink. I think that's really, really sad.*

I have friends who drink, but I wouldn't even consider it. I know that may seem just something to say, when actually, from knowing an alcoholic, I would really like to keep away from it.

I can't understand why people wouldn't listen, especially to people who know what they are talking about. Well, thanks for sticking up for what you believe in, because there are people out there who are listening.

Your friend,
Jennifer

Dear Mr. Nelson,

I think that what you're doing is very wonderful, to devote this part of your life talking to teenagers, and trying to make a difference in our lives. I have heard many, many lectures in my time but, truthfully, yours made the most effect on me. I, as well as the rest of the teenagers who have the privilege of hearing your speech are very, very lucky.

I'm trying to recover from a line of serious drugs. I'm totally off the acid and LSD, but recovering from pot, cigarettes and alcohol is going to be the hardest part. All of my friends drink and smoke, so it is very hard for me to quit. I'm also known for the "Massive Parties" and so my friends make me feel like this is my job to pick the party place, call all the people, and get all the drugs and alcohol.

I have not done this for two months now, and I feel really good about myself. The one thing that I do is never, never get in a car with anyone who has had the slightest amount of alcohol (even my parents).

I would very much like to become a member of SADD. I would love to do anything I can to help in any way.

Thank you so much, Mr. Nelson. You have helped me to make some very hard questions seem easier to answer.

Thanks again,
Amy

Dear Mr. Nelson,

I have been blessed with a family who do not drink or abuse any other substances, and I, myself, have made a decision not to drink. I've seen what can happen in car accidents and it scares me. I play sports; athletics are my life and if I lost my legs, I don't know what I'd do.

Thank you for coming to my school and other schools to talk to us, because from some of the letters you read to us, people need you. I respect you for coming on your time to help us realize we can change lives.

I have never drank, and all I can do is wonder why others do. I have fun being high on life. Why can't others? I care, and I want you and others to know I am a friend, and "Friends Don't Let Friends Drive Drunk." None of my friends are going anywhere drunk if I can help it.

Thank you!
Bernadette

Dear Mr. Nelson,

People all over the world say they care. Well, I'm happy to say that you do more than care. You actually take action and most people don't do that. I would just like to tell you "Thanks," and that the work you are doing is very admirable.

When you let us read those letters, I was intrigued by the rape case. If you still write her I hope you can tell her she is not alone, and I hope she is doing okay.

Personally, I think teenagers just are plain smart but often are afraid to use it. I hope you and others can bring it out. Thanks for the gallant effort.

Cheryl

Mr. Nelson,

I do not drink, and I haven't any intentions of drinking in the future. I really wanted to let you know how much I love what you're doing for my generation.

Although I don't drink, some of my friends do. I really worry about them, and I try my best to discourage them from drinking, but they tell me I don't understand because I don't drink. I want to know if there's something I can do. You see, I don't even go to parties where drugs and alcohol will be present. I wish there was a way I could chauffeur all drunk people home after a party.

I'm also worried about some of my friends while they're at home because their parents drink. They won't say anything to their parents in fear of getting punished, and I feel very uncomfortable in their houses.

They know they are always welcome at my house at any time, but I feel even that isn't enough for me to do to help them. I've seen drunk drivers on the road while I'm driving, and they scare me. I hope you can stop a good portion of drunk driving. If you have any comments that can help me, please write.

Thank you,
Maci

Dear Mr. Ken Nelson,

I think drinking is a very bad thing to do. Why? Because my cousins drink and drive, and I want information to help those people. Please, can you send me information to help those people who drink and drive.

You are a very good person and believable.

Ott

Dear Mr. Nelson,

None of my family or I have any kind of drinking problem. I just wanted to write you this letter to thank you for talking to us about drinking and driving.

I know drinking is wrong, but I didn't think that if you stayed somewhere or if you were home it is that big of a deal. But, I guess if you do it every weekend or every day, you can get addicted.

I have drank once or twice before, but it was nothing really. I went to a doubles party and got a little buzz but that's all. It's been a long time since I've even had a drink. I'm glad I'm not a drinker.

Everyone I'm ever around, friends and family, don't drink. Maybe once in a while, but they don't drive, so I really don't know what it's like for kids or parents with a drinking problem, and I'm glad.

Well, thank you for coming to our school and giving us information on drunk driving. I know if my friends are ever drunk and are going to drive, I won't let them drive, and if they do, I will not get in the car.

Could you please send me something on SADD.

Thanks for coming,
Shelly

Dear Mr. Nelson,

My name is Lori, and I really do appreciate what you are doing. I can't give you a story or anything. My friends don't drink and neither do I. But, just in case something ever did come up I would like some information about SADD.

Thank you,
Lori

Mr. Nelson,

I'm not a drinker, never have been and never will. I believe totally in the saying, "Friends Don't Let Friends Drive Drunk." When I get my license I plan on always being the designated driver. When it comes to peer pressure for drinking, I'm very strong. I'd just like to say, "Keep up the good work!" I appreciate your efforts. Please send me some information on SADD.

Thanks for caring,
Michelle

Dear Mr. Nelson,

Hi. You might remember me. My name is Kristin. You came here during the summer of 1990 to talk to our class. I was the one who wrote to you about my friend's mom who got killed by a drunk driver who got off with "manslaughter."

When I joined SADD you sent me a lot of information on SADD. The information really helped me to understand about drinking and driving. It's wrong.

I recently got my license. Never in my life will I ever drink and drive or get in a car with a person who is intoxicated. That's a promise.

Sincerely,
Kristin

Dear Mr. Nelson,

I just wanted to say thanks for the inspiration that you have on all those adolescents all over the state.

I may seem out of my age range, but I think it's really important that the adolescents of our society today should realize just how important and valuable their lives are. I mean it's like, when they have a problem, they either turn to drugs or alcohol. Then that could lead to something worse like harder drugs or drunk driving.

There's just so much influence out there, you know. There are so many bands out there, and they just drink right in front of the cameras. Then here we have little adolescents who want to be cool like them and do it, too.

I mean, it's not fair! These kids are supposed to set the pace or our future. What kind of a future will we have if these kids continue to constantly punish themselves under this influence?

If I could, I would tell these kids that they should go for their goals. They should break these bad habits of theirs and go out and fulfill their dreams. If you have patience, willpower, determination and perseverance, you can do it. Don't let anything get in your way. Have confidence in yourself. Believe in yourself.

Again, thank you for being such an inspiration for these kids and good luck on your crusade. I fully believe in your mission.

"Unsigned"

Dear Mr. Nelson,

It's amazing just listening to a person with a high point warning and telling them to be aware. It's real great that you see many schools and try your best to influence each individual what bad things drinking could do, and how to help your friends. Every student letting in the light you bring to them will show them the right way.

People like you make me want to thank you in the best way, and that way is to take in what you told us and say it loud to everyone else. Say it loud!

Sincerely,
Clark

Mr. Nelson,

I really enjoyed your discussion. My grandfather and step-grandfather were both alcoholics, and I have friends who drank heavily until we talked to them.

I really don't understand why kids or adults start drinking. They see the effects and still do it. I don't suffer from peer pressure, so I guess I don't understand.

Because, if people are my friends, they won't pressure me, and I don't listen to people who aren't my friends or aren't nice to me. Keep up the good work.

Thank you,
Melissa

Dear Mr. Nelson,

Thank you very much for coming and talking to us today. I'm lucky, none of my family drinks except my grandma and my cousin, but they very rarely drink, and they don't drive drunk, ever. Also, none of my friends drink. I really feel strongly about drinking, and I would like to be a member of SADD.

Thank you for your time. Most adults at this school and in this town don't care too much about teenagers.

Sincerely,
Jennifer

Mr. Nelson

I really appreciate what you're doing. You speak very well. I've never drank alcohol before in my life. I'm dead set against it.

I do know what people go through, though. I've been pressured many times to drink and go to parties. I've found the best way to avoid alcohol and other drugs is to stay away from the temptation.

I still don't understand why people turn to alcohol for any reason. It doesn't make sense. Just because your friends do it is probably the stupidest reason I've ever heard.

Once again, I am thankful for you coming to our school and talking to us. You're a very nice man. I hope life treats you well.

See you later,
Kolleen

Dear Mr. Nelson,

I just want to say that I really appreciate the speaking that you do. I think that it will really help those who have serious drinking problems.

I don't have any problems like that. I'm what you'd call "straight." I don't drink, I don't do drugs, and I'm not quite driving yet (I'm almost 16 . . . June).

But the reason I'm writing is because I do have friends who drink and drive. It scares me. They do it all the time, not because they like it so much, they want to have a reputation and want to be a realistic rebel. I have been scorned and despised by these people because I've let them know I care.

I once was really good friends with Richard but something happened, and I lost a friend. He told me he was going to go out, drink, and have a good time. Before he left, I told him I really cared about him, and I told him if he was going to drink to be safe and careful. He said "Alright."

Later that week, someone called his house and told his mom about his drinking. He immediately accused me of getting him in trouble.

I never told his mom, but he never believed me, and I've never talked to him since. There were so many reasons why I should've called, but I valued his friendship so much, it would hurt me to see him in trouble.

Thanks for letting me write about this, and for listening to us. You've been great!

Yours truly,
Kelly

Mr. Nelson,

What's up? How have you been doing? I'm very interested in the club SADD. I want to get more involved with this club. I want to show other students that drinking and driving don't mix.

I don't have a problem or anything, I just want to help. Can you send me a poster, button or bumper sticker to prove that I'm out to help students to not drive drunk?

I'm really against it. I don't think it's right, but for people who do, I want to help them or prevent them from hurting others. I want to help.

Sincerely yours,
Katie

Dear Mr. Nelson,

I don't have a problem or anything. It's just that I get scared when I hear about drinking. I feel bad for the kids that do have problems.

I'm only 15 years old, but I hang around the juniors and seniors. All my friends go to parties every weekend and sometimes I go with them. I have never drank except for one time, but that was nothing, I didn't even get buzzed. I could have gotten drunk if I wanted to, but I thought to myself, "What's the point!" Hey, I have a great life ahead of me and I don't ever want to ruin it by drinking.

But that one night that I did try, the next day I felt so bad, I truly felt like crying. I don't know why. I guess drinking and I don't mix.

My dad's parents never really did drink. My parents both gave up drinking because they said it wasn't right for them to tell us to say "No" when they drink. I'm glad you came!

Thanks,
Laura

Mr. Nelson,

Thanks for being who you are. Because of people like you who care, you set a great goal for us to help ourselves. I'm grateful that you care so much to help us talk some sense into some of our thick heads.

Although I never drank, and I hope I never will, I have tasted alcohol two or three times in my 15 years, but I never did like it so I'm not worried.

I hope that all of us will be able to look up to you to help us through, and I'm thankful for your commitment and heart of nothing but pure gold.

The film is right, a world that can put men on the moon should be able to stop drunk drivers. Why not? Do we just not care enough? But people like you give hope to people like me that maybe there is a way to stop people from driving drunk. Right now, it's a long shot, but there's always hope because of you.

Thanks a lot! We need more Mr. Nelsons in the world.

Very grateful,
Ann

Dear Mr. Nelson,

Don't think I am involved with drinking, I'm not. I just don't understand how people can stand something that tends to taste so terrible, makes them lose control of their body (not to mention their mind), and so on. Now, if they liked what they just ate, and liked it so much they wanted to taste it again. (Ha! Ha!).

I refuse to drink, period! I would like some information on SADD. Also, if I'm a designated driver, can I get pulled over if I have my drunk friends in the car?

Sincerely yours,
Emily

Mr. Nelson,

I've heard a lot about SADD but don't know much about it. I am a Christian, and I do not drink. When I was in 8th grade, I knew an older man who drank. He didn't get drunk, though. He told me not to drink, but if I did, to be honest with my parents. He let me have a sip so I'd know what it was about.

I decided I wouldn't drink because I didn't like the taste. I also knew what it did to people. My parents are very supportive of me. I want to encourage others not to drink.

In the letters I read, it seemed like people felt like they were alone, that they were the only ones who were drinking or doing drugs. They need to know there are people who care.

Sometimes you need to look for someone you least expect will be there for you. Will you please send me some information about SADD so I can help other people?

Monique

Mr. Nelson,

I just want to say thank you for coming. It's great to know people like you are out there. I know what it's like living through alcoholism. My father is an alcoholic and drug addict, still using, and I have a lot of best friends who think it's great to party with drugs. It kills me to see what they could be headed for.

Myself, I've never done drugs (Thank God), and I try very hard to help my friends. I know what's out there, and after I've lived through a lot of pain and a lot of hurt, I just want to try to let other people know there is a lot more to life than alcohol and drugs. I'm totally against it, and I would please like some more information about SADD.

Thank you so much for your time.

Jamie

Dear Mr. Nelson,

After reading all those letters, it makes me think, I have never had a drink of alcohol and never will. You may not believe me because most people don't, but you see, my friends would never pressure me to do something, or else they are not even my friends.

My boyfriend used to really get messed up in alcohol. When I met him later he told me I really turned his life around because of the attitude I had. After a time, he quit drinking.

All I want to say is you can make a difference. You don't hurt anyone but yourself when you drink, and who cares what others say? It's your life and you are the one in control of it. You should be able to make your own decisions.

I will always be there for others, but I've made the decision not to associate with the kind of crowd or attend parties that contain alcohol.

All of my uncles and grandparents drink, and my grandpa died from it. One of my uncles has been in prison now for a long time for drunk driving. I would like to do all I can to discourage others from falling into these traps. Please send me as much information as possible on SADD.

Starr

Dear Mr. Nelson,

I've never really drank before except for trying it a few times. I hate the taste so it's easy for me to push it away.

I have a cousin who's living with me whose mother killed herself. His father, who he had never really known, agreed to take him in. Well, he is a very bad alcoholic and has a drug problem. He beat him and kicked him out onto the streets. He was only 10 years old. My family agreed to take him, and he's been with us for over four years, and I wouldn't give him up for the world.

I feel that children of drunk parents are the victims, and they need the right people to tell them it's not their fault. Alcohol runs in my family, and thank God my mom broke the chain when she had two children. I want to thank you for your concern in this world.

I'm wanting to get into talking or helping younger kids to learn about those serious problems our nation is having. Is there any way or info that could be given to me about these programs? I would seriously like to be a part of any one the programs. I just don't know how to get into it. Can you help?

I love children, and their safety is very important to me. Thanks for your concern!!

> *Sincerely,*
> *Jessica*

Dear Mr. Nelson,

I think your talk was great. After reading some of those letters, I realized that not one was from a student who didn't drink. I don't drink. I want to say you don't have to drink to be cool.

If your friends can't accept you for who you are, then they aren't your friends. Just remember that drinking isn't going to bring you anywhere but down.

Thanks for helping me understand more. Please write back.

> *Mia*

Dear Mr. Nelson,

I just wanted to express that I'm very interested in being involved in SADD. I enjoy joining such clubs, and I figure that being a member of this club will help keep me staying sober (I've never been drunk and hopefully never will!).

Please, if you could find the time, send me all the information you can on SADD. I appreciate the fact you take a lot of time for this!

Thank you, and I'll be looking forward to your letter.

> *Sarah*

Dear Mr. Nelson,

All these letters I have read remind me of someone I know or me. I have many friends who drink and do drugs. When I'm with them, they ask me if I want some. I always refuse the offer. Sometimes, I can't help it; I want to try it so badly.

I've never done any drinking or drugs before. I always try to help my friends quit their habit. I lecture to all of them. All of my friends who are addicted come from broken homes. They have no one to persuade them to go the right way. I feel it is my responsibility to quit and get their life together.

When you come and talk to us in our class, it's really good. You may not be able to stop drinking completely, but at least you know you are doing your best to help save lives.

I would like to thank you for sharing your feelings with us.

> *Thank you,*
> *Lyle*

Dear Mr. Nelson,

I don't have any problems with alcohol, but some of my classmates do. If there was any way I could help them I would, but I need to know how.

First, I'm lucky that none of my friends I hang out with drink. I feel that they won't start in the near future. Could you send me some more information on SADD, so if any of my friends or close family drink, I could help them?

I think it's a good thing you go throughout all those high schools and talk with all of those students. I think you have helped many kids who need serious help with their drinking problems. I hope that you will keep going to all those high schools and talking about this deadly drug.

Your friend,
Suzanne

Dear Mr. Nelson,

I don't drink, and I don't intend to drink. The more I hear about drunk drivers and the results of drinking, the more I hate it.

I have an uncle who smokes, drinks, and chews. It hurts me to see one of my family turned to such a low state. He's had this habit ever since he was twelve. He never stopped. He's starting to lose his memory, and he gets skin diseases. He always talks to me like I'm five years old. It's very hard to see him like that.

I hope no one should get in such a state. I urge my friends and kids my age not to drink.

Thank you for coming. Please send me more info about SADD. I would like to see alcohol movies and letters to keep away from it.

Thanks for listening,
Hillary

Hi Mr. Nelson,

Well, I'm writing to you while you're speaking to us. I don't have a problem like that at all! I've never drank, smoked, or anything like that.

It's true what's said about peer pressure. If you don't drink, you're considered a geek, but I could care less about what people think about me because I'm not here to please them.

Well, I guess I just wanted to tell you that you don't need a beer to have a good time. I've gone to parties and stayed out'till 2:00 in the morning and not got in trouble because my parents trust me and know I don't drink. I guess the reason is because I've never given them any room to think I drink or smoke.

I don't care if I'm considered a geek because I'll tell you one thing, at least little geeky comes home happy, remembering the fun time I had, while cool you goes home throwing up and feeling stupid. BYE!

Sincerely,
Maribel

Mr. Nelson,

I don't drink, I don't believe in drugs, and I don't want to have sex until I'm married. I think it's very sad that so many kids drink, smoke, or do drugs. But, as you know, in small towns there's nothing to do. So, lots of people I know drink, do drugs and have sex. Some of my friends got raped when they were very young.

The pressure put on us kids is immeasurable. I admit I've drank once. My friend at that party really got drunk. She knew she would drink, so she asked me to make sure she didn't get into any trouble. At the party we both drank. I didn't have too much because I promised that friend I'd look out for her.

While she was drunk, she had guys all over her. I took her out, and I told the guys to leave her alone. She yelled at me and told me I had no business telling her what she could and couldn't do.

I understood that it was the alcohol talking (she thanked me afterwards). Anyway, after hearing and reading those letters, I just wanted someone to hear from another student that you don't have to drink to be cool. I've never found a good reason to drink. I don't do it, only once.

I get urged, but I don't. I also don't say anything to my friends. They all want to be accepted. One time at a dance, two of my very close friends left to get alcohol. I couldn't find them, and it was a long while. I really started getting worried. I even started crying. Then, I knew why parents get so upset.

They came back and saw me crying. I told them why. They threw the alcohol away. I'm glad they did. Then, for some reason I don't know, I asked if they kept any. We found some and all took a drink, then threw it away. Can you tell me why I did that? I'm so scared I'll be pressured into something I don't want to do.

Usually, I say "No-o," but I'm afraid that one day I'll break down and say "Yes." Please tell everyone that if someone cool says you have to drink to hang around with them, maybe they're not so cool, or not going to be such good friends as you like.

Please send me some SADD information. Thank you for noticing that I had a lot to say!

Jacqueline

Mr. Nelson,

I would like to say you have a great job. I'm really glad that you came and talked to us today. It was interesting reading all those letters and seeing how many teenagers are really trying to do something to help their problems.

I don't drink or do drugs, and I'm really proud of myself. I'm glad that my parents do not let me go to parties. I don't think I'd like to go to parties anyway, because from what I hear, the only reason to go to parties is to get drunk or do drugs and get high.

I don't see why people could be so STUPID! My dad has let me try a wine cooler before. I liked the taste of the wine cooler, but it did nothing for me. My parents are proud of me because I have not gotten into any trouble at all.

Thank you so much,
Vikki

Dear Mr. Nelson,

I was really glad that you came to our school today. I say this because, personally, I wanted to get involved in SADD and MADD. I can remember my uncle was a heavy drinker and drove all over the place, but, thank God, he never killed anyone. But, yes, he did kill himself.

No one in my family has a problem, but I want to get involved, so I could stop those who haven't started. Maybe by getting involved, even a little bit, I can get the word out to my close friends and family who might need it. My parents would like to get involved.

Sincerely,
Jaiyash

Dear Mr. Nelson,

I'm 15 years old right now, and I know how it feels when you are inside a car with someone who is under the influence of alcohol, because my father always gets drunk when we go to parties.

I have never drank alcohol before in my life. Instead, I do the one thing I enjoy the most, and that is to play baseball or any other sport as long as I'm away from alcohol, drugs, cigarettes, and also people who get drunk, which is the one thing I hate the most since I remember.

I also want you to know that I really enjoyed your presentation, and I would like some more information about SADD, because I know this will be one of the ways to stop deaths due to drunk driving. I would not like to see someone I love get killed because of drunk driving, or killed by someone who drives under the influence. Thank you for coming.

Sincerely,
Elias

Mr. Nelson,

Hello, my name is Tanya, and I don't drink, but I know people who do. I've been in several positions where I've had to get into a car with a person who was drunk.

Well, I really think you're a great person to take time out from your schedule to come and talk to us high school students. I really feel you've gotten your point across to me and to other people in this room.

I think getting drunk is dumb, and a bunch of people who do it think so, too. They do it to fit in with others. I would like to learn more about this SADD and MADD; so if you have enough information, could you send me some?

Thanks for your time.

Your friend,
Tanya

Dear Mr. Nelson,

Thank you for coming and educating our class about SADD. I have always wanted to get into this group. I don't drink at all. I think it's stupid, and not right at all.

Even though I don't drink, I'm sure others in my class do. I hope you've made as much of an impact on them as you have on me. Bringing those letters helped, too. It made this problem a reality to me. Getting something that someone else our age wrote makes a big difference.

Thanks,
Barbara

Dear Mr. Nelson,

I've read some letters about people wanting to quit drinking, getting raped, and so on. I don't believe in drinking, and I've never drank before and never will. But as I listen, I think of a friend last year who always drank and got so drunk that she sometimes came to school still drunk.

She was a special friend, and I care for her still, even though we don't talk as much. I talked to her about her drinking last year, and I'm happy because this year she's not drinking.

I'm in the 9th grade right now, and I feel great knowing that I did something right. But the point that I wanted to make to everyone who will read this letter is, if you're a true friend, you'll never let drinking overcome you and your dearest friend when it comes to driving, because when you realize you could have done something, it's too late.

I think, Mr. Nelson, what you're saying is sad but true. I wish all those students who have problems will get help soon. I like to say I'm proud to support SADD because if I didn't, my special friend would have died last year.

Thanks for coming to our class.

Sincerely yours,
Christina

It took a student to remind me (via her letter) that she hadn't read any letters from someone who didn't have a problem. She wanted me to know that she was a non-drinker and had a lot of fun at parties without including alcohol. She assured me there were lots more like her. From that date on, I sorted out and included at least one "no problem letter."

I found that yes, she was correct. Once that door was opened, other writers told me I didn't need to worry about them. Some who said they hadn't started drinking, did confess that they recognized the temptation that was facing them, and feared they might give in, but mainly their concerns seemed to be there friends' situations. How could they help their friends escape from the alcohol/drug plight they found themselves in? How could they convince their friends to not begin drinking at all?

Many complimented their parents' roles in setting good examples. It's difficult to evaluate the level of impact, from reading only a few dozen letters, that parents and older siblings have on teenagers through their caring words, firm standards, and responsible actions. The writers left no doubt that it's a positive influence.

Observations:

An early decision was necessary as to how best to respond to the letters handed to me at the conclusion of my classroom programs. Many writers, especially the girls, included their phone numbers. Some asked that I call them to talk. Others, of course, certainly did not want me to make any contact with their home.

For me, a natural letter writer, the decision was easy. My phone number has never appeared on any letters or material given or mailed to students. The last thing I want is to receive a call from a distraught teenager pleading for an answer as to how to handle a drinking boyfriend or an alcoholic parent.

Let them put it in writing. They need time to think through a difficult situation. Writing forces that effort. I needed time to think through my response as well. Then, they can read and re-read my response letters, as many have said they have done, and hopefully get some helpful suggestions. Letters via the postal service were delivered for many years unless the writers requested otherwise. More recently, all response letters to teenagers were delivered to their teacher, with a request that he or she hand them out personally.

A hypothetical scenario from giving my phone number to teenagers follows, and disturbs me even more than the fear of an occasional distraught teenager's call. Suppose I wasn't at home and my message machine recorded a name and phone number with a young female voice requesting a return call? In this pretend scene, a brief message indicated she wanted to talk with me about her boyfriend's drinking problem.

So, I pick up the phone and dial. A man's voice answers. Picture the following conversation developing:

"Hello, this is Ken Nelson. Is Julie there? She asked me to call."

"What do you want to talk with her about? Who are you?"

"I was a guest speaker at her class last Tuesday. It was Mr. Johnson's health class."

"Why should she call you? I don't understand."

"The subject of my lecture was alcohol abuse and alcohol-driving. Julie apparently wanted to talk about a situation with alcohol she had with her boyfriend . . . (a pause) . . . It's not abnormal. Lots of kids have written and asked me for suggestions about problems they were facing."

"Who are you? Are you a policeman or counselor, or something? I didn't know her boyfriend had an alcohol problem. Why didn't Julie talk to us about it?"

"To answer your first question, no, I'm not a policemen or counselor, just a volunteer speaker for MADD and SADD who teenagers feel they can open up to. I've been a parent of teenagers, too. I don't know why they don't always go to their parents for some answers."

"I still don't like it. She only fifteen and she's our daughter. I'll kick the hell out of her boyfriend if he's trying to get Julie started on alcohol. We can handle this!"

"Well, fine. Will you tell her I called, please?"

I think this uncomfortable call, although a hypothetical situation, illustrates why I've never given out my phone number to students.

I have leaned on MADD for the one statistic I use in my talks to impress upon students the magnitude of damage already done by drunk driving in this nation. The stage is set when I request a show of hands of those who had heard of grandfathers, uncles, fathers, or older brothers or sisters who had served in either WWII, the Korean War, or the Vietnam war. Often as many as seventy percent of hands shoot up. Very surprising to me, the number of raised hands was always significantly greater in rural area schools than those in urban areas.

I remind my listeners that a lot of people died in these wars, and that almost five hundred twenty thousand families received letters from the defense department telling them that their young person wasn't ever coming home. Some students shake their heads in disbelief when I follow this statistic by saying:

> While you're still thinking about this tragic loss of lives from these wars, did it possibly occur to you that during this same period of time, from the start of WWII to the end of the Vietnam War, drunk driving killed far more of our people than all of those three wars put together?

Again, I lean on their emotions:

> Will you make your own personal resolution that you're not going to get involved in an activity that is going to cause your folks and your family to have to do without you? Parents just never get over the loss of a child in these drunk driving crashes.

Then it is time for the fifteen minute video.

My large SADD banner that I had designed from a bumper sticker has been hung, taped or tacked on the front wall of every classroom where I deliver a lecture. It proclaims that FRIENDS DON'T LET FRIENDS

DRIVE DRUNK. At some point during my program, I often ask, "Will you consider taking this slogan and keeping it for your own during the fifty or sixty years you'll be driving a car?"

A statistic from SADD confirms that teenagers have rallied around this appeal to look out for each other. Following the video I explain the significance of this statistic that I print in large numbers on the blackboard adjacent to the banner:

```
                                                    (15-19 yrs. old)
1981 -------------------------------------------------- 6,280 deaths
1999 -------------------------------------------------- 2,228 deaths
Now--------------------------------------------------- about 2300 deaths[1]
```

I say:

> In 1981, the year SADD began, (MADD started a year earlier) 6,280 teenagers died in automobile crashes that they caused. They were the drinkers, they were the drivers, and they caused the crashes in which they died, or they killed another teenager. Adults were not involved at all in these statistics.
>
> Now let's move ahead: Even with more young drivers, look what happened! The deaths of teenagers caused by drinking teenage drivers dropped by almost 4,000 a year. Do you realize the impact of these figures? It means that each year now four thousand less sets of parents have to suffer through the loss of their teenager in the situations I've described. You can feel awfully good about what teens ahead of you have helped accomplish.

What has caused this highly significant drop in the number of these tragic losses of young lives? Who should get credit?

The early and strong role that MADD, SADD and many other private and governmental organizations have had in reducing overall alcohol

---

[1]   The author is confident that the 1981 number of 6,280 deaths for 15-19 year olds was provided to SADD by NHTSA, as well as was the 2228 number for 1999. The "now" number of 2,300 is an estimate, based on the most current statistics available, which more often cover the 16-20 year old group rather than the narrower range of 15-19 year old drivers.

impaired driving deaths has to be recognized. They brought the attention of our nation to a deadly problem that was growing worse, and forced action.

Few would question the impact of raising the minimum drinking age to 21 on a national level. Tighter rules for new drivers in many states, with an emphasis on zero alcohol tolerance, could certainly be a factor.

Not so effective have been the efforts to reduce drunk driving by adult repeat offenders. Harsher measures now openly debated, including impounding vehicles and installing ignition devices, may become widely used to target this group. Courts may impose longer jail terms.

Our law enforcement continues to try and identify and remove drinking drivers from our roads before another tragedy happens. I encourage my young listeners to give their parents or adult friends the California Highway Patrol's (CHP) brochure on using a Designated Driver and also the one on Sobriety Checkpoints.

But then, I remind my classroom audiences that they must recognize their own unique power. Teenager decisions themselves may well have been the greatest factor in this striking reduction of alcohol-related young deaths caused by teenage drivers who had been drinking. I say:

> No one knows better than those of you sitting right here that when you're fourteen to seventeen years old, and at parties where there is alcohol, your parents aren't going to be there holding your hands, cautioning you not to drink or begging you not to ride home with a drunk friend. You're making your own decisions, good or bad, and that's the way it should be.

I point out two good decisions that I feel teenagers have made since 1981: They helped design SADD's Contract for Life, calling for a commitment between a young person and a caring, dependable adult. Many tens of thousands of these Contracts have been handed to members of my young audiences who have asked for them.

Secondly, and perhaps most important, my listeners are reminded that their age group's commitment to look out for each other in difficult party situations, a key part of SADD's philosophy, became a national commitment of millions of teenagers. As true friends, each would do their best to make sure that their friend did not get into a car with someone who had been drinking. As I tell them,

Whether you drink at parties is not the prime issue. You will make your own decisions and I hope you will follow our laws. When you carry the SADD I.D. card that I'll make up for you, you are making a commitment that you will do your best to insure your friends' safety. At one of those parties you may turn out to be the only person in this world who can prove that you are a true friend to that friend of yours.

SADD's speaker at the 1998 annual convention held in Washington, D.C. that year, confirmed that the dramatic reduction in teenage deaths had been accomplished. They challenged the three hundred high school leaders and their adult sponsors to reach for a new goal: 2,000 by 2000.

Was it reached? Did the deaths of our 15-19 year old teenagers, where the young people, often including the drinking drivers as well as the innocent victims, drop under 2,000? No, it didn't and it hasn't yet, but seems to be hovering around 2300 each year, even with the addition of new drivers. Is it still a success story? Yes, but it's a work in progress.

What challenge can I leave with these students that is optimistic but accepts reality? The fifty-five minute program is about over, and they're tired.

SADD's goal for the years ahead is still to reduce the number of these deaths to below two thousand a year. This will happen only if those of you in this room, who will be the drivers in the years ahead, will make the same commitment as those before you did, but do even a better job of looking out for each other. You alone have that power. If you do this, the goal can yet be reached.

It's important too to acknowledge to my young audiences that many adults have pitched in to help reduce the overall deaths from drunk driving. Asking if students remember the video and the staged crash into a tree, followed by the statement that 25,000 people die in drunk driving crashes each year,[2] I note that this has changed too, and write additional numbers

---

[2]   The 25,000 number very likely was composed of what was and still is defined as "alcohol related" situations. At the time the video was made, few, if any, state legislatures had defined a BAC level of .08% as being drunk while driving.

on the blackboard to accentuate the positive trend: Alcohol related crashes caused 17,602 deaths in 2006, according to the National Highway Traffic Safety Administration (NHTSA). Thirteen-thousand, four-hundred and ninety-one of these deaths were recorded where one or both drivers had a BAC level of .08% or higher. Heads nod affirmatively in the class when I ask, "That's a pretty fair change isn't it?" But they aren't allowed too much feel-good time, as I continue:

> Let's look at it another way for just a minute. Thirteen-thousand, four-hundred and ninety-one needless deaths because someone chose to violate our laws and drive when drunk!

Now, shaking heads replaces the nods.

Most teenagers, understandably, want to be part of something that's currently popular. Few want to go it alone. Many will follow if close friends or the in crowd lead. None want to be left out and feel completely isolated.

The letters you've read demonstrate all of these traits in our young people. Some have led to destructive decisions; the same traits have also helped create healthy situations. Our teens are also impatient. They want to have things happen now! Just ask their mothers about this fact of life.

Our teenagers are listening and thinking. They have many more challenges and serous decisions to make than my generation of teens in the 1930s did.

The final minutes of my hour in each class are devoted to soliciting individual memberships in SADD. This is the time I find out if my audience has found me to be believable, honest, caring, and persuasive.

It took only a few students early on to ask me how soon they would receive their SADD I.D. Cards to convince me that I needed to take advantage of the sometimes annoying teenager trait of impatience. Was that fair? It surely worked well. I added a sentence when holding up the blank applications. I tell them:

> For those of you who fill out applications, I'll take them home, and tonight and tomorrow morning I'll make up personal I.D. cards for you. I should be able to get them all done and in the mail to your teacher by noon not more than two days from now.

The concept of SADD, that of caring enough about each other to take the time to look out for friends in potential alcohol-driving situations, seemed to appeal to many of the 160,000 young people who gave me the courtesy of quietly listening. A fifty minute program, during which I lean on their emotions awfully hard, has to tax even the best students' attention span.

Students today have no shortage of accurate information on alcohol use and the consequences of getting involved with the numerous other mind-altering drugs. Health classrooms are loaded with current, readable books on the subject. Teachers have become very knowledgeable. Most are not bashful about telling it like it is.

Are our young people responding? The thousands of responses and letters given to me indicate that many are. We sometimes get mixed indicators. Only time will provide answers. Teenagers will always be teenagers, and we've all been there once.

At the time of this writing, more than 81,000 have chosen to fill out the applications. Almost all were mailed their cards on the schedule that was promised. Many teachers commented on the value they saw in being able to hand their students the cards while my time with them was still fresh in their minds.

Although only a handful of MADD and SADD leaders have ever sat through one of my more than 4,700 lectures, I've made it a point to keep them posted as to speaking schedules and summaries of my activities. Recognition of my efforts by these two organizations have always been generous, in the form of letters, plaques and trophies that arrived regularly over the twenty-eight year period. Their support has been far more than a volunteer has any right to expect, and has always helped to keep me pumped up for another year's work.

On a half-dozen occasions, I typed up the prior year's spontaneous letters, ranging in number from 100 to 250, and delivered a package to both MADD and SADD. Their strong affirmation triggered the idea of eventually making this unique collection of candid, honest, and revealing letters from our teenagers available to a much broader group of readers. In *Dear Mr. Nelson* I have had the privilege of sharing with you a book of written expressions that may never be duplicated again.

ACKNOWLEDGEMENTS

It is important that the following people be recognized for their contribution in making possible the final draft of *Dear Mr. Nelson*. Some have helped with editing, some with very usable suggestions, and others with many hours of typing and computer skills. All supplied encouragement. Their names are, in alphabetical order: Suzanna Anderson, Ross, CA; Bruce Black, Oakland, CA; Darren W. Hurst, Justin S. Hurst, and Kenneth A. Hurst, all of Granite Bay, CA; Amy McAndrews, Manteca, CA; Donna McBride, Casa Grande, AZ; Robin Martin of Two Songbirds Press, Orangevale, CA; Patricia D. Nelson, Sacramento, CA; and Nanette Rigby, Madera, CA.

My deepest appreciation goes to MADD (Mothers Against Drunk Driving), and to SADD (Students Against Destructive Decisions). These two organizations provided me with the opportunity for a third career, now spanning more than twenty-eight years.

Although I purposefully never leaned on either group for financial help, their complimentary messages, floods of awards, and numerous plaques were more than enough continuing incentive to pursue my volunteer speaking for them.

Looking back, it would seem an unlikely partnership for a man who had already completed two careers. One covered the age from nine to twenty-one, milking cows, shocking hay, and shoveling cow manure. After a three and a half year break for World War Two, followed by an equal period at the University of California in Berkeley, paid for by wonderful taxpayers and exiting as a soil scientist, my second career of thirty years was spent in the farm fertilizer industry.

After I got over the stage fright from facing live audiences, the more than two decades of representing SADD and MADD at high schools in northern California and western Nevada became my most rewarding career of all.

Being able to claim that I represented two such nationally respected organizations kept the doors open and invitations flowing in. It was only after years into this speaking project that I developed my own reputation as an "honest broker" with teenagers and their teachers.

I am proud that still today, after all these years, each class audience I visit faces their blackboard on which is written this introduction: KEN NELSON, representing MADD & SADD.

ABOUT THE AUTHOR

Kenneth E. Nelson

Born in 1921, a farm boy during the depression years, the author spent three and a half years in WWII and was the Communications officer on LST 784, landing Marines and their "Long Toms" on the Iwo Jima beach at age twenty-four. He graduated from UC Berkeley with a degree in Soil Science in 1950, and has been a Sacramento resident for half a century.

Nelson's first book, *Thoughts of a Boy Growing Up*, was a memoir dedicated to his seven grandchildren, who constantly asked him to "tell us what it was like when you were a boy." This book, built around depression era experiences and observations, is no longer in print. Copies were delivered to all of California's 1000 senior high school libraries.

Promised soon, from iUniverse, is his first piece of fiction, a novel titled *Neighbors: A Summer/Winter Affair*, about a 75-year old staid widower and a young, divorced, amorous and unpredictable neighbor.

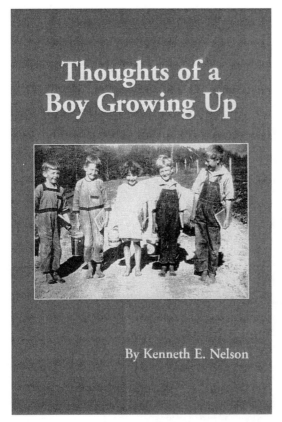

Pictured, l. to r., the author, his older brother Roy Nelson, Mildred Lindley, Jack Smith, and Leland Hadley—the total second and third grade classes at the Upper Mattole school in Humboldt County, California. Circa 1928.

Awarded to the author at a luncheon ceremony on May 24, 2000 also recognizing efforts of members of the area's police forces, sheriff's departments and the CHP in combatting and reducing drunk driving. The event was co-sponsored by MADD and the California Office of Traffic Safety.

Pictured is the Lifetime Achievement Award presented on July 12, 1998, in Washington D.C. to Kenneth E. Nelson by Students Against Destructive Decisions' (SADD) Executive Director Stephen Wallace.

The plaque was in recognition of seventeen years of volunteer speaking on the issues of alcohol abuse and alcohol-driving as those related to teenagers.

Beginning with his first address to student audiences at Burbank High School in Sacramento, CA, in December 1981, Nelson had given over four thousand such presentations. His audiences were mainly individual class size groups and totaled over 150,000 teenagers.

The author's Lifetime Achievement Award was only the second ever presented by SADD.